ECONOMIC AND FINANCIAL INTEGRATION IN SOUTH ASIA

This book analyses the current state and potential of economic and financial integration in South Asia, which has emerged as one of the most dynamic regions of the world. It looks at how regional convergences and cooperation would reinforce ties amongst the diverse economies of South Asia in the changing global economic landscape.

Drawing on empirical research, the book looks at the degree of economic and financial integration in South Asia, which according to the World Bank includes the least integrated regions in the world, and explores the fundamental factors that drive integration amongst these countries. It offers important insights into the financial landscape of the region, as well as the dynamics of the interlinkages in the banking system, the stock markets, and the debt markets. The book examines the role of bilateral trade in augmenting regional economic ties, the opportunities for growth these will foster, and the major challenges and roadblocks for the leaders of the region. It also provides an overview of China's role in South Asia's financial integration and the interdependence of these economies for economic opportunities, macroeconomic and financial stability, jobs, sustainable growth, and inclusive development.

Detailed and insightful, this book will be of great interest to investors and regional policymakers. It will also be of interest to researchers and students of economics, public and foreign policy, finance, international relations, and South Asia studies.

Sanjay Sehgal is currently a Professor of Finance and the Head of the Department of Financial Studies, University of Delhi, India. He has 29 years' teaching experience in the field of investment management, financial derivatives, corporate finance, and financial econometrics. He has taught courses in finance at LSE and ESC Pau, France, as well as delivered academic and research seminars at Vancouver Island University, Canada, the Universities of Nottingham and Leicester, and more. Prof. Sehgal has written a research book, completed eight major research projects, and published more than 150 research papers in international and national refereed journals.

Wasim Ahmad is currently working as an Assistant Professor and as PK Kelkar Faculty Fellow in the Department of Economic Sciences, Indian Institute of Technology Kanpur. His research areas are financial economics, macroeconomics, and applied econometrics. Dr. Ahmad has also been awarded the Subir Chowdhury Postdoctoral Fellowship at the London School of Economics and Political Science for the period 2019–2020. He was the Co-Principal Investigator of the ICSSR, Govt. of India, sponsored major research project. Dr. Ahmad's research work has appeared in the leading journals of economics and finance.

Piyush Pandey is an Assistant Professor in the area of Finance in Shailesh J. Mehta School of Management, IIT Bombay. His research and teaching interests include financial derivatives, investment management, market microstructure, and banking. He has published his research work in international peer-reviewed economics and finance journals. He is also actively involved in corporate consulting having consulted JLLSFG on a real estate finance project and a wealth management firm on profitable investment strategies. He has worked as a Research Assistant of the ICSSR, Govt. of India, sponsored major research project.

Sakshi Saini is an Assistant Professor at the Institute of Economic Growth, Delhi. She is pursuing a PhD in the Department of Financial Studies, University of Delhi. She has completed a Master's in Economics from Jawaharlal Nehru University and has worked as a Research Assistant of the ICSSR sponsored major research project. She has presented papers at many national and international conferences, and has published research articles in peer-reviewed journals. Her research interests are international finance, monetary economics, and applied econometrics.

ECONOMIC AND FINANCIAL INTEGRATION IN SOUTH ASIA

A Contemporary Perspective

Sanjay Sehgal, Wasim Ahmad, Piyush Pandey and Sakshi Saini

LONDON AND NEW YORK

First published 2021
by Routledge
2 Park Square, Milton Park, Abingdon, Oxon OX14 4RN

and by Routledge
52 Vanderbilt Avenue, New York, NY 10017

Routledge is an imprint of the Taylor & Francis Group, an informa business

© 2021 Sanjay Sehgal, Wasim Ahmad, Piyush Pandey
and Sakshi Saini

The right of Sanjay Sehgal, Wasim Ahmad, Piyush Pandey and
Sakshi Saini to be identified as authors of this work has been
asserted by them in accordance with sections 77 and 78 of the
Copyright, Designs and Patents Act 1988.

British Library Cataloguing-in-Publication Data
A catalogue record for this book is available from the British Library

Library of Congress Cataloging-in-Publication Data
A catalog record has been requested for this book

ISBN: 978-0-8153-8013-9 (hbk)
ISBN: 978-1-003-09756-3 (ebk)

Typeset in Sabon
by codeMantra

CONTENTS

v

FIGURES

TABLES

CONTRIBUTORS

Rishman Jot Kaur Chahal is a PhD Candidate in the Department of Economic Sciences, Indian Institute of Technology (IIT) Kanpur. Her research areas are institutional economics, corporate finance, and macroeconomics. She has Master's in Economics from Madras School of Economics. She has presented her doctoral work at leading conferences in economics and finance, and has publications in leading journals to her credit.

Mahendra Kumar Singh is currently pursuing a PhD in the Department of Economics at Iowa State University, USA. His research areas include development economics and international trade. He has an MSc in Economics from the Department of Economic Sciences, Indian Institute of Technology (IIT) Kanpur.

PREFACE

The coming of the new political executive in India in 2014 was noted by media for being the first ever swearing-in of an Indian Prime Minister to have been attended by the heads of all SAARC countries. The foreign policy of the then government of the biggest economy of South Asia, i.e. India was coined by media as *"Neighbourhood First"* policy. Subsequent years saw the talk of SAARC satellite and Development Bank of SAARC to further strengthen the regional cooperation. It was at this time that Indian Council of Social Sciences and Research (ICSSR) awarded a major sponsored research project named *"Financial Integration in the SAARC region: An Empirical Study"* to the authors of this book to study the current state of economic and financial integration of the South Asian countries and provide policy suggestions thereon to strengthen the same. This book is the research output of the academic work conducted by the authors in this regard, and is a first comprehensive study of its kind for this region to bring forward the contemporary dimensions of *South Asian Integration*.

It is of particular importance to study the regional integration in South Asia at a time when new USA political executive shuns regional trade agreements in favour of bilateral ones. More so when global economic gravity is shifting to the east and 21st century is believed to be *"The Asian Century"*, South Asia has been accorded as one of the most dynamic regions of the world (ironically it is also the least integrated region in the world) by World Bank, growing at a remarkable rate of 7.1% over the last decade. Regional cooperation in South Asia can rally around the grouping of *Association of South East Asian Nations* (ASEAN) to emerge as torchbearers of multilateralism for economic growth and development of Asia as a whole.

This book provides greater insights into the several aspects of the economic and financial integration in the South Asian economies that would be valuable for regional policymakers, investors, the academic community mainly comprising of students of international economics and finance.

ACKNOWLEDGEMENTS

This book is an outcome of Indian Council of Social Science Research (ICSSR), Government of India, sponsored research project entitled "Financial Integration in the SAARC Region: Empirical Analysis & Policy Issues". We would like to sincerely thank ICSSR for providing us the financial support to facilitate research undertaken by us. We are grateful to the continuous academic guidance of Prof. N.R. Bhanumurthy, National Institute of Public Finance and Policy (NIPFP), and Prof. P.K. Jain, Department of Management Studies (DMS), Indian Institute of Technology (IIT) Delhi, during the course of the research. We earnestly thank policymakers, financial market participants, and academicians who generously helped us in executing the primary survey for this study by filing questionnaires regarding the dynamics of South Asian Integration. We also thank Dr. Tarunika Jain, Mr. Mahendra Kumar Singh, Ms. Rishman Jot Kaur Chahal, Dr. Priyanshi Gupta, Mr. Gagan Sharma and Dr. Shirin Rais for their contributions in carrying out this research.

The research papers carved out from this study were presented in many national and international conferences, and we were immensely benefitted from the suggestions received from these conference participants who provided us new and different insights into our work. We would also like to thank participants of the research seminar on "Financial Integration in the SAARC Region" which was organized by the Department of Financial Studies, University of Delhi, in association with the Department of Humanities and Social Sciences, IIT Kanpur, on 1 April 2017 to disseminate research findings of our work besides providing a platform for interaction among academicians, students, researchers who are working on similar area to present their work in the form of academic dialogue. The seminar helped us better understand various dimensions of South Asian Integration and appreciate its unique nature and complexity.

We would like to acknowledge the infrastructural support provided by the University of Delhi South Campus, IIT Kanpur, and IIT Bombay for carrying out this research. We are also grateful to the continuous encouragement and support received from Prof. Vimal Kumar, Head, Department of Economic Sciences, IIT Kanpur, and Prof. Shivganesh Bhargava, Head, Shailesh J. Mehta School of Management, IIT Bombay. We also appreciate assistance of Mr. Y.M. Dua, working as project staff for extending his administrative support.

We express our sincere gratitude to the anonymous referees who gave their constructive comments and suggestions that helped us improve the manuscript of this book in many aspects. We reserve the final word of thanks to the editorial team at Routledge India – Shoma Choudhury, Brinda Sen, Shloka Chauhan, and their colleagues – who approved our work and gave their consent to come out with a book on this very relevant and contemporary subject.

ABBREVIATIONS

ABMI	Asian Bond Market Initiative
ADB	Asian Development Bank
ADCC	Asymmetric Dynamic Conditional Correlation
ANOVA	Analysis of Variance
AR	Autoregression
ASEAN	Association of South East Asian Nations
BBIN	Bangladesh, Bhutan, India, Nepal
BCIM	Bangladesh-China-India-Myanmar
BIMSTEC	Bay of Bengal Initiative for Multi-Sectoral Technical and Economic Cooperation
CPEC	China-Pakistan Economic Corridor
CPIS	Coordinated Portfolio Investment Survey
DCC	Dynamic Conditional Correlation
EGARCH	Exponential Generalized Autoregressive Conditional Heteroscedasticity
EU	European Union
F&O	Futures and Options
FEV	Forecast Error Variance
FX	Foreign Exchange
GARCH	Generalized Autoregressive Conditional Heteroscedasticity
GDP	Gross Domestic Product
HDI	Human Development Index
IBSA	India, Brazil and South Africa
ICRG	International Country Risk Guide
IFM	Inference Function for Margin
IFS	International Financial Statistics
IMF	International Monetary Fund
LL	Log Likelihood
MGARCH	Multivariate Generalized Autoregressive Conditional Heteroscedasticity
MSR	Maritime Silk Road
NAFTA	North American Free Trade Agreement

NPA	Non-Performing Asset
OTC	Over the Counter
PNB	Punjab National Bank
RMB	Renminbi
SAARC	South Asian Association for Regional Cooperation
SAEU	South Asian Economic Union
SAFE	South Asian Federation of Exchanges
SAFTA	South Asian Free Trade Area
SAPTA	SAARC Preferential Trading Agreement
SAR	Spatial Autoregressive Model
SARSO	South Asian Regional Standards Organization
SASRF	South Asian Securities Regulators' Forum
SATIS	SAARC Agreement on Trade in Services
SAWTEE	South Asia Watch on Trade, Economics and Environment
SDF	SAARC Development Fund
SDM	Spatial Durbin Model
SEM	Spatial Error Model
TPP	Trans-Pacific Partnership
UNCTAD	United Nations Conference on Trade and Development
UNDP	United Nations Development Programme
UNESCAP	United Nations Economic and Social Commission for Asia and the Pacific
VAR	Vector Autoregression
WDI	World Development Indicators
WEF	World Economic Forum
WITS	World Integrated Trade Solution
WTO	World Trade Organization

INTRODUCTION

The phenomenon of *economic regionalism* stemming from a common vision of an integrated community is an overarching reality of the present world. *Regional integration* reinforces ties amongst a set of diverse economies so as to provide avenues for economic opportunities, sustainable growth, financial stability and inclusive development. But of late with the coming to power of new polity in the US which has sparked off a wave of de-globalization leading to trade wars with China, withdrawal of the US from *Trans-Pacific Partnership (TPP)* and protectionist measures amongst others, there is a growing consensus amongst Asian leaders for regional integration and greater financial cooperation. *Emerging market economies* (EMEs) have become much more integrated into the world economy due to trade openness, financial liberalization and mobility of factors of production leading to global value chains. South Asia, a diverse region of heterogeneous countries, formally initiated a regional integration process with the formation of the *South Asian Association of Regional Cooperation* (SAARC) in 1985. Until the late 1970s, these countries followed high protectionist trade policies and maintained strict capital controls. But with the changing global economic landscape, South Asian countries have embraced outward-oriented strategies and have increasingly acknowledged that regional approaches are quintessential to accomplish their developmental challenges. They have undertaken several regional initiatives since the inception of SAARC to achieve closer cooperation and integration. Recently, South Asia has been accorded as one of the most dynamic regions of the world by the World Bank, growing at a remarkable rate of 7.1% over the last decade. In spite of the global headwinds, World Bank believes that South Asia will hold on to its top spot as the world's fastest growing region, with growth rate pegged at 7% in 2019, then 7.1% in 2020 and 2021. This growth while still robust reflects continued strong consumption and investment, supported by favourable financial conditions and improving external demand. This region needs to increase its exports to sustain its high growth and reach its full economic potential. According to World Bank, South Asia

1

has the world's largest working age population, a quarter of the world's middle-class consumers, the largest number of poor and undernourished in the world, and several fragile states of global geopolitical importance signifying immense opportunities that can help in harnessing its enormous potential. Globally, the region is also gaining significance as indicated by the list of its observer countries i.e. Australia, China, European Union, Iran, Japan, Republic of Korea, Mauritius, Myanmar and the US that are engaged in collaborative ventures with SAARC.

The region, however, remains one of the least integrated into the world albeit after three decades since the formation of SAARC. Although it is comprised of countries which share a common history, heritage, culture and contiguity, economic and political differences have not permitted SAARC initiatives to achieve desired results and are major impediments in the way for realizing stronger integration amongst the SAARC members. Given the increasing emphasis on closer regional cooperation particularly in Asia with the formation of ASEAN (*Association of South East Asian Nations*) Economic Community (AEC) in 2015, it is an opportune time for the political leadership of the SAARC countries to steer their way through their political standoffs and embrace an open regionalism and institutional change that can help make South Asia an active partner in Asian economic integration and global economy. SAARC has dedicated the decade 2010–2020 to the intra-regional connectivity which can help propel growth, peace and prosperity in the region. It has also emphasized that the process of regional integration in trade, economic and financial sectors should be expedited. As global economic gravity shifts to the east and 21st century is believed to be "The Asian Century", the policymakers of the SAARC region are convinced to accelerate the regional integration amongst them so as to emerge as a countervailing power to the western economies and lend their support to the ASEAN regional grouping. According to the World Bank, to ensure growth in the long run, the region needs to integrate further with international markets so as to create more jobs and boost prosperity for its people.

To further integrate into the international markets, it is warranted to first study the connectedness of this region as a whole, and hence, this book provides a comprehensive analysis of the current state of economic and financial integration of the South Asian countries and further explores the underlying determinants that might drive the process of integration. It might look counterintuitive for a region which is least intra-regionally connected (trade within the bloc vis- à-vis trade with the world) to even explore the financial market linkages. But we must understand that these countries share a common history, heritage, culture and contiguity, and hence can learn from the financial markets and systems prevailing in India, the biggest economy of this region which has fairly well regulated, sophisticated and competitive markets systems with respect to global standards. Also, the savings rate of SAARC member countries is high and that combined with the young demographics means long working life with longer-term inflation-beating investments which could help to increase the capital market penetration in these countries. Besides a large consumer base, SAARC members are keen on building production capabilities in both factory and knowledge sectors to create value chain opportunities leading to the expansion of corporate sectors which would further result in market activity in those countries. Also, the developmental needs and priorities in these economies will be fulfilled by the banks of these respective countries as they are the biggest source of credit, and hence, the dynamics of the banking system has to be studied so as to share the best practices amongst each other. This book is the research output of the academic work conducted by the authors in the form of a major sponsored research project funded by ICSSR named "Financial Integration in the SAARC region: An Empirical Study". This book provides greater insights into the several contemporary aspects of the economic and financial integration in the South Asian economies that would be valuable for regional policymakers, investors, the academic community mainly comprising of students of international economics and finance.

Chapter 1 presents a brief overview of the process of South Asian Integration. It introduces the South Asian region and then proceeds to explain the international experiences of regional integration while highlighting the South Asian initiatives in this regards. Further, it presents the backdrop of the opportunities and challenges for regional integration in South Asia. In Chapter 2, the degree of economic and financial integration is examined by conducting a primary survey of market participants, policymakers and academia. Along with empirical research necessitated to study the existing levels of economic and financial integration in the South Asian region, views of the opinion leaders regarding the process of integration in the region were virtually missing. Hence, the authors examine the perceived level of economic and financial integration, and further explore the fundamental factors that drive integration amongst the SAARC members by adopting a survey-based approach. Chapter 3 examines the possible determinants of the economic integration of SAARC countries. It introduces the macroeconomic dimension of economic integration by combining the dynamic correlation-based business cycle synchronization measures with the major macroeconomic indicators. Chapter 4 introduces the role of bilateral trade in augmenting the process of economic integration. It works on the bilateral export and import data created for the analysis and introduces a host of regulatory and socio-economic factors to examine the impact of these factors on bilateral trade of SAARC countries. This chapter provides evidence on the major factors which determine the bilateral trade of SAARC countries. Chapter 5 introduces the credit-growth framework for SAARC countries by examining the business cycle and financial cycle interactions under the time-varying framework for SAARC member countries. Economic and trade linkages between SAARC member countries lay the conceptual ground for subsequent chapters dealing with financial integration between SAARC countries. Underdeveloped and rigidly fragmented financial markets will be countercyclical for effective mobilization of financial resources within the region thereby hampering economic growth and development of the region. *Financial integration* is examined for both financial markets – i.e. equity, debt and currency segments – and the banking system in Chapters 6–9, respectively. Given China's increasing foothold in the South Asian region and its pitch for membership in SAARC, Chapter 10 assesses its level of integration with the South Asian countries to analyse its objective case for inclusion in SAARC. Drawing upon the results, this book endeavours to provide policy suggestions for these member countries to expedite the process of economic and financial integration and reap full potential from regional cooperation.

Given the social, economic and geopolitical importance of this region, the contribution of the book shall prove to be a valuable resource for investors, policymakers and academic community, particularly from this region. The study has important implications for international portfolio managers as it provides useful insights to engage in effective risk management and asset allocation. For policymakers, it shall be of particular relevance in the light of the growing number of regional cooperation initiatives worldwide for achieving political influence, enhanced linkages amongst economies as well as developing a coordinated response to global shocks. It will help the policymakers to see the viability of the SAARC region as a whole to achieve developmental objectives and regional growth and cooperation. The study shall be instructive and provide strong arguments for the SAARC group members and specifically for India to come out of their political standoffs and collaborate in efforts of policy realignment to bring dynamism into this region thereby promoting regional integration. From the academic point of view, the book bridges an important gap in the literature as it is the first study of its kind that comprehensively analyses the economic and financial integration of the South Asian region. Further, the book can also prove useful for students of international economics and finance, particularly interested in studying regional integration as it will introduce them to its economic and financial dimensions.

The scope of the book lies in the very essence of the concept of economic regionalism which in academic parlance is the engine of economic growth and development for any region. Winds of de-globalization are blowing in the west fanned by political leaders to claim power in their domestic constituency and are a challenge to Asian countries' shared commitment to "open regionalism". In this context, when ASEAN is taking great strides to anchor the expectations of the east in what is otherwise described as the *"Asian Century"*, SAARC bloc with its more than two decades of existence seems to be in deep slumber. It's important to study and analyse this existential dilemma of SAARC beyond the qualitative perception of its obsolescence to make South Asia, which is one of the most dynamic (in economic, social and political aspects) regional groups of the world, an active partner in the Asian growth story. Hence, this book is a first attempt to provide a quantitative foundation to help understand the extent of various dimensions of economic and financial integration of South Asia.

Taking cognizance of the rich academic literature on similar work conducted for other regional groupings of the world, the authors take note and therefore apply suitable research methods and analyse the empirical results in the given context of South Asia and suggest policy suggestions thereon to drive the process of integration in this region leading to economic growth and development. Given the current state of the willingness of its policymakers and maturity of the economic and financial sector of these countries, some ideas may be implementable now, while some may be implementable in the future as the political ill-will settles down. However, the objective is to start deliberation on even the ideas of the future, since even that takes time to materialize. It is a first comprehensive study of its kind for this region to bring forward the various dimensions of South Asian Integration and help readers appreciate its unique nature and complexity. More importantly, in the given political economy context, where multilateralism is being increasingly substituted by bilateral and unilateral arrangements, the role of regional blocs particularly in the east is looked upon to act as catalysts for economic growth and development. Further, it is important to ascertain the relevance of SAARC or provide policymakers with a future challenge to leverage another platform i.e. *BIMSTEC*[1] to lend support to the larger ASEAN grouping to contribute to the success story of the *"Asian Century"*.

Note

1 The Bay of Bengal Initiative for Multi-Sectoral Technical and Economic Co-operation (BIMSTEC) is an international organization of sectoral cooperation amongst seven nations in Bay of Bengal – Bangladesh, India, Myanmar, Sri Lanka, Thailand, Nepal and Bhutan.

1

SOUTH ASIAN INTEGRATION

An overview

Sanjay Sehgal, Sakshi Saini and Piyush Pandey

South Asian region

South Asia is a diverse region encompassing eight countries, namely, Afghanistan, Bangladesh, Bhutan, India, Maldives, Nepal, Pakistan and Sri Lanka that are heterogeneous in terms of their geography, demography and economic size. India accounts for more than 75% of the region's combined population and Gross Domestic Product (GDP) as of 2015.[1] The other largest economies of South Asia, Pakistan and Bangladesh, respectively, account for nearly 10% and 7% of South Asia's GDP, and 11% and 9% of its population. The smaller countries of the region are either landlocked (Afghanistan, Bhutan and Nepal) or island economies (the Maldives and Sri Lanka) that contribute less than 3% to South Asia's GDP and population.[2] Owing to its sizable territory, huge population growth and the rapid pace of economic growth, India clearly dominates South Asian region having contiguous (land or maritime) borders with every South Asian country (except Afghanistan). Despite varied characteristics, the countries of the region are unified by their common history, cultural affinity and geographic proximity. Cohesiveness amongst the countries also springs from similarities in terms of their colonial rule legacy and planned approach to development after independence.

Post-independence, South Asian countries adopted import substitution policy with heavy trade protection, practised strict exchange rate controls and discouraged flow of foreign capital. Further, there was the heavy intervention of the state in economic activity and the entry of the private sector was highly repressed. This development strategy resulted in the sluggish growth of these economies with low productivity, moderate level of industrialization and weak export performance. South Asia started embracing outward-oriented development policies only after the 1980s thereby registering remarkable average GDP growth of 5.7% during 1980–2000, which further accelerated to 6.5% during 2000–2007.[3] Today, South Asia is the fastest growing region of the world with the average annual growth rate of 7% in 2015 outpacing East Asia and the Pacific (World Bank, 2016a).

In spite of the global headwinds, World Bank believes that South Asia will hold on to its top spot as the world's fastest growing region, with growth rate pegged at 7% in 2019, then 7.1% in 2020 and 2021. Over the past years, South Asia's economic growth has been impressive and is gaining sustained momentum owing to its gradual implementation of macroeconomic reforms. The consistent increase in the economic growth of the region is led by strong domestic consumption, and not by exports or by capital accumulation. The Gross Fixed Capital Formation has dwindled since the beginning of the century, and private investment remained stagnant over the years thereby raising the question on sustainability of South Asia's economic growth in the long run (World Bank, 2016b).

The region has shown resilience to the economic and financial turmoil that grappled the world economies. The countries remained immune to the impact of the Global Financial Crisis and have also defied recent China's slowdown and diverging monetary policy of advanced economies to sustain its growth rate. However, the resilience of South Asian economies resulted not from their strong macroeconomic fundamentals, robust institutions and proactive policies, but due to their moderate exposure to an international environment that made them less vulnerable at times of global turbulence. The economies of the region are also characterized by poor governance, weak regulatory framework, lack of infrastructure and inefficient financial intermediation.

Along with highest economic growth rate, South Asian region also has the highest population density across all regions with a combined population of 1.89 billion (about one-fourth of the world's population) as of 2017 and the highest concentration of poor in the world.[4] Further, Human Development Index (HDI) value of the South Asian region is on an average 0.621, lower than the world average of 0.717[5] which can be attributed to rampant poverty, high mortality, low literacy and malnourishment amongst a large section of its population. The countries have inadequate infrastructure such as sanitation and access to electricity to meet the basic needs of its population. About 55% and 27% of South Asia's combined population lacks access to sanitation and electricity, respectively. Further, South Asian countries have a low level of financial inclusion with only 46% of its population having bank accounts (UNESCAP, 2016).

Prolonged political change and uncertainty have gripped the South Asian economies. Political and security landscape in Afghanistan is persistently deteriorating due to political crisis and armed conflicts. Bangladesh has dealt with long-standing political conflicts, terrorism and security threats. Nepal also faces political and security issues due to Maoist insurgency, frequent changes of governments, and persistent protests and strikes even after the promulgation of the constitution. Pakistan in its history has oscillated between military rule and democracy, making it politically unstable. The country has continually confronted political turmoil, civil conflicts and security threats posed by military forces and terrorist activities. The political dynamics of these countries have strong repercussions on their macroeconomic and financial stability.

Regional integration: international experience and South Asian initiatives

The past few decades have witnessed an increasing number of regional agreements aimed at integrating the economies in the same region owing to geographical and cultural proximity. The primary focus areas of such agreements revolve around removing barriers to free trade and increasing the free movement of labour and capital across national borders. Some of the cooperation arrangements have become highly evolved such as *European Monetary Union* (EMU) which has completed economic and financial integration and is taking policy measures to correct the fault lines in the aftermath of crisis instead of embarking upon disintegration. North America has set up *North American Free Trade Agreement* (NAFTA) which, in terms of combined purchasing power parity of the nominal GDP of its members (the USA, Canada and Mexico), was the largest trade bloc in the world in 2013. South America has set up the *South American Common Market* (MERCOSUR) which is an economic and political agreement among six major South American countries to promote free trade and movement of goods, people and currency. Similarly, Africa has set up the *African Union* (AU) consisting of 54 African states. The Gulf Cooperation Council (GCC) is a regional economic and political union consisting of countries of the *Persian Gulf* (Bahrain, Kuwait, Oman, Qatar, Saudi Arabia and the UAE) except Iraq which was formed in 1981. Similar to the *European Currency Unit* (ECU) which was used as a nominal medium of exchange in the EU before the introduction of Euro, businesses in the Gulf area transact using a basket of GCC currencies. In the Asian context, *Association of Southeast Asian Nations* (ASEAN) is the healthiest and most integrated regional organization in South East Asia comprising of Brunei, Cambodia, Indonesia, Laos, Malaysia, Myanmar, the Philippines, Singapore, Thailand and Vietnam. The ASEAN was established in 1967 in Bangkok with the signing of the ASEAN Declaration (*Bangkok Declaration*). It has promoted cooperation and integration for its members to help accelerate the economic growth, social progress and cultural development in the region. Recently the establishment of the *ASEAN Economic Community* (AEC) in 2015 is a major milestone in the regional economic integration agenda in ASEAN, offering opportunities in the form of a huge market of US$2.6 trillion and over 622 million people. ASEAN grouping will play a pivotal role to establish what is being termed as the Asian century.

South Asian countries were prompted to have a strong institutional framework for achieving closer integration when regionalism started to take shape around the world. Initially, Bangladesh mooted the need for a comprehensive regional framework in 1980 to attain mutual peace, progress and prosperity in the region. The proposal was endorsed by smaller countries of the region including Bhutan, Maldives, Nepal and Sri Lanka, while India and Pakistan were sceptical because of their concerns regarding security. Sensitive to India and Pakistan's concern, Bangladesh excluded all references to security matters and suggested only non-political and noncontroversial areas for cooperation in their draft proposal (Dash, 1996). *South Asian Association for Regional Cooperation* (SAARC) was finally established when the Heads of State or Government of all seven countries came together to sign SAARC charter in 1985. Afghanistan later became the eighth member in 2007. Formation of SAARC thus marked the beginning of regional cooperation and integration initiatives of the South Asian countries. As underlined in SAARC Charter, the alliance amongst the countries was formed with the objective to promote of welfare, economic prosperity, social and cultural development, collective self-reliance, collaboration and assistance amongst the member countries. Bilateral and contentious issues were prudently excluded from its purview as they were believed to be an obstruction in the way of multilateral cooperation initiatives of the region (Pattanaik, 2006). SAARC strives to collaborate on specific areas of cooperation including human resource development, tourism, agriculture and rural development, environment, economic, trade and finance, social affairs, poverty alleviation, transport, science and technology, education, security and culture.

SAARC countries have taken several initiatives in achieving closer integration among the member nations. It has provided a regional platform for policymakers to meet regularly to discuss vision and agenda for cooperation, and build consensus to deal with social, economic and developmental issues. At the outset, the identified areas of cooperation were agriculture and rural development, health and population, science and technology, transport, sports, and arts and culture. Ministerial and senior official level meetings were organized on regular intervals to identify and discuss issues, and coordinate programs and policies. However, SAARC countries could not achieve much in terms of regional cooperation as identified areas for regional cooperation were mainly social, cultural or developmental that did not have regional imperative (Pattanaik, 2006).

South Asian countries began to consider economic and trade cooperation only after they started liberalizing their economies in the wake of increased globalization. In 1992, the SAARC Chamber of Commerce and Industry was established to promote trade, service, industry and agriculture by providing a platform for entrepreneurs of the region to develop strong business linkages. Specifically, on the trade front, SAPTA (*SAARC Preferential Trading Agreement*), signed in 1993, became the stepping stone to promote mutual trade and economic cooperation by working out trade and tariff policies amongst the member countries. Product coverage and tariff liberalization were limited under SAPTA thereby providing little scope for regional trade integration. Therefore, to further strengthen the economic and trade integration and extending the scope of SAPTA, *South Asian Free Trade Area* (SAFTA) agreement was ratified in 2004 for progressively moving towards free trade area through the free movement of goods and removal of trade barriers. SAFTA, which came into force in 2006, included trade facilitation elements and switched the tariff liberalization process from a positive to a negative list approach (Rodríguez-Delgado, 2007). It also compensated for revenue losses for the least developed countries of the region in the event of tariff reductions (Baunsgaard and Keen, 2005). Trade in services and investments was ruled out from the ambit of SAFTA. Therefore, the *SAARC Agreement on Trade in Services* (SATIS) was later signed by the SAARC member countries in 2010 to liberalize trade in the service sector. SATIS is an important step towards regional economic integration of South Asia as the economies of the region are largely driven by their services sector, and hence, it provides immense scope for augmenting trade in services.

SAARC countries have also embarked on several initiatives to foster financial cooperation and integration. A regional network of SAARC Central Bank Governors and Finance Secretaries called *SAARCFINANCE* was formed in 1998 so as to foster cooperation in macroeconomic policies, synchronize banking legislation and practices; collaborate among central banks and finance ministries; share ideas, information and experiences; undertake monetary and exchange cooperation; investigate global financial developments; and promote research on economic and financial issues among the SAARC member countries. *SAARCFINANCE* provides for the involvement of financial institutions in its activities like conducting research, training and seminar thereby creating an arrangement for networking of these institutions within the region. Meetings of the coordinators that are appointed by Central Bank of each country are conducted regularly to promote cooperation among central banks and its financial and monetary policies. For promoting the development of securities markets, encouraging cross-border listings and achieving greater harmonization among the member countries, *South Asian Federation of Exchanges* (SAFE) was established in 2000. Later in 2005, a forum of securities regulatory bodies of South Asian countries called *South Asian Securities Regulators' Forum* (SASRF) was formed to further enhance the cooperation and exchange of information among the regulators of these countries. The forum provides for securities regulators' support for encouraging cross-border listing and trading in the region and other development projects of SAFE. Further, Reserve Bank of India also announced a currency swap arrangement worth US$2 billion to the SAARC nations in 2015 in both foreign and Indian currency to enhance financial integration and stability in the region.

SAARC has taken a significant initiative to meet its developmental needs. A fund mechanism, called SAARC Development Fund (SDF), was launched in 1998 to support and promote social, economic and infrastructure development projects in the region through its three windows. Social window funds projects relating to education, health, human resource development, etc., for poverty alleviation and social development. Economic window supports projects that focus on trade and industrial development, agriculture, services, and science and technology. Energy, power, transportation, telecommunications, environment, tourism and other infrastructure areas are funded by infrastructure window. SDF aims for regional growth and development by leveraging funds, providing grants and technical assistance for projects that are of strategic importance to SAARC.

Opportunities and challenges of South Asian regional integration

South Asia emerged as the fastest growing region of the world in 2015 and is expected to experience continued growth acceleration (well above 7%) over the coming years (World Bank, 2016a). With the world's largest working age population, a quarter of the world's middle-class consumers, the largest number of poor and undernourished in the world, and several fragile states of global geopolitical importance (World Bank, 2014b), the region has immense opportunities that can act as a resource to harness its enormous potential. The potential to further propel development and integration of South Asia also lies in its geography. Highest population density of South Asia across all regions and better access to markets can benefit the firms of the region to take advantage of agglomeration economies (Ghani and Ahmed, 2009: Chapter 1). Further, geographic proximity of South Asia to oil-rich Gulf, Central Asia and South-East Asia provides a strategic location to the region to further augment trade with the neighbouring regions.

South Asian regional integration suffers from formidable challenges that are economic as well as political. The intra-region trade of South Asia has remained very low over the past decades. Its share of intra-regional trade is just 5% of total trade of the region and less than 2% of its GDP, while that of ASEAN (Association of South East Asian Nations) is 25% and 20%, respectively (The Asia Foundation, 2016). There are several factors that have resulted in low trade amongst the South Asian countries. These include high tariffs for "sensitive goods" that have been excluded from tariff liberalization, complex non-tariff barriers, poor institutions (such as the lack of e-filing of trade documents), inadequate infrastructure (like lack of a modern warehouse or container handling facility or food testing laboratory at the border) and the absence of a transit trade arrangement despite of geographical congruity of the South Asian countries (De, 2011). Even the transition from preferential trade (that is, SAPTA) to free trade agreement (that is, SAFTA) has not been instrumental in boosting intra-regional trade of South Asia and realizing its full trade potential. SAFTA is not comprehensive given its scope which is limited to goods and does not include services, investment and other non-border market access issues. Further, it exempts plenty of goods from tariff liberalization that is included in the sensitive list (Sally, 2006). SAFTA also excludes cooperation in granting transit facilities and development of transport infrastructure which are essential for a free trade regime (Dubey, 2007). Rules of Origin under SAFTA are rigid, thereby restricting the formation of regional value chains (UNESCAP, 2017). In addition, South Asian countries lack well-established and well-functioning regulatory and institutional frameworks required to support trade liberalization, especially in services (Ahmed and Kumar, 2014).

Regional integration continues to be restrained because of the political differences amongst the member countries that have not permitted economic and welfare gains from regional integration to take precedence in policy matters, thereby stifling the way towards closer cooperation and integration of the region. The hurdle in achieving regional cooperation lies in the lack of commitment of the member countries to resolve their political conflicts through dialogue and develop cordial relation amongst them. Bilateral political animosity between India and Pakistan has been at the forefront of regional political dynamics of South Asia that has impinged upon the integration initiatives of the region. Amidst the escalating political disputes, rising subservient activities and cross-border terrorism in the region, 19th SAARC Summit was called off which was to be hosted in Islamabad, Pakistan, in November 2016 due to non-participation of India and other member countries (including Bangladesh, Bhutan and Afghanistan) that expressed concerns regarding peace and security in the region. This provides ample evidence that the bilateral contentious issues of the member countries that were purposely kept outside the scope of regional integration so that they do not hinder SAARC's regional initiatives are actually derailing its multilateral initiatives. Security has been a pivotal concern of the South Asian countries even prior to the inception of SAARC three decades back. The countries of the region do not have a common security concern to unite them; rather, security threats are within the region which is manifesting into mistrust and suspicion, thereby making regional cooperation an arduous task (Pattanaik, 2010).

Internal political dynamics of the South Asian economies have also hampered their growth prospects and regional integration. The economic growth of Afghanistan has remained stagnant over the past years because of political uncertainty and armed conflicts. Nepal's economy is also languishing because of political instability. Though Bangladesh has registered stable economic growth in the past few years, it also confronts the unstable political environment due to protests and strikes. Serious political and security threats in Pakistan are dampening its economic activity. Amidst the political uncertainty in the majority of the South Asian countries, regional cooperation and integration remain a daunting challenge.

The asymmetric power balance in the region has also posed challenges for closer cooperation and integration amongst the South Asian countries. High growth trajectory, relatively huge industrial base, growing population, strong political leadership and advantageous central geographic position of India in the region have made other South Asian countries circumspect of its regional hegemony. To counter this, South Asian countries have been deliberating China's membership in SAARC which can act as a potential countervailing force to mediate long-standing dominance of India and maintain a strategic balance in the region. India, on the other hand, is apprehensive of China's inclusion as it can possibly reduce its leverage in the region. The political and strategic interests of SAARC member countries, predominantly guided by political motives, are therefore conflicting. Considering the perspective of the region as a whole, China's rising economic influence in the region cannot be ignored. The argument in favour of China's inclusion in SAARC is put forth on the grounds of its increasing trade and investment linkages in the region which is surpassing India as the major trade and investment partner of majority of the South Asian countries. However, a major consideration against China's entry is that it can create power tussle in the region which may further destabilize political relations amongst the countries, thereby hampering the region's progress and integration. Given the opposing arguments with regard to China's membership, its inclusion in SAARC still remains a matter of ongoing debate.

Recent developments

The concept of Economic Regionalism which is a key to openness and growth has thus seen much resistance with the largely unexpected election of Donald Trump as President of the USA which has overturned many assumptions and expectations about the future of multilateral regional groupings. The present polity in the USA has shown resistance to globalization and signalled an increasingly nationalist, isolationist and protectionist policy, wherein there is uncertainty surrounding regional trade deals like the TPP[6] and its ongoing trade war with China. Though the underlying concerns of the USA largely remain geopolitical and geo-strategic it is sure to challenge the institutional and alliance relationship in Asia. Asia's shared commitment to "open regionalism" makes Asian regionalism an important counter-narrative and alternative model to the west anchoring around the ASEAN group. As global economic gravity shifts to the east and 21st century is believed to be *The Asian Century*, "open regionalism" should be the central pillar of this ecosystem, in which China, India and East Asian countries (Japan & Korea) should be encouraged to participate with ASEAN as bulwark to ensure economic growth and development of the region. Of particular interest is the scope and relevance of another subgrouping in Asia i.e. SAARC which is of social, economic and geopolitical importance in the region but is the least integrated region of the world primarily dwarfed by the political tensions between the two biggest members of the group i.e. India and Pakistan. The coming of the new political executive in India in 2014 was noted by media for being the first ever swearing-in of an Indian Prime Minister to have been attended by the heads of all SAARC countries. The foreign policy of the then government of the biggest economy of South Asia i.e. India was coined by media as "*Neighbourhood First*" policy. Subsequent years saw the talk of SAARC satellite and Development Bank of SAARC to further strengthen the regional cooperation. But again power-asymmetry and lack of common strategic thinking make South Asia an unusually fragile strategic environment particularly highly bellicose relationship between India and Pakistan. In this backdrop, China launched "*First China-South Asia Cooperation Forum*" (CSACF)[7] in Yunnan Province in July 2018 to bring South Asia and China together on one platform. China's CSACF initiative comes at a time when the SAARC has been going through the throes of an existential dilemma, and hence, this book sets an ambitious agenda to study the current state of economic and financial integration of the South Asian countries and further explore the underlying determinants that might drive the process of integration. Given the political economy of the member countries, it is a first comprehensive study of its kind for this region to bring forward the various dimensions of South Asian Integration and help readers appreciate its unique nature and complexity.

Concluding remarks

South Asia is a unique region encompassing small and big economies at a different stage of their economic development. The economies of the region began their regional integration initiatives three decades back with signing of an accord leading to the formation of SAARC in 1985. The objective was to have a regional framework that can help economies attain mutual progress, notwithstanding the pervading asymmetries amongst them in terms of their geography, demography and economic size. SAARC has provided a platform for policymakers to meet regularly to discuss vision and agenda for cooperation and build consensus to deal with social and economic issues. The countries of the region have also taken several initiatives to enhance regional cooperation and integration amongst them. Ratification of SAPTA, SAFTA and SATIS to promote trade in goods and services, respectively; establishment of SAARCFINANCE network to share experiences on macroeconomic policy issues; and creation of SDF as a funding mechanism to support development projects, etc., exemplify the palpable initiatives taken by the SAARC countries towards closer cooperation and integration.

The countries also made the transition in their planned approach to development by introduction of macroeconomic reforms post-1980s to adopt outward-oriented development policies which enhanced their growth prospects. With these efforts, the region has become the fastest growing region in the world. Cooperation amongst the countries, however, has been moving at a lumbering pace owing to the obstruction caused by complex tariff and non-tariff barriers. Apart from a cautious outlook towards trade liberalization, poor infrastructure and weak governance also impinge on South Asian regional integration. The functioning of SAARC is also undermined by the political dynamics of the region. Political animosity amongst the member countries has made larger regional benefits subservient. As global economic gravity shifts to the east and 21st century is believed to be *"The Asian Century"*, it is an opportune time for the political leadership of the SAARC countries to steer their way through their political stand-offs and embrace an open regionalism and institutional change which can help make South Asia an active partner in Asian economic integration and global economy.

Notes

1 Source: World Bank, Authors' Calculations.
2 Source: World Bank, Authors' Calculations.
3 Ghani and Ahmed, 2009: Chapter 1.
4 Source: World Bank.
5 Source: Human Development Index (HDI) Report, 2016.
6 The Trans-Pacific Partnership (TPP), also called the Trans-Pacific Partnership Agreement, is a defunct proposed trade agreement between Australia, Brunei, Canada, Chile, Japan, Malaysia, Mexico, New Zealand, Peru, Singapore, Vietnam and the USA signed on 4 February 2016, which was not ratified as required and did not take effect. After the USA withdrew its signature, the agreement could not enter into force. The remaining nations negotiated a new trade agreement called Comprehensive and Progressive Agreement for Trans-Pacific Partnership, which incorporates most of the provisions of the TPP and which entered into force on 30 December 2018.
7 Over 400 ministers, senior officials, delegates and media representatives from all SAARC member-states except Bhutan plus Myanmar and Vietnam from South-East Asia attended the meeting of First China-South Asia Cooperation Forum (CSACF) in Yunnan Province on 15 June 2018. India's presence and participation at the CSACF, though, was at the Consul-General level for this forum.

2

ECONOMIC AND FINANCIAL INTEGRATION IN THE SOUTH ASIAN REGION

A survey

Sanjay Sehgal, Sakshi Saini and Piyush Pandey

Introduction

South Asia, a diverse region of heterogeneous countries, began regional cooperation initiatives three decades back with signing of an accord leading to the formation of South Asian Association for Regional Cooperation (SAARC) with a firm belief that a comprehensive regional framework would help the countries to attain mutual progress, notwithstanding the pervading asymmetries among them in terms of their geography, demography and economic size. Cooperation amongst the countries, however, has been moving at a lumbering pace owing to the obstruction caused by complex trade barriers, poor infrastructure and weak institutions. Enduring political conflicts between the two major countries – India and Pakistan – further punctuates the cooperation amongst the SAARC countries. Amidst the vast economic gaps and long-standing political disharmony, the progress of SAARC in achieving regional integration has been modest so far. The regional bloc started to gain momentum as the countries gradually removed their high trade barriers and capital controls with changing global economic landscape. Ratification of South Asia Preferential Trade Agreement (SAPTA), South Asian Free Trade Area (SAFTA) and SAARC Agreement on Trade in Services (SATIS) to promote trade in goods and services, respectively; establishment of SAARCFINANCE network to share experiences on macroeconomic policy issues; and creation of SAARC Development Fund (SDF) as a funding mechanism to support development projects, etc., exemplify the palpable initiatives taken by the SAARC countries to achieve closer cooperation and integration. It has also provided a platform for policymakers to meet regularly to discuss vision and agenda for cooperation and build consensus to deal with social, economic and political issues. However, SAARC countries need to address the formidable challenges that impede their way in realization of integration and the subsequent gains arising from it in forms of high production efficiency, decreased costs and enhanced investment opportunities. Solidarity among the SAARC countries is foremost in making regional integration a positive sum game, and India being at the strong position in the SAARC region needs to spearhead the cooperation. Against this backdrop, it becomes especially important to study the present level of India's integration with each of the SAARC country and the major drivers so that they can be emphasized for strengthening regional integration.

While empirical research has been undertaken on analysing economic and financial integration, the literature on the views of opinion leaders regarding integration in the South Asian region is virtually missing. In this chapter, we follow survey-based approach to examine economic and financial integration (including capital and currency markets as well as the banking system), and explore the fundamental factors that drive integration. We solicit perceptions of opinion leaders like market players, policymakers and subject experts on the extent of integration and factors driving the process of integration among the SAARC countries. We believe that empirical results alone are not sufficient in providing decisive inputs for forming an integrated development strategy for a region, views of the opinion leaders are as critical in cohesive policy formulations. The survey-based approach along with the empirical analysis undertaken in subsequent chapters will be helpful to provide a broad framework in providing useful insights in forging greater regional integration among the South Asian countries.

Survey methodology

Questionnaire design

We prepare two sets of well-structured questionnaire – one specifically for the opinion leaders of India and another for rest of the SAARC countries. Both questionnaires comprise five sections: (1) economic and trade integration, (2) capital (stock and bond) market integration, (3) currency market integration, (4) banking system integration and (5) policy suggestions. Sections 1 and 5 of the questionnaire, i.e. the section on economic and trade integration and policy suggestions, are expected to be filled by all participants, while the other three sections relating to financial integration are intended for the participants who have an exposure to the particular segment of the financial system. Sections 1–4 include one general item measuring the views of opinion leaders about the present level of integration (with respect to every SAARC country in India-specific questionnaire, and with respect to India in the SAARC-specific questionnaire) on a five-point Likert scale (ranging from 1 "not integrated" to 5 "very integrated"). Further, we include an item listing a set of plausible factors strengthening the process of integration under their respective section on integration, compiled from academic and empirical literature and experts' suggestions. The perceived importance of each factor, common in both the questionnaires, is again measured on a five-point Likert scale (ranging from 1 "not important" to 5 "very important"). We also ask one open-ended question under each section to identify additional factors that may impact integration in detail. In Section 5, we list certain policy suggestions to seek respondents' view regarding their importance in strengthening integration amongst the SAARC countries. These policy suggestions have been compiled from theoretical and empirical literature and vetted from subject matter experts. Finally, we ask an open-ended question to seek any other comment or suggestion to enhance integration in the region. While drafting the questionnaire, special emphasis is given to provide simple instructions, formulate questions that are easily comprehensible and avoid any misleading, ambiguous or superfluous interpretations, and also the length of questionnaire to increase the response rate. Also, we pre-test the questionnaire on three potential participants of the survey prior to administering it and solicit suggestions from them. Pre-testing a questionnaire is usually done to better understand the strengths and weakness of the questionnaire so as to achieve better results. Based upon the feedback received from the experts, we include other possible factors that can strengthen financial integration in the region and remove any inconsistency and/or interpretability of questionnaire. Many redundant questions as identified in pre-testing were removed/ modified.

Data collection

We conduct an online questionnaire survey amongst the opinion leaders of the South Asian countries to gauge their views on the extent of economic and financial integration among the SAARC countries and the determinants driving the process. Because of the lack of availability of a standardized comprehensive database of market representatives, policymakers and subject experts required for the present study, we prepare a list of economic, financial and educational institutions for each SAARC country. Potential participants having affiliation of such institutions are then identified, and questionnaire is mailed to them on the email ids available on the website of their respective institutions.

Apparently, the major drawback of a mailed questionnaire survey is that responses depend upon the willingness of participants to volunteer for the survey, leading to low response rate. Therefore, to enhance the credibility of the survey and its response rate, we mail the questionnaire to 380 potential participants along with a cover letter highlighting the study for which the survey is conducted and its objectives. Confidentiality and acknowledgement of their responses is also assured in the cover letter. To further increase the response rate for the survey, we send four reminders after specific intervals to the non-respondents. The questionnaire received a total of 29 responses thereby achieving a response rate of 7.6%. Majority of the responses are received from India followed by Pakistan, while no response is received from Afghanistan. Since all the respondents do not necessarily belong to capital or currency market or the banking system, the number of responses we receive under these sections is lower than the total number of responses. The number of responses we have received may not be encouraging, but our study though not that exhaustive due to small sample size provides foundational analysis of the views of opinion leaders of the South Asian region that is imperative in understanding the state of regional integration and possible factors that can be emphasized to strengthen it.

Data consistency

To increase the accuracy of evaluating a survey it is pertinent to check reliability of its measures i.e. the extent to which they are free from error and yield consistent results (Peter, 1979). We conduct reliability analysis to test the internal consistency of the data obtained from the primary survey using Coefficient Alpha (Cronbach, 1951), which is the most widely used technique to gauge reliability. High internal consistency is indicated by high score of the coefficient. The value of the coefficient lies between 0 and 1, and generally 0.7 is deemed as an acceptable reliability coefficient (Nunnally, 1978). Reliability analysis is conducted on the data we obtain from the set of economic and trade integration, capital market integration, banking system integration and currency market integration factors that seek respondent's view on the importance of each factor on a five-point likert style ranking. We find Cronbach's Alpha coefficient for each set of factors (economic and trade integration, capital market integration, banking system integration and currency market integration) to be much higher than 0.7, indicating high level of internal consistency amongst them.

Methodology

Analysis of the survey responses to examine the present level of economic and financial integration in the SAARC region and the factors determining it is predominantly carried out through descriptive statistics and frequency charts. Statistical test is employed to assess differences in the perceived importance of the factors determining integration across the SAARC countries. Analysis of Variance (ANOVA) is a well-known parametric test to examine the difference between the means of two and more unrelated groups in a data set, but requires data to be drawn from a normally distributed population and variance across the groups to be equal. Therefore, we first examine the assumptions of normality and homogeneity of variance using Shapiro-Wilk and Levene's test, respectively. If these assumptions are satisfied, ANOVA can be employed to investigate any differences in the views of opinion leaders across countries regarding the importance of factors strengthening integration. Shapiro-Wilk test demonstrates that all economic and financial integration factors are not normally distributed. Therefore, we shall use Kruskal-Wallis one-way ANOVA by ranks test (Kruskal and Wallis, 1952), a non-parametric alternative to ANOVA that does not require assumption of normality and is also not affected by the violation of homogeneity of variance assumption.

Present level of economic and financial integration in South Asia

Being the largest economy of South Asia in terms of geography, demography and economic size, India has the most profound role to play in accomplishing its vision and agenda of well-integrated economic and financial system. In this light, we conduct a primary survey to examine the present level of economic integration and financial integration in capital and currency markets and the banking system of each South Asian country with respect to India. Present level of economic integration of India with respect to each SAARC country as opined by the respondents is presented in Figure 2.1.

The level of integration of Afghanistan and Pakistan with India is perceived to be quite low as majority of the respondents feel that the countries are either less integrated or not integrated. About half of the respondents have moderate opinion about the level of integration between Maldives and India, but barring those respondents majority of the remaining believe integration of Maldives with India is low. Further, half of the respondents feel Bangladesh and Sri Lanka are economically integrated with India. India's integration has been regarded

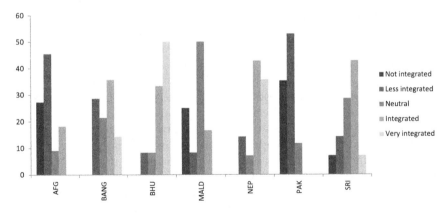

Figure 2.1 Present Level of Economic and Trade Integration of SAARC Countries with India.

Source: Authors' Conducted Survey Calculations.

Note: AFG, BANG, BHU, MALD, NEP, PAK and SRI denote Afghanistan, Bangladesh, Bhutan, Maldives, Nepal, Pakistan and Sri Lanka, respectively.

to be the highest with Bhutan and Nepal by majority of the respondents. Trade intensity[1] of SAARC countries vis-à-vis India corroborates the perception of opinion leaders regarding the level of economic and trade integration.

As illustrated in Figure 2.2, Bhutan and Nepal have strong trade intensity with respect to India which is on an average 72% and 57%, respectively, since the operationalization of SAFTA in 2004. Thus, these two countries are perceived to be highly economically integrated with India by majority of the respondents. Being landlocked countries, both trade primarily with India so much so that it is their largest export and import partner. Trade intensity of Afghanistan and Pakistan with India is low (on an average 6.3% and 2.9%, respectively) as compared to rest of the SAARC countries (refer Figure 2.2), explaining their low level of perceived integration with India. Political disharmony between Pakistan and India not just stifles trade between the two countries, but also hampers trade between Afghanistan and India that relies on land transit via Pakistan for market access.[2]

Capital markets in the SAARC region have made very considerable progress during the last 20 years. India is the only member country having functioning capital markets with structures and regulations based on international best practices. As depicted in Figure 2.3, level of integration of capital markets of India with respect to majorly all member countries is viewed to be extremely low. Strict capital controls, absence of information and standards for market development, low levels of markets awareness,

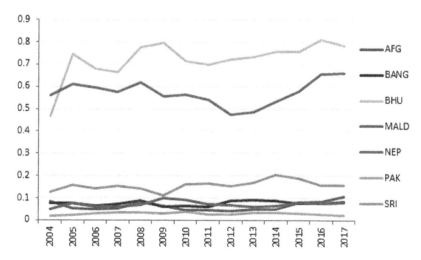

Figure 2.2 Trade Intensity of SAARC Countries with India.
Source: UNCTAD, Authors' Calculations.

Notes: (a) Trade Intensity of country *i* with India is calculated as total trade of country *i* with India divided by total trade of country *i* with the world. (b) AFG, BANG, BHU, MALD, NEP, PAK and SRI denote Afghanistan, Bangladesh, Bhutan, Maldives, Nepal, Pakistan and Sri Lanka, respectively.

lack of regulatory and enforcement capacity in the capital markets of the South Asian countries substantiate the uniform perception of almost negligible capital market integration amongst the opinion leaders.

As regards currency market integration, majority of the respondents view India's integration to be absent with respect to Afghanistan, Maldives and Pakistan, and low with respect to Bangladesh and Sri Lanka (refer Figure 2.4). On the other hand, Bhutan and Nepal are perceived to be integrated by majority of the respondents. Findings are roughly similar for banking system integration (refer Figure 2.5).

Perceived integration of the currency markets of Bhutan and Nepal with India can be attributed to the pegged exchange rate regime of the countries against Indian Rupee. Possible linkages amongst the banking system of Bhutan and Nepal with India can be ascribed to the cross-border arrangements of Indian public sector banks with the banks of the two countries. State Bank of India has 55% ownership in Nepal State Bank of India, which is the first Indo-Nepal joint venture in the banking system of Nepal. Another major public sector bank of India – Punjab National Bank (PNB) also has a joint venture with Everest Bank, Nepal (20% shareholding), and Druk PNB Bank, Bhutan (51% shareholding). Overall, the perceived level of economic and financial integration of Afghanistan with respect to India lags behind rest of the SAARC countries, while India's economic and financial integration with Nepal and Bhutan is perceived to be the highest among all SAARC countries.

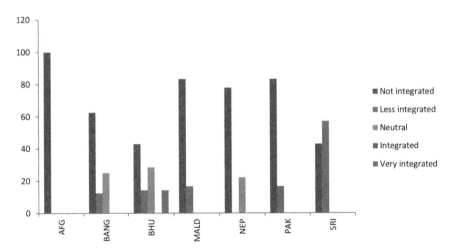

Figure 2.3 Present Level of Capital Market Integration of SAARC Countries with India.

Source: Authors' Conducted Survey Calculations.

Note: AFG, BANG, BHU, MALD, NEP, PAK and SRI denote Afghanistan, Bangladesh, Bhutan, Maldives, Nepal, Pakistan and Sri Lanka, respectively.

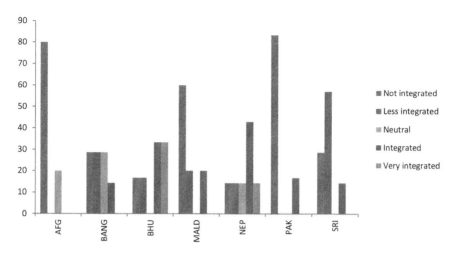

Figure 2.4 Present Level of Currency Market Integration of SAARC Countries with India.

Source: Authors' Conducted Survey Calculations.

Note: AFG, BANG, BHU, MALD, NEP, PAK and SRI denote Afghanistan, Bangladesh, Bhutan, Maldives, Nepal, Pakistan and Sri Lanka, respectively.

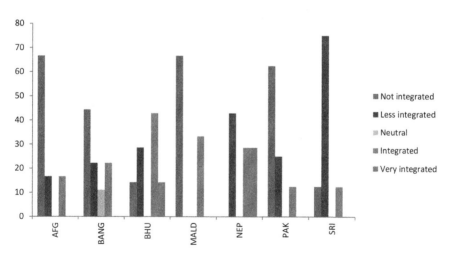

Figure 2.5 Present Level of Banking System Integration of SAARC Countries with India.

Source: Authors' Conducted Survey Calculations.

Note: AFG, BANG, BHU, MALD, NEP, PAK and SRI denote Afghanistan, Bangladesh, Bhutan, Maldives, Nepal, Pakistan and Sri Lanka, respectively.

Fundamental determinants strengthening economic and financial integration

We investigate fundamental determinants of economic and financial integration in the South Asian region by taking into account plausible variables influencing integration that have been discerned in the prior studies. Academic literature has widely recognized economic integration not just as a concept, but a process encompassing five sequential steps to complete integration as outlined by Balassa (1961). The five stages constitute (a) free trade area, (b) customs union, (c) common market, (d) economic union and (e) monetary union, with the degree of integration intensifying at every stage. Enhanced trade network among the countries along with focus on removal of barriers to trade is therefore the foremost step of integrating economies. Increased trade intensity among the countries also leads to business cycle co-movements across them (Frankel and Rose, 1998) and thereby catalyzing economic integration among them. As noted by Balassa (1961), the benefits from integration become even more substantial for developing countries which may experience higher growth rates as compared to the developed ones. Further, convergence in macroeconomic policies (viz. fiscal and monetary) implies reduced economic fluctuations in the countries and is expected to spur integration among them by contributing to subsequent establishment of economic and monetary union. Legal and social institutions as understood by governance structure of a country also play an important role in promoting heightened economic cooperation and integration (Owen, 2013).

Several market-related variables as the potential drivers of financial integration have been used in the literature. Financial market integration implies increase in the capital flows and greater tendency for prices and returns on traded financial assets in different countries to converge (De Brouwer, 1999). Therefore, internationalization of financial markets (i.e. flow of assets from one market to another) and synchronization of prices, returns and interest rates are expected to promote integration in the capital markets. A developed and well-performing capital market induces integration among the countries by attracting foreign investors and increasing portfolio investment flows (Vo and Daly, 2007). Additionally, reduction in the domestic transaction costs facilitates cross-border asset trade, leading to financial integration (Lane and Milesi-Ferretti, 2003). Financial integration is also fostered by a well-developed and resilient banking system. Performance of banks is closely associated with capital adequacy, and credit risk (as measured by level of non-performing loans) is therefore expected to impact integration in the banking system. In currency segment of the financial market, size of foreign exchange reserves and financial exposure of the countries play an important role in driving exchange rate movements across countries (Fratzscher, 2009). Differences in corporate governance and institutional structures and tax and accounting framework may impede the integration of financial market. Therefore, harmonization of tax policies, regulations and governance structures diminishes these differences by lowering information costs thereby promoting financial market integration (Buch and Heinrich, 2002).

A comprehensive list of factors strengthening economic integration and integration in capital, banking and currency segment of financial market identified after an extensive review of literature is presented in Table 2.1.

Collective responses of the opinion leaders reveal that high trade openness (measured as Total Trade as a percentage of GDP) and trade linkages (proportion of country's trade with India in its total trade with the world) between the countries are unanimously considered to play vital role in expediting the process of economic and trade integration (refer Figure 2.6). Quality of governance,[3] high economic growth and development (measured by GDP growth rate and per capita Real GDP) and business cycle synchronization are other major factors considered to be important in expediting economic integration in comparison to other factors.

To examine the perceptual differences amongst the opinion leaders of the region, we first ascertain the appropriateness of the statistical test to be employed by investigating the assumptions of ANOVA test. We conduct Levene's test to examine homogeneity of variances across the groups and Shapiro-Wilk test to check for normality. Results reveal heterogeneity of variances and non-normality of the data; hence, we employ Kruskal-Wallis one-way ANOVA by ranks test to test whether the perception regarding fundamental determinants driving integration differs across the sample countries. The sample countries considered for Kruskal-Wallis test analysis are Bangladesh, India, Nepal, Pakistan and Sri Lanka. Responses from rest of the countries and SAARC secretariat are grouped together under "others" category.

Kruskal-Wallis test statistics[4] indicate that there is uniformity in the perception of opinion leaders across all the SAARC countries regarding the importance of trade openness (χ^2 (5) = 4.236, p = 0.52) and trade linkages (χ^2 (5) = 5.632, p = 0.34) as the factors strengthening economic integration. Trade among the countries is foremost in attaining closer cooperation and integration in a region. Despite foreign policy reforms introduced by the SAARC countries to facilitate intra-regional trade through dismantling of tariff and non-tariff barriers, regional trade of SAARC remains abysmally low in comparison to other regional trade blocks.

As indicated by Figure 2.7, the regional trade intensity (total trade amongst the member countries/total trade of member countries with the world) is lowest for SAARC region (hovering around 0.05%) compared to other regional economic blocs. Therefore, opinion leaders have recognized the need to augment trade and reduce the barriers so as to provide impetus to economic integration in the region. Kruskal-Wallis test statistic for quality of governance (χ^2 (5) = 10.041, p = 0.07) indicates that its perception differs across countries, with the lowest mean rank assigned by opinion

Table 2.1 Determinants of Economic and Financial Integration

Category	Determinants of Integration	Reference Studies
Economic and trade	High economic growth and development (measured as GDP growth rate and per capita GDP)	Vo and Daly (2007); Guesmi et al. (2013); Ng et al. (2013)
	Business cycle synchronization and level of industrial growth	Buttner and Hayo (2011); Guesmi et al. (2013)
	Favourable external position	Guesmi et al. (2013)
	Convergence in inflation rate	Vo and Daly (2007); Huoy and Goh (2007)
	Convergence in short-term interest rates	Huoy and Goh (2007); Guesmi et al. (2013)
	Fiscal position (based upon Budget Balance)	Arfaoui and Abaoub (2010)
	Trade openness (total trade as % of GDP, trade flows, trade tariff)	Vo and Daly (2007); Guesmi et al. (2013)
	Trade linkages (total trade between the two countries)	Frankel and Rose (1998); Vo and Daly (2007); Guesmi et al. (2013); Huoy and Goh (2007)
	Quality of governance (institutional, legal and regulatory environment)	Owen (2013); Vo and Daly (2007); Ng et al. (2013)
	Low foreign exchange volatility	Huoy and Goh (2007); Guesmi et al. (2013)
	Level of economic liquidity (broad money supply to total reserves)	Brunnermeier et al. 2008
Capital market	Capital market development (existence of market infrastructure institutions)	Vo and Daly (2007); Büttner and Hayo (2011); Ng et al. (2013)
	Synchronization of capital market regulation and trading practices	Ng et al. (2013)
	Synchronization of stock returns and market cycles	Abad and Chulia (2014)
	Synchronization of interest rates	Balli et al. (2013)
	Capital market liquidity	Kim et al. (2005); Wang and Moore (2008); Balli et al. (2013)
	Capital market growth performance (price earnings ratio and dividend yield)	Bekaert et al. (2005); Huoy and Goh (2007); Guesmi et al. (2013)
	Capital market volatility (volatility of market return)	Abad and Chulia (2014); Huoy and Goh (2007)
	Level of market internationalization	Delphi Technique
	Costs of trading	Lane and Milesi-Ferretti (2003)
	Accounting and tax policies (tax on portfolio income and repatriation laws)	Lee et al. (2011)
	Corporate governance and disclosure policies	Ng et al. (2013)

Category	Determinants of Integration	Reference Studies
Currency market	Acceptance of reciprocal currencies as legal tender	Delphi Technique
	Size of the financial sector	Delphi Technique
	Foreign exchange reserves	Fratzscher (2009)
	Quality of governance	Buch and Heinrich (2002)
	Regional cooperation arrangement	Delphi Technique
	Capital account convertibility	Delphi Technique
	Regional arrangements to control black money and money laundering	Delphi Technique
Banking system	Banking sector development (deposit to GDP, credit to GDP)	Lane and Milesi-Ferretti (2008)
	Banking sector credit risk (level of NPA)	Delphi Technique
	Convergence in deposit rates for household	Delphi Technique
	Convergence in deposit rates for non-banking financial corporations	Delphi Technique
	Capital adequacy ratio	Delphi Technique
	Private credit extended by banks to GDP ratio (%)	Delphi Technique
	Synchronization of banking regulations and practices	Delphi Technique
	Corporate governance and disclosure policies	Ng et al. (2013)

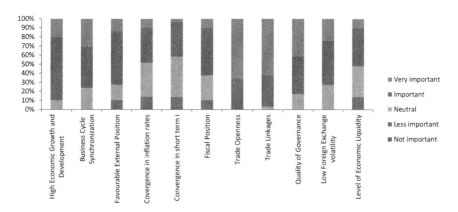

Figure 2.6 Factors Strengthening Economic and Trade Integration amongst SAARC Countries.

Source: Authors' Conducted Survey Calculations.

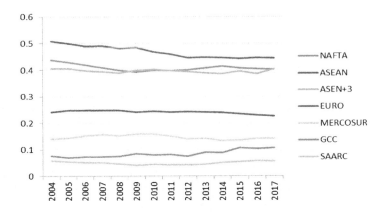

Figure 2.7 Regional Trade Intensity of Major Regional Blocs.
Source: UNCTAD, Authors' Calculations.

Notes: (a) Trade Intensity of a regional bloc *i* is calculated as total trade within the regional bloc *i* divided by total trade of regional bloc *i* with the world. (b) ASEAN is Association of South East Asian Nations. ASEAN+3 bloc is ASEAN member bloc plus China, Japan and South Korea. EURO represents the Eurozone. MERCOSUR is trading bloc in Latin America, and NAFTA is trading bloc in North America. GCC is Gulf Cooperation Council which is regional intergovernmental political and economic union consisting of Arab states of Persian Gulf except Iraq.

leaders of Pakistan, while high growth and development and convergence in the business cycles are uniformly perceived to be important by the respondents across countries.

As regards capital market integration, market institutional development, synchronization of capital market regulation and trading practices, and accounting and tax policies are considered to be very important by majority of the respondents (refer Figure 2.8). Capital markets of the SAARC countries, except India, are still underdeveloped, and there are significant divergences in their regulations and taxation policies. As opined by the respondents, development of capital markets, alignment of regulatory structure and simplification of accounting and tax policies are crucial to trigger capital market integration in the SAARC region. There is significant disparity in the perception of opinion leaders across countries regarding capital market development as a driver of integration, as reflected by the Kruskal-Wallis test statistic (χ^2 (5) = 11.781, p = 0.04). Particularly, the leaders of India and Sri Lanka ascribe high rank to capital market development as a driver of capital market integration.

In case of currency markets, predominantly all factors are perceived to be important in strengthening integration as depicted in Figure 2.9. Regional cooperation arrangement is considered to be very important in strengthening linkages among the currency markets by majority of the respondents,

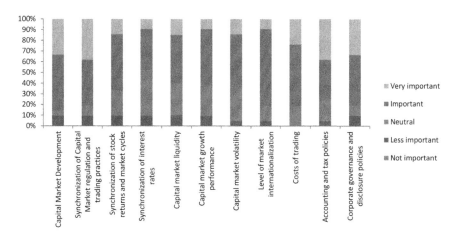

Figure 2.8 Factors Strengthening Capital Market Integration amongst SAARC Countries.

Source: Authors' Conducted Survey Calculations.

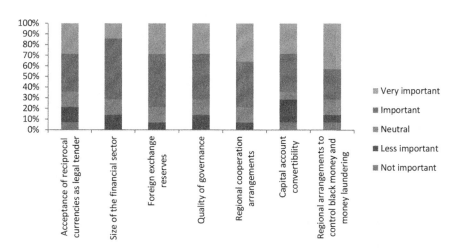

Figure 2.9 Factors Strengthening Currency Market Integration amongst SAARC Countries.

Source: Authors' Conducted Survey Calculations.

followed by level of foreign exchange reserves (refer Figure 2.9). Cooperation agreements among the countries are essential to propel integration among the countries. However, SAARC countries have not been able to do much on this front to enhance currency linkages among themselves. The

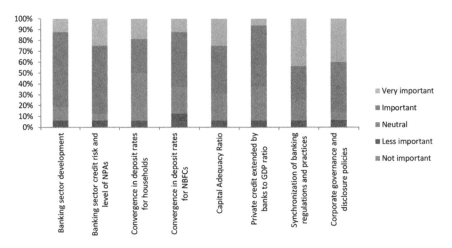

Figure 2.10 Factors Strengthening Banking System Integration amongst SAARC Countries.
Source: Authors' Conducted Survey Calculations.

only notable initiative till date has been the currency swap arrangement offered by India to provide short-term foreign exchange liquidity requirements of Member States.

Figure 2.10 illustrates perceived importance of banking market integration factors. Apparently, banking sector development, credit risk and level of Non-Performing Assets (NPA), and corporate governance and disclosure policies have been opined to be important in strengthening banking system integration. Kruskal-Wallis test results reveal uniformity in the perceived importance of these factors across countries. The perception of the opinion leaders is uniform in spite of the fact that the banking system of the region is characterized by wide variation in the level of development (as measured by bank credit and liquid liabilities relative to GDP) across the member countries (see Arora and Ratnasiri, 2014).

Summary and policy suggestions

In this chapter, we examine the perceived level of economic and financial integration, and explore the fundamental factors that drive integration amongst the SAARC countries by adopting a survey-based approach. We solicit perceptions of market participants, policymakers and subject experts on the extent of economic, trade and financial integration (involving capital, banking and currency segments) and factors driving the process of integration amongst the SAARC countries through a mailed question-naire. We believe that empirical results alone are not sufficient in providing decisive inputs for forming an integrated development strategy for a region, views of the opinion leaders are as critical in cohesive policy formulations. Survey findings reveal that the perceived level of economic and financial integration of India with the exception of Nepal and Bhutan lags behind rest of the SAARC countries. Results from the survey-based approach to explore fundamental factors which drive integration found high trade openness and trade linkages amongst the countries to play vital role in expediting the process of economic and trade integration for majority of South Asian countries. As regards capital market integration, market institutional development, synchronization of capital market regulation and trading practices, and accounting and tax policies are considered to be very important by majority of the respondents. In case of currency market, regional cooperation arrangements are considered to be very important in strengthening linkages amongst the currency markets. Banking sector development, credit risk and level of NPA, and corporate governance and disclosure policies have been opined to be important in strengthening banking system integration.

Given the low level of economic and financial integration in the region, it is pertinent that the countries work with unanimity to intensify regional cooperation and integration. Enhancing trade policy cooperation is considered to be very important by opinion leaders in facilitating trade and thereby triggering trade integration among them. SAARC region performs poorly in comparison with other regional blocks on trade parameters owing to the low level of bilateral trade among the countries in the region. Bilateral trade between India and Pakistan is the lowest among all SAARC countries owing to the political acrimony and conflicts, therefore the countries need to resolve mutual animosity to pave way for better economic relations. Further, harmonizing macroeconomic policies is required to mitigate the effect of external shocks that can potentially harm economic growth and stability of the region. Opinion leaders have also indicated the importance of cultural cooperation among the South Asian countries. Limited people to people interaction has withheld SAARC's enormous potential for cultural exchange and cooperation albeit shared history, culture and civilization of its member nations. Therefore, it is imperative to increase people to people contact through easing visa restrictions, building platforms for knowledge exchange, promoting tourism, bilateral currency convertibility, etc., so as to strengthen cultural affinities among them. SAARC countries further need to expedite their financial sector openness and enhance its awareness and further development to create structures and systems for functional financial markets.

Notes

1 Trade intensity of each SAARC country vis-à-vis India is computed by dividing country's trade with India by that of the world.
2 Recently, India has signed Chabahar port land transit agreement with Afghanistan and Iran that will provide trade links between India and Afghanistan thereby fostering trade between the two.
3 World Governance Indicators (WGI) defines quality of governance on the basis of six dimensions: Voice and Accountability, Political Stability and Absence of Violence, Government Effectiveness, Regulatory Quality, Rule of Law and Control of Corruption.
4 Results of Kruskal-Wallis test are not presented due to brevity of space, but are available on request.

3

ON THE DETERMINANTS OF ECONOMIC INTEGRATION IN SAARC COUNTRIES

A macroeconomic perspective

Wasim Ahmad, Sanjay Sehgal and Rishman Jot Kaur Chahal

Introduction

This chapter provides a detailed account of the major determinants of economic integration for SAARC countries. The primary purpose is to find whether there is a possibility of economic cooperation among SAARC nations and to what extent economic, monetary, fiscal and trade factors explain the economic integration process of these countries. In South Asia, SAARC as an economic bloc occupies a central place from regional development and trade expansion perspectives. It is a regional group which consists of eight sovereign nations. Most member nations share common cultural, economic and historical backgrounds. It is also a home of 1/5 of the global population with a total contribution of around 6% in the global economic output (Central Bank of Sri Lanka (CBS), 2008). But SAARC remains a low-priority region for international trade and investment because of the high cross-border conflicts, economic disputes and huge trust deficit between member nations. Among the SAARC members, India is the most significant partner because of its size of the economy and geographical area followed by Pakistan and Bangladesh.

In the last two decades, South Asia has emerged as one of the essential drivers of Asian growth and development. As a result, the importance of SAARC has also increased. To foster the process of economic integration and even to break the shackles of the perpetuation of underdevelopment, SAARC countries have undertaken some policy initiatives including the South Asian Preferential Trade Agreement (SAPTA) implemented in April 1995, SAARCFINANCE implemented in 1998 and South Asia Free Trade Agreement (SAFTA) implemented in July 2006. But despite these policy measures, the region has still not been able to seek the attention of the global community as other regional or economic interest groups such as G7, ASEAN (Association of South East Asian Nations), BRICS (Brazil,

33

Russia, India, China and South Africa) and IBSA (India, Brazil and South Africa). More importantly, at the time when emerging economies are gaining a great deal of attention of policymakers and global investors, it is vital that the significant attributes of South Asian region must be examined in the light of recent global economic order.

In the last two decades, the South Asian countries have experienced a moderately increased level of economic integration within the SAARC and between SAARC and the world economy. The liberalization measures undertaken during the 1990s have yielded dividend on business cycle synchronization (BCS). In the global economic set-up, South Asian economies are conventionally believed to be less economically integrated because of their conventional economic orientation. SAARC in this regard is no exception as its members' countries exhibit weak economic interdependence owing to their social and economic differences. One of the reasons could be because of the adverse terms of trade with members nations which our analysis may also reveal. However, the trade linkages with China, Japan and the USA have increased over the years, and this is also one of the research objectives of this chapter.

In this chapter, we examine the primary determinants of the economic integration of five SAARC countries, viz., Bangladesh, India, Nepal, Pakistan and Sri Lanka. To analyse and assess the impact of economic factors on economic integration, we select the variables based on their relevance in the South Asian economic set-up. For example, we do not consider exchange rate because of their limited role in the regional financial transactions. We also include the USA as a controlling factor in our analysis and to confirm whether there was any exogenous impact of global financial crisis (2008–2009) on economic integration of SAARC countries. Specifically, the analysis in this chapter adds a new dimension to the literature by answering the following questions: What are the possible determinants of the economic integration of SAARC countries and between SAARC and other major regional trading partners? How firmly the macro and financial factors explain the linkages between financial flows and the interdependence of their business cycles? Is there any decoupling effect of these determinants on economic integration? How strongly does the heightened economic uncertainty arising in China and the USA impact the strength of economic integration of SAARC nations?

In South Asian context, these questions are pertinent especially in an era of growing regionalism across Asian countries as it is believed that economic integration through bilateral trade and regional cooperation may help to achieve high growth and development in the SAARC region. Strengthening of economic relations through different channels (monetary and fiscal policies interdependence, financial liberalization, trade agreements and external interdependence) across the South Asian region raises the possibility of spillover effects from one country to another. For the survival of SAARC as a relevant regional block, the high macroeconomic interdependence across member nations seems a pre-requisite (see Khan and Khan, 2003). Our analysis in this respect may help understand the possibilities for macroeconomic cooperation.

Related literature

In the literature, studies have examined three channels that determine the determinants of the economic integration of developed, developing and even less developed economies.[1] The first channel is the economic or policy channel. In this regard, the cross-country growth spillovers often determine the bilateral business cycle interdependence. For example, Clark and Wincoop (2001) use the Hedorick and Prescott (HP)-filtered Gross Domestic Product (GDP) series and calculate the bivariate correlation between host and partner countries. Their study reports that the policy overlapping does not affect the extent of business cycle interdependence. Second is about trade channel which determines the regional economic integration through bidirectional trade of goods and services. This channel is also one of the conventional channels through which economies impact each other. The notable studies in this direction are Frankel and Rose (1998), Clark and Wincoop (2001), Imbs (2004, 2006, 2010), Baxter and Kouparitsas (2004), Inklaar et al. (2008) and Cerqueira and Martins (2009). The study of Imbs (2004, 2006) suggests that the countries with similar levels of industrial development are more synchronous than the countries with heterogeneous industrial structures and specializations though it was later contested by the Baxter and Kouparitsas (2004) and Clark and Wincoop (2001).

The third channel is the financial channel that deals with the international flow of financial capital, cross-border credit transfers and equity and bond market movements. Influential studies in this line of research are Imbs (2006), Kose et al. (2012) and Kalemli-Ozcan et al. (2003, 2013). Using effortless econometric techniques of Ordinary Least Squares and Instrumental Variable (IV) regression, Kalemli-Ozcan et al. (2003) find that the countries with a higher degree of financial integration have better production specializations and limited BCS. The findings of this study were further contrasted by Imbs (2004). The study finds that the extent of financial integration has a stronger effect on the business cycle interdependence between two nations. In the case of developing economies, Kose et al. (2003) report that the financially open economies have synchronized cycles with the G7 countries. Studies have examined the positive spillover effects of foreign direct investment (FDI) in the economic integration via BCS in the light of production specialization (see Jansen and Stockman, 2004; Buch and Lipponer, 2005; García-Herrero and Ruiz, 2008; Hsu et al. 2011).

Concerning Asia, Crosby (2003) reports the limited impact of trade and macroeconomic determinants on the business cycle co-movements of

Asia-Pacific region. Rana (2007) further contradicts this study and indicates the positive effect of trade on the economic integration of East Asia post-AFTA (ASEAN Free Trade Area). In a similar line, Moneta and Rüffer (2009) find that the trade, oil price and exchange rate indeed determine the economic integration of East Asia. He and Liao (2012) stress on the influential role of the vertical trade integration on the business cycle correlation of emerging Asian countries. Their study reports that the supply-side factors contribute more than the demand-side factors in explaining the business cycle movements. Imbs (2011) examine the trade intensity and financial openness on the BCS of East Asia. The study finds that these two factors indeed play a significant role in the business cycle comovement. Kim and Kim (2013) find that capital flows are positively correlated within Asia-Pacific region and explain the determinants of BCS. Sethapramote (2015) examines the role of economic policy linkages in case of ASEAN countries. Using the quarterly data on six ASEAN nations with three macroeconomic (growth of real GDP, the consumer price index and nominal exports) and three policy variables (exchange rate policy, fiscal policy and monetary policy), the study finds that exports and monetary policy variable significantly explain the business cycle movements, whereas the impact of financial integration remains insignificant. Dai (2014) examines the possible determinants underlying the synchronization of business cycles between Asia and China, Japan and the USA. Using a large number of economic and financial variables, the study finds that the trade, financial, monetary and fiscal variables significantly explain the business cycle correlation between the sample countries.

However, although there are a sufficient number of studies in case of East Asia and Asia-Pacific region, the research on economic integration in case of South Asia is scanty and warrants immediate attention owing to its rising influence on the global economic set-up. In the case of South Asia, Saxena (2005) examines the issue of possible transformation of SAARC as a common currency area. Taking the case of India, Pakistan and Sri Lanka, using structural vector autoregression approach, this study reports that the limited impacts and high adjustments in demand and supply shocks can provide an ideal scenario for common currency area in SAARC. However, to the best of our knowledge, the examination of possible determinants of BCS of SAARC nations along with their regional partners such as China and India has not been investigated. This chapter is an attempt to fill this void.

Data description and econometric approach

We use quarterly data for this analysis. The sample covers five SAARC countries, viz., Bangladesh, India, Nepal, Pakistan and Sri Lanka. The dataset covers the period from 1991:Q1 to 2015:Q4.[2] We also include China in our analysis because of its rising influence in the SAARC region and even as a control variable in the regression estimation.

The econometric scheme of this chapter follows the three-step procedure. In the first step, we calculate the output gap using HP filter of sample countries (see Frankel and Rose, 1998; Clark and Wincoop, 2001).[3] To calculate the output gap, we use the real GDP data retrieved from the World Bank database. In the second step, we apply Dynamic Conditional Correlation (DCC) approach of Engle (2002) on the output gap of five countries and China. We apply this method to obtain the bilateral time-varying conditional correlations. The time-varying conditional correlations are used by several studies to measure the economic and financial integration across different economic indicators and asset classes (see Sethapramote, 2015; Perego and Vermeulen, 2016; Lukmanova and Tondl, 2017, among others). In the third step, after retrieving the conditional correlations from DCC estimates, we specify the following regression:

$$\text{Corr}_{ij,t} = \text{const}_i + \text{BCS}_{ij,t}\beta_i + \Delta\text{BM}_{ij,t}\delta_i + \Delta\text{TRADE}_{ij,t}\phi_i + \\ \Delta\text{FDI}_{ij,t}\nu_i + \Delta\text{DEBT}_{ij,t}\lambda_i + \Delta\text{INF}_{ij,t}\eta_i + \text{Control}_{i,t}\theta_i + \nu_t$$

where $\text{Corr}_{ij,t}$ is the bilateral DCCs between two countries' output gaps. $\text{BCS}_{ij,t}$ represents the BCS which takes the value 1 when output gaps of two countries exhibit the same signs and –1 otherwise. $\Delta\text{BM}_{ij,t}$ is the differences in broad money as a % of GDP between country i and country j. $\Delta\text{TRADE}_{ij,t}$ is the pairwise export difference between country i and country j, respectively. Seemingly, $\Delta\text{FDI}_{ij,t}$ and $\Delta\text{INF}_{ij,t}$ are differences in FDI and inflation between country i and country j, respectively. $\Delta\text{DEBT}_{ij,t}$ is the difference between total external debt of country i and country j. $\text{Control}_{i,t}$ represent the economic uncertainties of China, the USA and the competitiveness index of Asia. We also include the global real economic activity index of Kilian (2009) in the control variables list.[4] ν_t is the residual. We consider these variables to capture the impact of economic, monetary and trade channels, and also the impact of exogenous shocks received from China, the USA and Asia as control factors.[5] We consider broad money (M_2 as % of GDP) to capture the effect of monetary policy on the BCS. According to Agénor et al. (2000) there is a limited impact of pro-cyclical monetary aggregates on the overall output of the middle-income economies. In majority of the cases, it has been observed that monetary aggregates exhibit positive relationship with aggregate output of the economy. We include this variable to capture the impact of cross-country credit channel on economic integration (see State Bank of Pakistan, 2014). Since money supply is overly linked with general price level in the economy, we include the inflation variable in the model by considering the GDP deflator. We include this variable to capture the indirect effect on the bilateral trade of sample countries. The variations in bilateral trade often have visible impact on the overall growth of the economy. It has been often observed that in case of SAARC countries, the excessive domestic price upheavals force the member countries to undermine the differences and trade is facilitated. The inflationary trend also hints towards the choice of the monetary and fiscal tightening which in turn the impacts the strength of economic integration of the SAARC region.

To capture the impact of cross-country fiscal policy, we include total external debt for the sample countries. Total external debt includes the bilateral debt from governments and their agencies, and it also includes the loan assistance provided through central banks and official export credit agencies. To capture the extent of trade integration and its impact on the economic integration of SAARC countries, we consider the bilateral export difference between two countries. According to Volz (2010) FDI has a positive impact on the aggregate output fluctuations on the economy. Examining the case of East Asia, the study concludes that there are direct and positive impacts of FDI on output variations. Keeping this into account, we include FDI as % of GDP in the model to capture the flow of capital to check whether the variations in FDI explain the economic interdependence of SAARC nations.[6]

We include the policy uncertainty indices of China and the USA. This is done to infer upon the possible impact of economic uncertainty arising from these two regional and global economies on the bivariate conditional correlation of SAARC countries.[7] It is an important variable that can capture the news-based uncertainty resulting from an economy. However, we have retrieved the EPU series of China and the USA from Thomson DataStream, and it is available monthly and at lower frequencies. The last variable is essential from the regional perspective. We introduce the competitiveness index of Asia prepared by CESifo Asia. The index measures the overall business strength of the Asian economies. We include this variable to check whether the variable can explain the BCS of the SAARC nations. At last, we improvise our model by including the Kilian (2009) index of Global Real Economic Activity, which has been developed by taking into account the dry cargo single voyage ocean freight rates. Since our sample includes China and India and these two countries are representatives of demands for industrial goods, we consider the variable as the control in our regression.

Finally, we introduce the BCS variable which takes the value of 1 if the output gaps of two countries have the same sign and–1 if they have opposite signs (see Erb et al. 1994; Büttner and Hayo, 2011). We estimate this model with lag because of its binary nature. Following Lukmanova and Tondl (2017), we construct the bivariate series by using the log of the absolute difference between country pairs except for control variables. For example, $\Delta BM_{ij} = \log|\Delta BM_{it} - \Delta BM_{jt}|$. By doing this, we consider the dynamic interdependence of values between a pair of sample countries.[8]

Table 3.1A List of Variables

Variables	Name	Source
GDP	Gross Domestic Product, nominal deflated by GDP deflator of each country	Annual series from WDI-World Bank
BM	Broad money (% of GDP)	Annual series from WDI-World Bank
Trade	Difference between bilateral exports	CEIC economic database
FDI	Foreign direct investment, net inflows (% of GDP)	Annual series from WDI-World Bank
Debt	Total external debt (bilateral)	CEIC database
INF	Inflation, GDP deflator (annual %)	Annual series from WDI-World Bank
CHEPU	China Economic Uncertainty Index – news-based series	Quarterly series from Thomson DataStream
USEPU	The USA Economic Uncertainty Index – overall	Quarterly series from Thomson DataStream
ASIA	IFO, Asia, World Economic Survey (WES), problems the country is currently facing, lack of international competitiveness	Quarterly series from Thomson DataStream
GEAI	Global Economic Activity Index	Kilian (2009) from web source

Table 3.1B shows the descriptive statistics of four panels (A–D). The differences across economic and monetary exhibit common patterns, indicating the absence of an outlier in the series. The minimum value of differences across factors exhibits negative signs showing that the extent of dominance of one country over another, whereas the maximum values show the opposite trend. The standard deviation of all variables across panels provides evidence of limited variability. The variations of mean and standard deviation often play a crucial role in deciding whether the series is stationary. We have also plotted the output gaps of six sample countries (see Figure 3.1a–e). We find that the output gap between sample countries provides a clear picture of the movements of these economies. To confirm the real events, we briefly map the significant downturn phases of these economies. We find that for Bangladesh, the output gap can capture the business cycle movements of the economy. The periods of significant slumps are 2002–2003 and 2009–2010. A close appraisal reveals that during 2002–2003, Bangladesh's economy experienced a major downturn exacerbated by the twin shocks of high fiscal deficit and a deteriorating balance of payments.[9] The economy suffered from the second gloomy phase during 2009–2010 when the second phase of the global financial crisis (2008–2009) and its aftermath engulfed the economy through a secular decline in exports, remittances, tourism, external financing, and development assistance (see World

39

Table 3.1B Descriptive Statistics

Variable	Mean	Std. Dev.	Min	Max	Obs.
Panel A: Bangladesh with Nepal and Sri Lanka					
ΔBM	2.471	0.607	−0.171	3.532	160
ΔTRADE	0.104	1.680	−13.81	3.235	160
ΔFDI	−0.794	1.140	−7.108	0.940	160
ΔDEBT	1.019	1.404	−0.935	2.798	160
ΔINF	0.555	1.322	−4.455	2.625	160
Panel B: India with other SAARC countries					
ΔBM	2.573	1.024	−2.286	3.830	320
ΔTRADE	5.278	1.422	−0.738	7.492	320
ΔFDI	−0.635	1.045	−5.049	1.294	320
ΔDEBT	0.377	0.853	−1.691	1.510	320
ΔINF	0.586	1.082	−4.605	2.743	320
Panel C: Pakistan with other SAARC countries					
ΔBM	1.928	1.150	−2.664	3.817	240
ΔTRADE	35.673	50.166	−0.759	250.127	240
ΔFDI	−0.520	1.037	−4.240	1.291	240
ΔDEBT	0.993	1.236	0.524	3.961	240
ΔINF	0.718	1.142	−3.570	2.488	240
Panel D: China with other SAARC countries					
ΔBM	4.586	0.208	4.030	5.007	400
ΔTRADE	205.25	582.57	−3.036	3590.48	400
ΔFDI	1.252	0.928	−2.610	3.437	400
ΔDEBT	1.566	1.518	−0.518	4.613	400
ΔINF	1.342	0.836	−3.686	2.762	400
CHEPU	9.019	68.075	−108.022	161.433	400
USEPU	4.600	0.480	3.480	5.733	400
ASIA	4.62	0.301	4.145	5.374	400
GEAI	4.142	0.081	3.918	4.287	400

Note: The above table shows the descriptive statistics of sample variables. The table has been organized as per the combination of a number of countries and their respective possible pairs. For instance, Panel A includes only Nepal and Sri Lanka and likewise in other panels. ΔBM shows the difference in the money supply between the two countries. ΔTRADE is the pairwise export differences. ΔFDI is the difference between total FDI of country i and j. ΔDEBT is the difference between the total external debt of country i and j. Similarly, the ΔINF is again the inflation difference between country i and j. CHEPU, USEPU, ASIA, and GEAI indicate the China Economic Policy Uncertainty Index, US Economic Uncertainty Index, CESifo Asia Sentiment Index, and the Global Economic Activity Index prepared by Killian (2009).

Bank, 2009). Concerning India, we find that the output gap truly reflects the movements of the economy. The visible impact of the post-2008 global financial crisis is evident from the plot. Many studies report the contagion effect due to strong financial market linkages (see Ahmad et al. 2013).

Concerning Nepal, a close appraisal of economic history reveals that the economy experienced a severe downturn during 2001–2002, mainly on

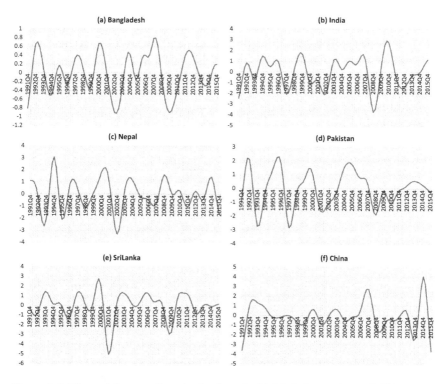

Figure 3.1 Plots of Output Gaps in the Sample SAARC Countries and China.
Source: Authors' Calculations.

account of political instability and Maoist violence, which eroded the business and investor confidence. The aftermath of 11 September 2001 (09/11) also impacted the economy externally (see Kogan Page, 2003). For Pakistan, the output gap of the economy exhibits two significant slumps during 1994–1995 and 1996–1997, mainly due to political uncertainty and vulnerable fiscal and external positions. The economy also experienced the foreign exchange crisis in October 1995 when the country had devalued its currency by 7%. The aimless budgetary management again worsened the situation and brought the economy to the brink of another foreign exchange crisis and led to the devaluation of the currency by 8.5%. The second phase of the downturn was mainly due to the political and constitutional crisis and the impact of the East-Asian crisis (1997) (see Bahadur, 1998; Khan, 1999).

For Sri Lanka, we find the case of a major slump during 2001–2002. The period is marked as the crisis period because of the failure of the central bank to defend the depreciating currency and adoption of the free-float exchange rate. These developments worsened economic woes. To rescue its economy, the government received a package of $530 million in April 2001 (see Kelegama, 2001). The other factors which contributed to the economic crisis were severe drought and the attack by Liberation Tigers of Tamil Eelam (LTTE) on major economic establishments (see Goodhand et al., 2011). In the case of China, we do not find the periods of significant downturns except during 2015–2016. In 2015, the Chinese economy recorded the slowest growth in 25 years. The economy achieved a growth rate of 6.9% in 2015.[10]

Empirical results

In this section, we examine the estimated results. We begin with the average DCCs reported in Table 3.2. The results suggest that there is a weak case of economic interdependence among SAARC countries and China. The correlation coefficients appear to be the reflection of the extent of economic integration these countries enjoy. In the case of India, we find that Nepal and Bangladesh exhibit a negative correlation. In the context of dependency theory, the possible explanation could be because of the large amount of economic assistance that India provides to these economies. The terms of trade between India and Bangladesh

Table 3.2 Dynamic Conditional Correlation Results

Variables	Coefficient	Std. Error	t-value	t-prob.
India/China	0.1537	0.1699	0.9050	0.3682
Nepal/China	0.1802	0.1416	1.2730	0.2069
Pakistan/China	−0.0548	0.1381	−0.3969	0.6925
Sri_Lanka/China	0.1874	0.1044	1.7960*	0.0763
Bangladesh/China	−0.0438	0.1250	−0.3505	0.7268
Nepal/India	−0.1760	0.1194	−1.4740	0.1443
Pakistan/India	0.0411	0.2114	0.1943	0.8464
Sri_Lanka/India	0.0820	0.1144	0.7171	0.4754
Bangladesh/India	−0.3002	0.1621	−1.8520*	0.0678
Pakistan/Nepal	−0.0933	0.1518	−0.6147	0.5405
Sri_Lanka/Nepal	−0.2000	0.1076	−1.8600*	0.0666
Bangladesh/Nepal	−0.1335	0.1331	−1.0030	0.3186
Sri_Lanka/Pakistan	−0.0362	0.1374	−0.2634	0.7929
Bangladesh/Pakistan	0.0077	0.1548	0.0497	0.9605
Bangladesh/Sri_Lanka	0.2494	0.1179	2.1160**	0.0375
α	0.7287	0.0562	12.970**	0.0000
β	0.1093	0.0816	1.3400	0.1841
No. Obs.	97			
Log-Likelihood	−440.249			

Note: ** and * denote the level of significance at 5% and better and below 10%, respectively. The estimated coefficients (α and β) of DCC model are significant, and their sum is less than 1, indicating that the DCCs are mean-reverting.

and between India and Nepal are highly skewed towards India. We will shed light on this issue in the subsequent section. The cases of negative association could also be seen between China and Pakistan. The descriptive statistics also show the high dependence of Pakistan on China. Surprisingly, Bangladesh, Pakistan and Sri Lanka exhibit a negative relationship with Nepal, suggesting a possibility of either one-sided dependence or limited interdependence. There is also a negative dependence between Pakistan and Sri Lanka. However, the correlation coefficient of Bangladesh with India and Sri Lanka with China and Bangladesh exhibits a statistically significant relationship. The sum of estimated coefficients α and β of DCC model is less than 1, suggesting that the DCCs are mean-reverting.

The estimated regression results are shown in Tables 3.3–3.7. As mentioned above, we estimate the regression model by considering the DCC calculated from the DCC model between country i and j as dependent and all other variables as independent variables, including controls. We estimate the model in a two-step procedure. In the first step, we estimate the fixed effects model by preparing four balanced panels. Table 3.3 shows the estimated results. The first panel exhibits the results of Bangladesh with Nepal and Sri Lanka. We find that ΔBM, ΔTRADE and ΔDEBT decouple the BCS process. On ΔBM, monetary policy in terms of monetary expansion does not seem to be in coordination for these countries. For instance, in the case of Nepal, the exchange rate is the main monetary policy variable, whereas, in the case of Bangladesh and Sri Lanka, it is the broad money. Besides, ΔTRADE and ΔDEBT variables, which exhibit the external debt and bilateral export difference of these nations, pick negative signs, confirming the decoupling effect. The possible explanation could be because of the wide difference in the magnitude of external debt. And the direction of exports and also the composition of fiscal variables of these groups of countries. According to Lukmanova and Tondl (2017), the accumulation of higher debt encourages higher fiscal spending, which in turn increases the financial stress and credit costs and also the budgetary consolidation. These adverse developments, in turn, result in the limited economic integration process. Mahmood et al. (2014) also state similar reasons in the forms of high fiscal and trade deficits and the saving-investment gap for the debt sustainability issue in Bangladesh and Sri Lanka.

Among all the variables, inflation is the only variable which appears to resurrect the BCS process. Goyal (2011) reports that the supply-side bottlenecks in these countries play a significant role in the rise of inflation. We shed light on this topic in the subsequent section.

In the second panel of India with Bangladesh, Nepal, Pakistan, and Sri Lanka, we find that the results of fixed effects are significant with BCS, ΔTRADE, ΔDEBT, and ΔINF. Interestingly, the coefficients of BCS and ΔTRADE pick positive sign, indicating an enforcing impact on economic integration. In

Table 3.3 Determinants of Economic Integration of SAARC: Panel Results

	(1)	(2)	(3)	(4)
Variables	Bangladesh	India	Pakistan	China
BCS	0.030	0.102***	0.054*	0.057**
	(0.036)	(0.033)	(0.031)	(0.023)
ΔBM	−0.317***	0.055	−0.086***	0.467***
	(0.072)	(0.038)	(0.020)	(0.110)
ΔDEBT	−0.138***	−0.170***	0.066***	−0.043**
	(0.028)	(0.039)	(0.025)	(0.021)
ΔFDI	0.004	0.008	−0.0078	0.139***
	(0.032)	(0.027)	(0.035)	(0.025)
ΔINF	0.074***	−0.111***	0.003***	0.0001***
	(0.022)	(0.016)	(0.000)	(0.000)
ΔTRADE	−0.129***	0.059*	−0.002	−0.115***
	(0.028)	(0.032)	(0.028)	(0.029)
CHEPU	−0.109	−0.021	0.040	−0.091**
	(0.109)	(0.098)	(0.109)	(0.041)
USEPU	0.366**	0.074	−0.244	0.435***
	(0.183)	(0.129)	(0.177)	(0.066)
ASIA	0.484	0.644*	0.932**	0.089
	(0.486)	(0.369)	(0.410)	(0.200)
GEAI	0.0004	0.001***	0.002***	−0.0001
	(0.000)	(0.000)	(0.000)	(0.000)
Constant	−2.059	−2.401	−3.057	−3.919***
	(2.261)	(1.710)	(1.995)	(0.940)
Obs.	160	320	240	400
R-Squared	0.393	0.273	0.24	0.235
Number of ID	2	4	3	5

Note: Standard errors shown in brackets.
*** denotes *p*-values less than 1% and better.
** denotes *p*-values less than 5% and better.
* denotes *p*-values less than 10% and better.

contrast, the coefficients of ΔDEBT and ΔINF exhibit negative signs confirming a decoupling effect. These results clearly signify the rising role of India in SAARC. The coefficient of BCS picks positive sign and shows a significant impact of BCS on India with the countries in panel. With respect to the magnitude of BCS coefficient, it is highest among all the panels, highlighting the presence of India in SAARC. Among all the macroeconomic variables, trade difference appears to be the major driver of economic integration between India and other SAARC members, excluding China. We provide more details on the signs of coefficients in the subsequent section.

The third panel of Pakistan consists of Bangladesh, Nepal, and Sri Lanka. We find that variables BCS, ΔDEBT, and ΔINF play a significant role in the BCS process as the coefficients of these two variables are positive and

Table 3.4 Determinants of Economic Integration of Bangladesh with Nepal and Sri Lanka

Variables	Bangladesh/Nepal	Bangladesh/Sri Lanka
BCS	0.087**	−0.006
	(0.037)	(0.031)
ΔBM	−0.931***	0.021
	(0.092)	(0.054)
ΔDEBT	−0.935***	0.116
	(0.338)	(0.128)
ΔFDI	0.057**	−0.014
	(0.026)	(0.019)
ΔINF	0.067	0.019**
	(0.041)	(0.008)
ΔTRADE	−0.102**	−0.048**
	(0.043)	(0.022)
CHEPU	0.269**	−0.320***
	(0.111)	(0.091)
USEPU	−0.295	0.909***
	(0.190)	(0.131)
ASIA	0.662	−0.418
	(0.529)	(0.370)
GEAI	−0.000	−0.001***
	(0.000)	(0.000)
Constant	2.115	−0.614
	(2.536)	(1.696)
R-Squared	0.769	0.588
F-statistic	50.73	20.63
Obs.	80	80

Note: Standard errors shown in brackets. Please refer to the footnote of Table 3.1 for variables' details.

*** denotes *p*-values less than 1% and better.

** denotes *p*-values less than 5% and better.

* denotes *p*-values less than 10% and better.

significant, implying that trade could play a vital role in fostering the process of economic integration. However, the decoupling effect is found for ΔBM, which signifies the lack of monetary integration. The fourth panel representing China, which comprises five countries such as Bangladesh, India, Nepal, Pakistan, and Sri Lanka, exhibits that recoupling effect on BCS. Among variables, BCS, ΔBM, ΔFDI, and ΔINF appear to play a significant role in the BCS process. The significance of the coefficient of these variables exhibits the process of economic integration.

Further details about this would be elaborated in the subsequent section. We find that ΔTRADE and ΔDEBT have a decoupling effect on the BCS process. The possible explanation could be because of the adverse terms of trade and debt positions of China with sample SAARC countries. The

Table 3.5 Determinants of Economic Integration of India with its SAARC Counterparts

Variables	India/Bangladesh	India/Nepal	India/Pakistan	India/Sri Lanka
BCS	0.084*	0.084**	0.097*	0.003
	(0.044)	(0.038)	(0.052)	(0.033)
ΔBM	−1.974***	0.176***	0.216***	0.459**
	(0.522)	(0.053)	(0.055)	(0.200)
ΔDEBT	4.091***	−3.568**	1.007***	−0.309
	(0.773)	(1.552)	(0.245)	(0.318)
ΔFDI	0.091**	−0.301***	0.018	−0.016
	(0.044)	(0.084)	(0.035)	(0.024)
ΔINF	−0.026	0.077**	−0.028	0.071
	(0.099)	(0.030)	(0.050)	(0.128)
ΔTRADE	−0.018	−0.034	0.066**	0.039
	(0.047)	(0.041)	(0.030)	(0.037)
CHEPU	−0.120	0.106	−0.326**	0.039
	(0.135)	(0.099)	(0.146)	(0.106)
USEPU	−0.398	−1.001***	0.537**	−0.163
	(0.254)	(0.185)	(0.234)	(0.188)
ASIA	−0.223	0.145	1.107**	0.611
	(0.585)	(0.566)	(0.549)	(0.372)
GEAI	0.003***	−0.0003	0.0003	0.0009
	(0.000)	(0.0004)	(0.0007)	(0.0008)
Constant	6.848*	7.932***	−4.743**	−3.713**
	(3.868)	(2.742)	(2.358)	(1.660)
R-Squared	0.651	0.775	0.662	0.690
F-statistic	14.1462	34.64	12.300	19.790
Obs.	80	80	80	80

Note: Standard errors shown in brackets. Please refer to the footnote of Table 3.1 for variables' details.
*** denotes *p*-values less than 1% and better.
** denotes *p*-values less than 5% and better
* denotes *p*-values less than 10% and better.

higher trade surplus of China encourages the rise in the import bill of these countries, which in turn leads to the adverse business cycle movements (see Lukmanova and Tondl, 2017).

However, we confirm these findings by estimating the bilateral regressions by decomposing the four panels shown in Table 3.3. Table 3.4 shows the results of Bangladesh with Nepal and Sri Lanka. The results suggest that among all the explanatory variables, BCS, ΔBM, ΔDEBT, ΔTRADE and ΔFDI are statistically significant for Nepal. For Nepal, there seems to be the decoupling effect overriding over the recoupling of the BCS process. Out of five macro variables statistically significant, we find that the coefficients of ΔBM, ΔDEBT, and ΔTRADE pick negative signs indicating the divergence in BCS process. Among all the variables, ΔFDI appears to be the only variable reinforcing the BCS process. For Sri Lanka, we find the

Table 3.6 Economic Integration of Pakistan with Bangladesh, Nepal and Sri Lanka

Variable	Pakistan/Bangladesh	Pakistan/Nepal	Pakistan/Sri Lanka
BCS	0.102*	0.017	0.063
	(0.057)	(0.038)	(0.067)
ΔBM	−0.141**	−0.016	−0.015
	(0.057)	(0.036)	(0.062)
ΔDEBT	−0.605*	0.360	0.760**
	(0.360)	(0.339)	(0.348)
ΔFDI	0.116**	0.061	−0.210***
	(0.052)	(0.055)	(0.066)
ΔINF	0.313***	0.059	0.109
	(0.097)	(0.038)	(0.085)
ΔTRADE	−0.056	−0.068	0.010
	(0.034)	(0.046)	(0.060)
CHEPU	−0.351	0.407***	−0.0302
	(0.211)	(0.114)	(0.159)
USEPU	0.070	−1.302***	0.902***
	(0.356)	(0.223)	(0.276)
ASIA	0.256	0.624	0.798
	(0.638)	(0.431)	(0.836)
GEAI	0.001	0.001**	0.002*
	(0.001)	(0.000)	(0.001)
Constant	0.230	0.377	−8.696**
	(3.252)	(2.202)	(4.095)
R-Squared	0.395	0.643	0.429
F-statistic	7.200	19.900	12.520
Obs.	80	80	80

Note: Standard errors shown in brackets. Please refer to the footnote of Table 3.1 for variables' details.
*** denotes p-values less than 1% and better.
** denotes p-values less than 5% and better.
* denotes p-values less than 10% and better.

significance of only the coefficients of ΔINF and ΔTRADE. The coefficient of ΔINF picks positive sign, whereas ΔTRADE shows a negative effect. The variable BCS is significant only in the case of Nepal, indicating the recoupling of business cycles. The negative sign of ΔBM suggests a lack of monetary policy coordination between Bangladesh and Nepal. However, the difference in ΔTRADE seems to have decoupling effects for both countries with Bangladesh. Among control variables, the results do not report the significance of any of these variables for Nepal, indicating that the heightened risk and uncertainty of China and the USA do not significantly determine the process of the economic integration of Bangladesh with Nepal. However, for Sri Lanka, we find that the economic policy uncertainties in China and the USA and even adverse movements in global output determine the BCS process between Bangladesh and Sri Lanka. Finally, it can

Table 3.7 Determinants of Economic Integration of China with SAARC Countries

Variable	China/ Bangladesh	China/ India	China/ Nepal	China/ Pakistan	China/Sri Lanka
BCS	0.041	−0.081**	0.044	−0.086**	−0.0042
	(0.034)	(0.033)	(0.045)	(0.033)	(0.036)
ΔBM	−2.299***	−0.241	1.309***	1.491***	0.357
	(0.545)	(0.390)	(0.478)	(0.215)	(0.308)
ΔDEBT	0.835***	−0.242	−1.220***	0.871***	0.224
	(0.199)	(0.228)	(0.315)	(0.222)	(0.201)
ΔFDI	−0.568***	−0.051	−0.270	0.375***	0.028
	(0.161)	(0.049)	(0.267)	(0.074)	(0.151)
ΔINF	0.000	0.056	−0.264***	0.0012	0.006
	(0.000)	(0.047)	(0.052)	(0.016)	(0.076)
ΔTRADE	−0.146***	0.0340	−0.042	−0.093	0.0076
	(0.040)	(0.045)	(0.062)	(0.057)	(0.050)
CHEPU	−0.212**	0.084	0.153	−0.053	−0.116
	(0.096)	(0.143)	(0.146)	(0.090)	(0.116)
USEPU	1.083***	0.019	−0.333	0.707***	0.117
	(0.196)	(0.146)	(0.220)	(0.139)	(0.171)
ASIA	2.097***	−1.887***	−0.354	0.196	0.912**
	(0.499)	(0.363)	(0.587)	(0.409)	(0.448)
GEAI	−0.002***	0.003***	−0.001**	0.0002	0.0005
	(0.000)	(0.000)	(0.000)	(0.000)	(0.000)
Constant	−2.559	8.118***	3.145	−11.390***	−5.385***
	(3.101)	(1.805)	(2.961)	(1.741)	(1.987)
R-Squared	0.713	0.543	0.612	0.762	0.291
F-statistic	14.37	15.37	15.370	36.240	3.660
Obs.	80	80	80	80	80

Note: Standard errors shown in brackets. Please refer to the footnote of Table 3.1 for variables' details.
*** denotes *p*-values less than 1% and better.
** denotes *p*-values less than 5% and better.
* denotes *p*-values less than 10% and better.

be concluded that due to geographical proximity, Bangladesh appears to be more economically integrated with Nepal than Sri Lanka.

Table 3.5 shows the results of India with Bangladesh, Nepal, Pakistan, and Sri Lanka. It appears that for India and Bangladesh, the coefficients of BCS, ΔDEBT, and ΔFDI pick positive signs and are statistically significant. These variables suggest that the process of economic integration between Bangladesh and India can be strengthened by the promotion of these variables. However, the coefficient of ΔBM picks a negative sign, indicating the lack of monetary policy interdependence. Among control variables, the coefficient of the Global Economic Activity Index (GEAI) shows a positive impact on the BCS process, implying that the variations in global economic output concentrated mainly in industrialized countries do have a significant effect on the BCS between India and Bangladesh. In the case of India and Nepal, we find that the coefficient of BCS picks a positive sign, and it is statistically significant, implying that there is a definite synergy between business cycles movements of these economies and economic integration. Among economic indicators, ΔBM and ΔINF exhibit a positive relationship with the BCS process, implying that the credit expansion could be the significant strength of economic integration, and the domestic demand could also enforce the economic integration process. The coefficients of ΔDEBT and ΔFDI pick negative sign indicating the case of either adverse terms of trade of Nepal with India or trade divergence. The higher external debt dependence of Nepal in India could be the possible reason for this. Among control variables, the results show that the US economic uncertainty appears to have a negative impact on the process of economic integration between India and Nepal.

However, one of the critical pairs that significantly determines the future of SAARC is the economic relationship between India and Pakistan. The political tension between India and Pakistan has recently derailed the economic priorities of SAARC. In this light, the regression results suggest that the coefficients of BCS, ΔBM, ΔDEBT, and ΔTRADE have enforcing effects on economic interdependence. Among control variables, we find the significant evidence of Chinese and the US economic uncertainty in explaining the economic integration process of India and Pakistan. Lastly, we examine the economic integration between India and Sri Lanka. It appears that the coefficient of BCS is not statistically significant, indicating a weak interdependence between these two countries. The economic variable, such as ΔBM is the only variable significant. It negatively determines the process of economic integration, implying that these countries must start a dialogue to foster the BCS process. The results suggest the case of divergence as both economies progress towards better economic integration. However, the control variables do not determine the process of economic integration between India and Sri Lanka as none of the variables are statistically significant.

Table 3.6 shows the results of Pakistan with Bangladesh, Nepal and Sri Lanka. We have done this analysis to analyse the relationship of Pakistan with its neighbors other than India. The results suggest that ΔBM and ΔDEBT have a decoupling effect on the BCS process, indicating either a lack of monetary policy coordination or the wide difference in the magnitude of the money supply between two nations. The variables which reinforce the BCS process appear to be the ΔFDI and ΔINF. It also means that there is a high chance that domestic conditions may play a vital role in the process of economic integration.

However, the variable BCS exhibits a positive and statistically significant only with Bangladesh and not with Nepal and Sri Lanka, indicating that there is a weak economic integration at the aggregated level. In case of Nepal and Sri Lanka, the level of economic integration seems to be significantly lower than Bangladesh. For Nepal, none of the variables are statistically significant. For Sri Lanka, we find that ΔFDI, which shows a negative correlation with economic integration between Pakistan and Sri Lanka, indicating a case of investment divergence as the economic integration progresses. ΔDEBT shows a positive relationship, exhibiting the case of external cooperation between the two countries. Among control variables, we find that the economic policy uncertainty in China, the USA and the variations in global economic activity impact the economic interdependence between Pakistan and Sri Lanka.

Table 3.7 shows the results of the economic integration of China with Bangladesh, India, Nepal, Pakistan, and Sri Lanka. We have done this analysis to find out the level of economic integration and the economic influence of China in the SAARC. For China and Bangladesh, the results suggest that the coefficients of ΔBM, ΔFDI, and ΔTRADE negative signs and are statistically significant explain the process of economic integration. It implies that the credit channel, FDI, and trade indeed have divergent effects on the BCS process between China and Bangladesh. However, external debt seems to be the only variable supporting the process of economic integration. The insignificant impact of BCS further substantiates these findings. However, in the case of India, we find weak economic interdependence. The coefficient of BCS picks a negative sign, and it is statistically significant, indicating a lack of BCS process.

Seemingly for China and Nepal, we find that only three macroeconomic variables significantly explain the process of BCS in either way. The coefficient of ΔBM picks a positive sign, indicating the monetary and credit smoothing. However, ΔDEBT and ΔINF exhibit a decoupling effect on the BCS process. In the context of economic integration, these results imply that the monetary policy has a vital role in the expansion of economic integration. For China and Pakistan, the coefficient of BCS exhibits a negative sign indicating a lack of BCS. Among macro variables, we find ΔBM, ΔDEBT, and ΔFDI resurrect the BCS process. The external debt and FDI seems to play a crucial role in augmenting the economic integration process.

However, the regression results of China with Sri Lanka exhibit weak economic interdependence in the equation as none of the variables significantly explain the economic integration process. Among control variables between China and SAARC countries, we find that except Nepal and Pakistan and Sri Lanka, the control variables significantly determine the process of economic integration. The most substantial effect of control variables is reported in the case of Bangladesh, where all variables significantly explain the process of economic integration.

We will further shed light on the implications and attempt to explain the sign and the meaning of statistical significance with recent developments and also through credible evidence. However, it is noteworthy that the regression results must be interpreted with caution as the estimated results exhibit low Adj. *R*-squared values. The possible explanation could be because of the exclusion of some of the relevant socio-economic variables. We do not include these variables in the regression because these variables will be part of our empirical approach in subsequent chapters in examining the process of economic, financial, and trade integration.

Comparison of regression results

In this section, we discuss the results explained above. The process of economic integration is indeed weak in these countries. There is also a visible level of asymmetry with respect to the signs of the possible determinants of economic integration. To avoid confusion, we focus more on the relevance of these results in the light of existing policy measures and the events that could explain the extent of economic integration among the sample SAARC countries in a more precise manner. The subsequent chapters will also cover different dimensions of economic integration, and to avoid overlapping, we stick to the economic and trade frameworks. We begin with the results of the economic integration of Bangladesh with Nepal and Sri Lanka. We find that some of the explanatory variables explain the economic integration of Bangladesh and Nepal. Even in the case of Bangladesh and Sri Lanka, the results report a similar outcome. Focusing on the determinants of Bangladesh and Nepal, the magnitudes of the differences between broad money supply and net exports are tilted towards Bangladesh, indicating that the size of the Bangladesh economy is larger than Nepal. In the light of policy development, the initiative of the Asian Development Bank (ADB) to create an economic cooperation group within SAARC popularly known as SASEC (South Asian Sub-Regional Economic Cooperation) comprising Bangladesh, Bhutan, India, and Nepal. It is also known as "*Growth Quadrangles*".[11] The priority areas of this group are energy, tourism, transport, trade, and investment. However, the coefficient of differences between exports of Bangladesh and Nepal indicates a negative relationship with economic integration. The possible explanation could be because of the size of trade which appears to be in favour of Bangladesh. The negative coefficient could be interpreted in the line of the prosperity of these countries. Since Bangladesh is the net exporter, the high economic growth implies lesser imports or trade diversion. In 2014–2015, Bangladesh had the export of worth $25 million to Nepal, whereas Nepal exported only $12.04 million.[12,13] However, FDI seems to be enforcing factor for economic integration between Bangladesh and Nepal. Scrutiny reveals that Nepal is also one of the recipients of FDI from Bangladesh. According to Nepal Rastra Bank (hereafter NRB, June 2018). Nepal received around 2.5 billion rupees worth of FDI from Bangladesh.

Concerning Bangladesh and Sri Lanka, the findings of above results should be seen in light of the efforts put forward by these two countries to strengthen the economic ties over the years. Bangladesh has always strived for a better economic relationship with Sri Lanka. This is evident from the fact that the economic agreements between these two countries have started way before the establishment of SAARC. The first economic agreement between these two nations was signed on 07 November 1979 in the area of economic and technical cooperation followed by agreement on avoidance of double taxation and fiscal evasion (19 December 1992) and an agreement on shipping services (10 June 2011). The moderately higher level of economic integration between these two nations could be seen as an amalgamation of these economic agreements.[14] In 2017, the process of economic integration had taken a new shape when both countries signed a free trade agreement (FTA) that included 14 different agreements covering the crucial areas such as agriculture, education, investment, shipping, and telecommunication.[15] It is anticipated that with the realization of all these agreements, the Sri Lankan economy will have access to BCIM (*Bangladesh, China, India and Myanmar*) regional economic corridor. The BCIM corridor will help to transport trade goods to Myanmar and North-eastern part of India and more importantly, to the ASEAN markets. The trade figures suggest that the bilateral trade between Bangladesh and Sri Lanka jumped by USD 67 million in 2014-15.[16] During 2017-2018, the trade between Bangladesh and Sri Lanka amounted to USD76 million. However, the regression results of these two nations suggest a strong call for credit channel coordination and cross-border investment. The negative coefficient of trade indicates the net trade deficit of Bangladesh with Sri Lanka. According to DCCI, the export of Bangladesh went up from USD 14.82 million in 2006–2007 to USD 30.45 million in 2015–2016, whereas the export of Sri Lanka during the same period has gone up from USD 16.37 million to USD 45.01 million.[17] Inflation seems to be an important driving factor, and this could be because of the nature of trading items. Bangladesh seems to import all the primary and industrial items from Sri Lanka, and in return, Bangladesh exports textiles, footwear, and jute products to Sri Lanka. The higher inflation difference indicates that the economy of Bangladesh is ahead to Sri Lanka as far as the inflation rate is concerned.

We now focus on the bilateral economic relationship of India with Bangladesh, Nepal, Pakistan and Sri Lanka. It is apparent from the results that economic integration of the Indian economy is moderately higher than Bangladesh within SAARC. Starting with India and Bangladesh, we find that the major drivers of economic integration appear to be the differences in external debt and FDI. Scrutiny reveals that Bangladesh and India signed the bilateral trade agreement in 1980, which was later amended and signed in March 2006 and was valid until March 2009. Bangladesh also occupies a prominent place on economic integration because of the geographical proximity and longest boundary sharing of 4,096 km (see Sengupta, 2007). The geographic proximity also encourages smuggling and informal trading, as reported by Chaudhari (1995). In 2011–2012, India's export to Bangladesh amounted to $5.84 billion. In return, Bangladesh's export to India was $584.64 million (see Balaji, 2016). Over the years, the trade imbalance of Bangladesh with India has increased. To reduce the imbalance, the Indian government removed the 46 items from the sensitive list, giving leeway to the Bangladesh exports. However, the controversy still surrounds on removing the non-trade barriers (NTBs). The economic integration between India and Bangladesh can also be seen in the economic aid that India provides to Bangladesh. India supports Bangladesh on many fronts, including development assistance and government aid. India has already offered the grant assistance of $37 million to Bangladesh to deal with the natural calamity that struck the country in 2007–2008. India also provides support to Bangladesh, mainly on multi-sectoral projects. Besides these, India also extends its support in the areas of infrastructure development and provides economic support through Lines of Credit and Advances. In April 2017, India extended two lines of credit to Bangladesh worth $5 billion. One of the lines is to support the 17 projects covering infrastructure and power.

Owing to its least developed country status, Bangladesh currently enjoys the Generalized Systems of Preferences, under which the goods produced and exported from the country attract duty-free and quota-free benefits. To attract FDI from India, Bangladesh has developed special economic zones for Indian investors in Mongla, Bheramara and Mirshorai.[18] The sectors in which Bangladesh needs special attention of Indian investors are electrical machinery and equipment, light engineering, vegetable/roots and tubers, agro-processing, automobiles, textiles and organic chemicals. In the services sector, ICT, pharmaceuticals, hospital and medical equipment, tourism and professional services offer good opportunities. However, India's export basket to Bangladesh includes cotton, sugar, cereals, vehicles, and accessories. And Bangladesh exports include textile fibers, paper yarn, fish, apparel, mineral fuels, salt, and cement.[19] These developments also make our results relevant as it appears that there is a cross-border investment between these two countries, and FDI plays an important role too.

Concerning India and Nepal, the regression results suggest that the monetary policy, external debt, FDI and inflation are the variables capable of making the economic integration possible in either way. The differences in exports and FDI appear to be a decoupling factor in economic integration process but it could also be due to the wide gap in terms of the magnitudes of these variables in both countries. Nepal is conventionally considered as one of the crucial allies of India with a shared border of over 1,850 km. Over the years, the economic interdependence between these two nations has increased substantially. The bilateral trade of Nepal with India has grown up from 29.8% in 1995–1996 to 61.2% in 2015–2016, which is almost $4.8 billion. Nepal's main imports from India are petroleum products, motor vehicles, rice and paddy, machinery and parts, medicine, cement, etc. On investment from the FDI route, India plays a strategic role as its corporations have a significant presence in the investment landscape of Nepal. Nepal received about 40% of FDI from India and the rest from others, including SAARC countries. Till 2016, more than 150 Indian firms had their subsidiaries in Nepal.[20] India is the most significant member of Nepal and also as a trading partner. India also extends developmental support to Nepal in the form of development assistance. To ensure better infrastructure development, India has given three lines of credit worth $100 million, $250 million and $1 billion in 2006–2007, 2011–2012 and 2013–2014, respectively. These developments are in line with the regression results obtained above. The Indian government has also extended, amounting to $750 million as a credit line to the Nepalese government for the re-development of the earthquake-devastated country.

Concerning India and Pakistan, the economic relationship between these two neighbouring nations has always been a matter of concern for other SAARC members. The cross-border conflict and high trust deficit make the economic relationship between these two countries an interesting case of study. According to the regression results shown in Table 3.5, broad money, external debt, and trade seem to be the major sources of economic integration between these two nations. During 2012–2013, Pakistan's export to India has seen a growth of 28% and amounted to $513 million. The export basket included mainly industrial inputs comprising of organic chemicals, raw cotton, metal scrap, and leather. Whereas India's export to Pakistan in the same period amounted to $319 million and recorded the export growth of 19%. However, the total export to Pakistan stood at $1.84 billion. The trade balance has always been in favour of India.[21] The Indian export basket includes cotton, vegetables, organic chemicals, sugar and sugar confectionery, waste of food industry, coffee, tea and meat, machinery boilers. The political unrest and high cost of cross-border trade between India and Pakistan have led to informal trade arrangements. In a recent study, it has been estimated that the volume of informal trade amounted to $4.71 billion. Of which India's export to Pakistan stood at $3.99 billion and from Pakistan to India at $0.72 billion (see Taneja and Bimal, 2016). The major routes of informal trade are Dubai, Iran (Bandar Abbas), Afghanistan and Amritsar (India). However, according to Taneja et al. (2013), the trade potential between India and Pakistan lies between $10.9 billion and $19.8 billion. India's trade potential seems to be in favour as its export potential accounts for $7.9 billion and imports $3 billion. Despite these figures, still, there exist some grey areas which need immediate attention, including the reciprocation of Most Favoured Nation (MFN) enjoyed by Pakistan since 1996. After the SAFTA agreement, the rationalization of tariffs is still due. The recent addition has been in the form of a grant of NDMA (non-discriminatory market access) by Pakistan.[22] Considering the rising concerns that Pakistan could face the debt trap, India must also explore the opportunity to help the neighbouring partner and rescues it.

Concerning India and Sri Lanka, the regression results reported in Table 3.5 suggest a worrying outlook as, except broad money difference, none of the variables are significant. However, we outline different initiatives in the areas of trade and commerce to understand the rising interdependence between these two countries. Sri Lanka has been an essential ally for India in SAARC. India is also the largest trading partner of Sri Lanka globally. The trade between these two countries is guided by the Indo-Sri Lanka Free Trade Agreement, which came into existence in 2000. Both countries enjoy a healthy trade relationship with the bilateral trade value increasing substantially from $658 million in 2000 to $3.6 billion in 2013. The terms of trade seem to be in favour of India as the bilateral trade deficit of Sri Lanka has increased from –$544 million in 2000 to –$2549.30 million in 2013.[23] Despite the high amount of formal trade, studies have shown that informal channels are operating from the Indian side to trade goods in Sri Lanka. The size of the informal trade seems to be almost a third of the total value of trade. The lower transaction costs seem to be the formidable reason for informal trade (see Taneja, 2002, 2004). India and Sri Lanka are also part of other economic and trade interest groups such as Asia-Pacific Trade Agreement (APTA), SAFTA in SAARC and BIMSTEC and Global System of Trade Preferences (GSTP). Besides trade relations, India is also one of the largest investors in Sri Lanka. India has so far invested $800 million with the presence of all the major Indian corporations. In 2013 alone, India's investment in Sri Lanka was worth $50.52 million. Indian investment is mainly concentrated in activities like retail, hospitals, telecom, petroleum, real estate, and industrial metals. In recent, the Indian economy has also witnessed the inflow of investment from companies operating in Sri Lanka. Some of the well-known companies include Ceylon Biscuits, Brandix and Carsons.

Apart from these economic relations, India also supports Sri Lankan economic prosperity. India also helps Sri Lanka through development credit.[24] In recent years, India is seeking another trade agreement named Economic and Technological Cooperation Agreement (ETCA) for better bilateral interaction and inclusion of services and investment in trade basket. The technical analysis of this pact is currently underway (Kadirgamar, 2016; Sen, 2018). The above report seems to agree with the regression results discussed above.

For Pakistan and Bangladesh, the regression results shown in Table 3.6 suggest the broad money, external debt, FDI, and Inflation as one of the major determinants of economic integration. An overview of history suggests that both countries share a shared history, shared heritage, and culture. Bangladesh, popularly known as East Pakistan was carved out from

Pakistan in 1971. Despite the FTA in 2004, both countries have limited trade interactions. Compared to India, Bangladesh's trade relation with Pakistan is not very significant. In 2014, Pakistan's export to Bangladesh was worth \$684 million and Bangladesh in return exported \$54.8 million.[25] However, Manzoor and Chaudhary (2017) report the rising role of Pakistan as one of the major FDI granters in Bangladesh. In 2014, Pakistan had FDI exposure of USD 135 million in Bangladesh. On policy coordination, both countries have given the least preference to each other with limited interactions even at the diplomatic level. The regression results also seem to be consistent with the above details.

Concerning Pakistan and Nepal, the regression results reported in Table 3.6 indicate no significant economic integration as the coefficient of none of the economic variables is significant. However, we do analyse the historical developments and the recent initiatives for our reader to understand the status of economic integration between these two countries. Scrutiny reveals that Pakistan and Nepal have always tried to enhance the process of economic integration through continuous interaction and consistent efforts at diplomacy level. The first trade agreement between Pakistan and Nepal was signed in 1962. The deal helped facilitate the trade between the nations with the rationalization of transaction costs and payments. Despite the disruptions due to the war between India and Pakistan, both countries remained cautious in fostering the process of economic integration. In 1966 opened a road network to Radhikapur from East Pakistan (erstwhile Bangladesh) (see Muhammad et al. 2015). After the creation of Bangladesh, the Pakistan and Nepal relationship was a big miss which both countries tried to materialize by signing a trade agreement in 1982. The recent figures suggest that the trade between both nations is indeed deficient compared to India.

India is the most significant trading partner with the export and import shares of around 65% followed by China, the UAE and Indonesia from January 2009 to December 2015.[26] Pakistan has only 0.1% of total imports in Nepal. On investment and commerce, economic relations are not impressive. The recent initiatives include the formation of the Joint Business Council (JBC) formed in 1996 to promote the trade, investment and transfer, though the outcome has so far been not impressive.[27] Similarly, the Confederation of Nepalese Industries (CNI) has also signed MoU with the Chambers of Commerce and Industries in Karachi, Lahore, to promote bilateral trade and investment.[28] The economic relationship between these two economies is not very encouraging because of the limited trade and formal interactions. The above analysis appears to agree with the regression results.

Concerning Pakistan and Sri Lanka, the regression results are shown in Table 3.6 suggest that the differences in debt and FDI could play a critical role in enforcing the process of economic integration between these two countries. An overview indicates that the first FTA came into operation in 2005. Since then, both countries have tried to normalize their business environment. The FTA granted access to local markets for both countries. Although with respect to trade, both countries have made significant progress, in recent years, the focus has been on FDI. According to the National Chamber of Commerce in Sri Lanka, Pakistan had planned to invest around USD 500 million in Sri Lanka in the areas such as agriculture, information technology (IT), textiles and construction.[29] However, in goods trade, goods such as cotton and cement from the Pakistan side and rubber and coconut product from the Sri Lankan side received 100% concessions. Consequently, the export from Pakistan increased from $154 million in 2004 to $316 million in 2013, though the share of Pakistan ranged between 1% and 2% of total imports of Pakistan.

In contrast, the export of Sri Lanka to Pakistan accounted for only 0.14% of the value of exports, increasing from $46 million to $63 million from 2004–2013. In April 2015, both countries outlined the plan to revamp the existing FTAs with more space for services and investments (see Pakistan Business Council, 2015).[30] In January 2016, Pakistan and Sri Lanka signed eight MoUs in the fields of health, education, trade, science and technology, tourism, gem and jewelry to increase the value of bilateral trade to $1 billion.[31] The external debt assistance could be an exciting area in which both countries can help each other.

Lastly, we examine the influence of China in the SAARC. Analysing Bangladesh, the results are shown in Table 3.7 exhibits the significant interdependence between the two countries. The variables such as debt, FDI and trade seem to be the major determinants of economic integration. Scrutiny of existing developments reveals that China has a strong presence in Bangladesh (see Sahoo, 2013a, b). The first formal economic engagement with China took place on 4 October 1974. Since then, these countries have strived for better economic ties. Over the years, Bangladesh has become the third-largest trading partner of China with export from China, amounting to $6324 million against $458 million in 2012–2013. Bangladesh has received a significant amount of FDI from China worth $1.42 billion. According to Sahoo (2013a, b), the slow progress of India-Bangladesh economic relations has given an immense opportunity for China to expand its presence. Bangladesh is also planning to create separate SEZs for Chinese investors. The enormous interest of China in the BCIM corridor has also provided the opportunity for further expansion of economic ties between these two nations.[32] These developments are sufficient to believe that the Chinese influence on Bangladesh is stronger than India.

In South Asia, China and India's relationship plays a decisive role in shaping the geopolitical order of the region (see Yuan, 2007). The regression results suggest that India does not seem to be strongly linked with China. However, we present historical facts that may help reveal the status of economic integration between the two countries. With the accession of China to WTO in 2001, the trade share of China has gone up elevenfold globally during 1998–2012 (see Mohanty, 2014). The extent of bilateral trade between India and China has been high, and the trade balance seems to be in favour of the Chinese counterpart. In 2015, the bilateral trade between China and India amounted to $70.4 billion, which increased from $41.85 billion in 2008. In 2015, India and China reported the bilateral exports of $8.86 billion and $61.54 billion, respectively. The unbalanced trading pattern has resulted in a huge trade deficit for India. The trade deficit has widened in recent years, and it has reached to $52.67 billion. The bilateral investment also seems to be in favour of China. India has received a total investment of $2.763 billion compared to $0.564 billion investment in China.[33]

Concerning China and Nepal, the regression results (Table 3.7) suggest that the differences in broad money, external debt, and inflation seem to play a crucial role in the augmentation of the economic integration process. Both countries have historically been in good terms with the first formal economic aid agreement in October 1956. Since then, both countries have given priorities to their mutual economic interests with the establishment of the Inter-governmental Economic and Trade Committee (IGETC) in October 1982. In 2009, they again formed the *"China-Nepal Comprehensive Cooperative Partnership"* to facilitate trade, grant aid, investment, and tourism. However, India dominates the trade landscape of Nepal with a share of more than 65% of the total trade followed by China (10%) in 2010–2011 (see Prasad, 2015). In November 2012, China and Nepal signed the agreement to allow the free export of 7,787 products. On investment, as the regression results exhibit a positive effect on economic integration, it appears right as there is a large amount of Chinese investment in water resources and infrastructure buildings. Nepal attracts the highest amount of FDI from China. China has also expressed the interest to spend more than $8.3 billion in Nepal, which was announced in Nepal Investment Summit held in March 2017. Some of the ongoing projects include Upper Trishuli Hydropower Project, Kathmandu Ring Road Improvement Project with Flyover Bridges, and Pokhara International Regional Airport.[34]

The economic relationship between China and Pakistan, the regression results are shown in Table 3.7, the differences in broad money, external debt, and FDI are prime drivers of economic integration between the two countries. Scrutiny reveals that both countries signed the preferential trade agreement (PTA) in November 2003, which came into existence in 2006. Subsequently, FTA was signed in 2007 in Islamabad. The FTA envisaged the rationalization of tariffs in a phase-wise manner from 2007 to 2011. In the first phase, it was planned 30% rationalization on products from both sides, followed by 90% of the goods in the second phase. Since then, both countries have closely collaborated to deepen economic and trade relations. The deal between China and Pakistan reached to $15.15 billion from $1 billion in 1998. By 2018, both countries have planned to increase the size of trade to $18 billion. The trade volume between both nations has increased by 18% from 2014–2015. To boost foreign investment, the Pakistan government has also earmarked areas for the development of SEZs for Chinese investors. The most significant economic decision between both the nations seems to be the agreement to create the China-Pakistan Economic Corridor (CPEC) funded by the Chinese government to link the road from northern Pakistan to western China.[35] Another major project undertaken by China in Pakistan is the development of the Gwadar port in Balochistan.[36] However, the trade agreements seem to be working in favour of China as it has access to the new market for its exports and energy supplies through Gwadar port (see Kumar, 2007).

Focussing on the China-Sri Lanka relationship, the regression results do not show the evidence of significant economic integration between the two countries during the sample period. However, a close survey of historical developments reveals that the first economic agreement between two nations was signed in 1962, known as *Economic and Technological Cooperation,* followed by a maritime agreement in 1963. Another agreement named Sino-Lanka Joint Commission for Economic and Trade Cooperation was signed in 1991. The economic ties between these two nations were further boosted by the eight bilateral agreements covering investment, services, trade, media, communication, agriculture, education and industry in 2007. Seeing the progress of healthy economic relations, these two nations have further signed the agreement on investment facilitation involving the central banks. Besides the trade linkages, China also provides development assistance through aid, technical knowledge transfer and investments in numerous products in Sri Lanka. However, like other SAARC countries, the trade agreements seem to be working in favour of China as it enjoys a large trade surplus. The share of Sri Lanka's imports from China increased by about 14% in 2012, whereas China's imports from Sri Lanka accounted for only 1.2% in the same period. In 2015, the import from China amounted to $3727 million and accounted for a 20% share in total imports of Sri Lanka.[37] Both the countries are also contemplating to have an FTA so that Sri Lanka can also utilize its full potential in the areas where it has a comparative advantage. In this regard, the Sri Lanka export council has shortlisted 500 products in which the country has a comparative advantage over China. However, the APTA has provided some space to accommodate the trade interest of Sri Lanka. In the last five years, China has expressed enormous interest in the Sri Lankan economy. It is evident from the fact that during 2005–2012, the Sri Lankan economy received the financial assistance of worth $5.1 billion. More than 94% of grants and loans welcomed by the Sri Lankan government have roots in China (see Kalegama, 2014).

Conclusion and final remarks

This chapter examines the possible determinants of the economic integration of SAARC countries, including China, for the period 1991–2015. Using a three-step empirical procedure, we conclude that the process of economic integration between SAARC countries is weak as a majority of macroeconomic variables failed to reveal the significant impact on the BCS variable. However, on the brighter side, the data reveals that in order to foster the process of economic integration, the monetary policy coordination, trade, FDI and external debt factor could play a significant role. We do not find consistent results of fiscal and monetary indicators, highlighting a significant regulatory gap. The growth spillovers are observable, which means that the high growth of large countries in a group provides positive synergy to regional integration. Within SAARC, India appears to be better integrated than its counterparts. However, at the regional level, China's influence on SAARC's economic landscape is visible except Sri Lanka, and in some cases, it even appears to be more dominant than India. The analysis of the regression results of China and India visibly explains the dominance of China in the SAARC. The geographical proximity and colossal infrastructural investment make China's presence stronger than India.

Based on the results of this chapter, we thus conclude that the political and economic landscapes of SAARC seem to be dependent upon the extraordinary economic interest of India. For the small economies, China has already created an alternative platform for a better bargain with India. Nevertheless, the massive infrastructural investment and coordinated efforts at the regional level can create the possibility of better economic cooperation of India with SAARC. However, among global variables, the economic uncertainties in China and the USA and the indicator of global economic activity seem to be conveniently explaining the economic integration of SAARC countries. It also allows us to believe that these countries have gradually started making a mark on the global map.

Notes

1 De Haan et al. (2008) provide an excellent review of studies on the BCS in case of European countries.
2 All the above series are available in a yearly format, and we have interpolated into quarterly using the appropriate method to generate a sufficient number of observations. However, for regression analysis, we adjust the sample period and conduct the analysis for the period 1996: Q1–2015: Q4.
3 To extract the output gaps, we obtain the cyclical components, deviated from the trend components with Lambda = 1600.
4 https://sites.google.com/site/lkilian2019/research/data-sets (accessed on 11 September 2019).
5 We do not control the model with any socio-economic and institutional indicators because these variables will be incorporated in the subsequent chapters to analyse the cases of business and financial cycle interdependence and bilateral trade.

6 For complete list of variables, please see Table 3.1A.

7 The economic policy uncertainty (EPU) index of Baker et al. (2016), available at http://www.policyuncertainty.com.

8 We assign zero to value which are very small and close to zero.

9 For more details, please refer: http://www.cpd.org.bd/downloads/IRBD/INT03-01.pdf (accessed on 21 October 2017).

10 Please see https://www.wsj.com/articles/china-economic-growth-slows-to-6-9-on-year-in-2015-1453169398 (accessed on 21 October 2017).

    See also https://www.economist.com/news/business-and-finance/21662092-china-sneezing-rest-world-rightly-nervous-causes-and-consequences-chinas (accessed on 21 October 2017).

11 See for details: https://www.adb.org/countries/subregional-programs/sasec. SASEC is also popularly called as BBIN group.

12 In 2015–2016, the export basket of Bangladesh included woven garments, knitwear, textiles, agricultural products, raw jute. Nepal in return exported the vegetable products, prepared foodstuffs, mineral products, wood and articles of woods, etc.

13 https://www.dhakachamber.com/Bilateral/Nepal-Bangladesh%20Bilateral%20Trade%20Statistics.pdf (accessed on 19th October 2017).

14 See for example: http://www.bhccolombo.lk/agreements/ (accessed on 19 October 2017).

15 http://www.dhakatribune.com/bangladesh/foreign-affairs/2017/07/14/pm-hasina-sirisena-hold-bilateral-talks/ (accessed on 19 October 2017).

16 See for details http://www.industry.gov.lk/web/images/pdf/xz150.pdf (accessed on 19 October 2017).

17 http://dhakachamber.com/bilateral-trade/saarc (accessed on 15th September 2019).

18 See for further details: http://www.livemint.com/Politics/vxvVONyVlbRr-wNnuvwhazK/Bangladesh-PM-Sheikh-Hasina-pitches-for-more-trade-channels.html (accessed on 20 October 2017). In April 2017, Bangladesh and India also signed the agreement to generate power by establishing Bangladesh India Friendship Power Company Limited (BIFPCL). The project will be funded by EXIM Bank of India and has the production capacity of 1,320 megawatt (MW), located in Maitree Power Project in Rampal, Bangladesh.

19 https://economictimes.indiatimes.com/news/economy/foreign-trade/india-bangladesh-trade-may-almost-double-to-10-billion-by-2018-cii/articleshow/37126716.cms (accessed on 20 October 2017).

20 See for further details: http://www.mea.gov.in/Portal/ForeignRelation/India_Nepal_Relations_11_04_2017.pdf (accessed on 20 October 2017).

21 See for details: https://tribune.com.pk/story/548768/trade-between-india-and-pakistan-surges-21-to-2-4-billion/ (accessed on 21 October 2017).

22 For further details, please refer Taneja, Ray and Devyani (2016) on India-Pakistan trade relations. Please see also http://indiapakistantrade.org/pdf/Data%20Sheet_India_Pakistan_2015.pdf (accessed on 21 October 2017).

23 Source: http://www.mumbai.mission.gov.lk/index.php/trade/indo-lanka-trade-relations (accessed on 21 October 2017).

24 See for details: http://mea.gov.in/portal/foreignrelation/sri_lanka.pdf (accessed by 21 October 2017).

25 See https://dailytimes.com.pk/44003/pakistans-diplomatic-relations-with-bangladesh/ and http://www.ipcs.org/article/bangladesh/pakistan-bangladesh-free-trade-agreement-1237.html (accessed by 21 October 2017).

26 See for further details: http://www.efourcore.com.np/tepcdatabank/country-wise.php (accessed on 21 October 2017).

27 http://pakembnepal.org.pk/pak-nepal-economic-relations/ (accessed on 21 Octobcr 2017).
http://pakembnepal.org.pk/pak-nepal-economic-relations/ (accessed on 21 October 2017).

28 https://www.srilankabusiness.com/news/pakistan-expects-to-invest.html (accessed on 15th September 2019).

29 See for details: http://www.reuters.com/article/sri-lanka-pakistan-sharif/sri-lanka-pakistan-to-include-services-in-trade-pact-idUSL3N14P38Z20160105 (accessed on 21 October 2017).

30 See for details: https://www.dawn.com/news/1230917 (accessed on 21 October 2017).

31 See http://internationalaffairsbd.com/bangladesh-china-economic-military-diplomatic-relations/ and http://bdembassybeijing.com/index.php/en/commerce-en/bangladesh-china-trade-and-economic-relations-en (accessed on 21 October 2017).

32 http://www.mea.gov.in/Portal/ForeignRelation/China_Jan_2016.pdf(accessed on 21 October 2017).

33 http://mofa.gov.np/nepal-china-relations/ (accessed on 21 October 2017).

34 For more details on CPEC: https://www2.deloitte.com/content/dam/Deloitte/pk/Documents/risk/pak-china-eco-corridor-deloittepk-noexp.pdf (accessed on 21 October 2017).

35 https://businessmirror.com.ph/new-economic-corridor-to-boost-pakistan-china-trade-relations/ and https://www.dawn.com/news/1254586 (accessed on 21 October 2017).

36 http://blogs.lse.ac.uk/southasia/2017/05/22/sri-lanka-china-trade-relations-time-to-focus-on-unexplored-chinese-markets/ (accessed on 21 October 2017).

4

FACTORS INFLUENCING THE SAARC'S BILATERAL TRADE

Evidence from spatial econometrics models

Wasim Ahmad, Sanjay Sehgal and Mahendra Kumar Singh

Introduction

In the previous chapter, we found the significant role of external economic factors, including trade as one of the major explicators of economic integration between SAARC nations. In this chapter, we examine the impact of political, social and economic factors on the bilateral trade of major SAARC nations. Specifically, using spatial econometric technique, we investigate whether the imports and exports of the SAARC region are affected by these factors. So far most of the existing studies have examined the impact of economic factors on trade under gravity framework, this chapter takes a different perspective and examines the possible determinants of bilateral trade under gravity-based spatial econometric modelling (see Srinivasan and Canonero, 1995; Hassan, 2001; Baysan et al. 2006; Akhter and Ghani, 2010; Saini, 2011; Kumar and Ahmed, 2015). One of the key features of the spatial modelling is that it helps explain the supply models such as Ricardian and Heckscher-Ohlin in a better way than the conventional gravity model. For instance, the interpretation of direct and indirect effects helps explain the spatial spillover effects which further provides a new direction to understand the extent of trade integration (see LeSage and Pace, 2009). The inclusion of a large set of unique economic, political and social risk factors in the spatial model also makes our analysis superior to the existing ones. In the recent past, the study of Hossain et al. (2012) has used the spatial framework to explain the impact of Information and Communication Technology (ICT) on the market access and trade for Bangladesh and India.

The main motivation for this chapter comes from the fact that despite the measures of regional cooperation and economic development, the SAARC region has not been able to harness the trade potential between member nations. Although the SAFTA (Agreement on South Asian Free Trade Area) and SATIS (*South Asian Agreement on Trade in Services*) implemented in 2006 and 2010, respectively, envisage the role of trade integration in the region between 2006 and 2016, but it has not been able to yet fully materialized due to several reasons (see Ahmad and Sehgal, 2017; Kanungo,

2017). The formidable reasons could be because of the geopolitical conflict and mistrust among member nations. The intra-SAARC trade stands out to be below 5% of the total trade, significantly lower than the 25% in the case of the Association of South East Economic Nations (ASEAN), Commonwealth of In'dependent States' (CIS) (20%) and European Union (EU) – 27 (around 59%) (Exim Bank of India, June, 2014). The figures of intra-regional exports and imports also are at 5.8% and 3.4%, respectively, lower than the other trading blocks. However, the implementation of SAFTA, SATIS and subsequent SAARC meetings has also paved the way for better regional and economic integration as the region has experienced a surge in trade expansion. One of the peculiar features of the SAARC region is that its smaller member countries are major drivers of trade and development as compared to the larger ones. For example, Bhutan and Nepal in SAARC trade mostly with India and other SAARC members, whereas India, Pakistan and Bangladesh have trade relations majorly with the rest of the world. The total exports of Bhutan and Nepal account for about 88% and 64%, respectively, mainly directed towards India. It implies that for smaller countries SAARC does provide a better platform for trade expansion. However, larger countries exhibit limited trade share in SAARC. India, Bangladesh and Sri Lanka account for less than 10% in the total exports of the SAARC region. The 18th SAARC Summit (2013) held in Nepal (Kathmandu) also stressed on the need for better regional cooperation and free trade facilitation. Utilization of SAARC development fund through economic and social windows was also emphasized.

Besides this, the analysis is also timely and important especially at the time when India along with Bangladesh is pushing for BIMSTEC (Bay of Bengal Initiative for Multi-Sectoral Technical and Economic Cooperation) than SAARC (see UNESCAP, 2016; Rahman and Grewal, 2017). According to UNESCAP (2016), the overlapping initiatives for regional integration include the Economic Cooperation Organization (ECO) in which Afghanistan and Pakistan are the SAARC members. This development has raised a serious concern for the survival of SAARC as an effective regional bloc in the South Asia region.[1] The possible explanation for such a tectonic shift in regional integration is primarily due to political interference and cross-border violence between India and Pakistan. Further, to keep Pakistan out of SAARC bloc, India has even signed a pact with Bangladesh, Bhutan and Nepal and has created an acronym as BBIN (Bangladesh, Bhutan, India and Nepal).[2] However, in the light of these developments, the outcome of this chapter could be seen as a major contribution to the design and development of future bilateral trade policy in the SAARC.

The remainder of the chapter is organized as follows. The second section reviews the existing literature. The third section is about methodology and data source. The fourth section discusses our empirical results, and the fifth section concludes with policy recommendations.

Related literature

Similar to our study, most of the studies in case of SAARC have used the gravity framework on a large number of factors to explain the major determinants of bilateral trade. Using the gravity model, Srinivasan (1994) and Srinivasan and Canonero (1995) examine the possible impact of SAPTA. Their study concluded that smaller countries in SAARC would be the prime beneficiaries of preferential trade facilitation. Further, Rajapakse and Arunatilleke (1997) examine the bilateral trade between Sri Lanka and the rest of the SAARC nations using the gravity model. Their study finds that there is enough potential for further expansion of trade after the removal of restrictive trade. Samaratunga (1999) examines the bilateral trade among SAARC nations. Using a gravity framework, the study finds that there are better trade potentials among member nations. Hassan (2001) examines the trade creation and trade diversion effects using the gravity model. The study reports in favour of trade creation without trade diversion with the rest of the world. Rahman et al. (2006) apply augmented gravity model to study the role of SAPTA in trade creation along with nine other regional trading blocs. The findings of the study suggest that there is the scope of extra intra-regional trade creation under SAPTA. Rodríguez-Delgado (2007) assesses the impact of SAFTA agreement from the perspective of regional trade facilitation. Using the gravity model approach, their study reports that there is a limited impact of SAFTA on regional trade flows. In contrast to this, the study of Dayal et al. (2008) comes out with the contrary outcomes and suggests that SAFTA has a huge potential for trade creation and regional cooperation in SAARC. In a different study, Banik and Gilbert (2008) examine the impact of trade costs on the trade flow in South Asia. Using a modified gravity approach, the study finds that the infrastructure bottlenecks, lack of regulations and weak regulatory institutions are formidable reasons for high trade costs. Among recent studies on SAARC, Moinuddin (2013) finds that the rationalization of tariff and non-tariff barriers will positively impact the intra-trade-bloc among SAARC nations. Kumar and Ahmed (2015) examine the major determinants of export and import across SAARC nations using gravity approach for the period 1985–2011. They find GDP and population as major determinants of export and import flows.

Methodology and data

Based on the nature of the research problem, the spatial dependence model can be specified in various ways. In this chapter, following Martinez-Zarzoso (2003), Anderson and van Wincoop (2004), Rose (2004), Elhorst (2012) and Chou et al. (2015), we apply the three versions of the spatial model to estimate the spatial panel data models. These three models are a spatial autoregressive model (SAR), spatial error model (SEM) and spatial Durbin model (SDM).[3]

Data

Based on the availability of yearly data, we choose the sample period from 1980 to 2015 for four major SAARC countries, viz., Bangladesh, India, Pakistan and Sri Lanka. The list of explanatory variables is analysed and discussed in the subsequent section, and is sourced from World Integrated Trade Solution (WITS), International Financial Statistics (IFS), World Development Indicators (WDI), International Country Risk Guide (ICRG), Human Development Reports published by United National Development Programme (UNDP) and Contiguous variables namely language and distance are retrieved from the CEPII database. Table 4.1 shows the list of variables (factors) considered. Table 4.2 exhibits the descriptive statistics of sample variables. We infer the absence of an outlier in the dataset. The explanation about the choice of explanatory variables is discussed in the next section.

Variable definitions

In this subsection, we explain some of the important explanatory variables. GDP_{it} and GDP_{jt} represent the GDP in year t of each of SAARC countries and their trade partners, respectively. We have selected these variables based on the findings of existing studies which suggest that there is a positive relationship between economic growth and exports and imports of a country. According to Chou et al. (2015), if the estimated coefficient of GDP in the exporting country is larger than the importing country, it means that the exporting country is the net exporter because of the home country effect. Following Egger (2002), Baltagi et al. (2003), Serlenga and Shin (2007) and Salim and Kabir (2010), we use RFE (relative factor endowments) to capture the extent of the difference in factor endowments between the two trading partner countries. Specifically, according to Kumar and Ahmed (2015), the RFE shows the comparative advantage of one country over another and it is calculated as the difference between the natural log of per-capita GDPs between exporting and importing countries. RFE takes a value of zero when there is equality of factor endowments, and higher magnitude implies a higher share of inter-industry trade compared to intra-industry trade.[4] POP_{it} and POP_{jt} are the populations of sample SAARC countries i and j in year t. $OPEN_{it}$ and $OPEN_{jt}$ measure the extent of trade openness (measured by trade as a percentage of GDP) in year t in a sample SAARC country and its trading partner, respectively (see Wu et al. 2007; Chou et al. 2015). Studies have concluded that economic openness is considered as a positive factor for bilateral trade and development (see Krueger, 1974; Bhagwati, 1991; Isham and Kaufmann, 1999; René and Mollick, 2012). HDI_{it} and HDI_{jt} show the human development index of a SAARC country i in the year t and the partner countries. The role of human development in augmenting trade

Table 4.1 Data and Variables' Description

Factors	Definition	Source	Remarks
EXP.	Bilateral export (real) (constant USD)	WITS IFS	
IMP	Bilateral import (real) (constant USD)	WITS IFS	
GDP	GDP at market prices (constant 2005 USD)	WDI	
RFE	Relative factor endowment [modulus of [pci(i) – pci(j)]	Authors' Calculation	See Kumar and Ahmed (2015)
POP	Population, total	WDI	
OPEN	Trade (% of GDP)	WDI	Openness (country's volume of trade (export-import)/ GDP)
REER	Real effective exchange rate index (2010 = 100)	WDI	See Salim (2015), a bilateral exchange rate could be calculated using triangular system WRT USD
REMIT.	Personal remittances, received (% of GDP)	WDI	Remittances (received as % of GDP)
M2	Money and quasi-money (M2) as % of GDP	WDI	
Private	Domestic credit to private sector by banks (% of GDP)	WDI	
Govt.	A-government stability	ICRG	
SOC	B-socioeconomic conditions	ICRG	
INV.	C-investment profile	ICRG	
Internal	D-internal conflict	ICRG	
External	E-external conflict	ICRG	
Corruption	F-corruption	ICRG	
Law	I-law and order	ICRG	
Democrat	K-democratic accountability	ICRG	
Burea	L-bureaucracy quality	ICRG	
HDI	Human development index	UN HDI	

Source: Authors.

and economic growth has been highlighted by the studies of Cohen and Soto (2007) and Mustafa et al. (2017). To take into account the extent of bilateral trade flows, we use $REER_{it}$ and $REER_{jt}$ as Real Effective Exchange Rate. In other words, we examine the impact of exchange rate fluctuations on the trade balance. Studies have shown that the exchange rate depreciation has a significant and positive impact on the trade balance (see Petrović and Gligorić, 2010). In the case of SAARC countries, Ahmed (2000) finds

Table 4.2 Descriptive Statistics

Variables	Mean	Std. Dev.	Minimum	Maximum
GDP	2.154e+11	3.407e+11	9.719e+09	1.598e+12
Remit	4.651	2.467	0.730	10.59
POP	3.287e+08	4.181e+08	1.560e+07	1.295e+09
OEN	40.42	19.43	12.01	88.64
HDI	0.523	0.106	0.386	0.757
EX.	52.82	28.17	11.36	130.6
M2	42.75	13.38	19.59	77.98
Private	26.41	9.194	8.799	51.87
GOVT	6.786	2.360	1.830	11.08
SOCIO	4.588	1.441	1	7.830
INV	6.302	1.500	2.420	9.330
Internal	6.084	2.542	0.01000	10.75
External	8.665	2.059	4	12
Corruption	2.278	0.846	0.01000	4
Burea	2.058	0.754	0.01000	3
Democrat	3.628	1.443	0.01000	6
Law	2.583	1.077	0.01000	4
RFE	0.360	0.301	0	1.040

Source: Authors.

Note: Please see Table 4.1 for variables' sources and description.

REER as one of the important determinants of trade flow in case of Bangladesh. Bandara and McGillivray (1998) in the case of South Asia examine and find exchange rate movements as an important determinant of bilateral trade flow. The sign and magnitude of REER will also help in examining the possibilities of forming a currency union in SAARC. According to Jayasuriya and Maskay (2010) and Forhad (2014), SAARC countries are one of the largest recipients of global remittances. However, in the literature, studies have come out with mixed outcomes. For example, according to Jawaid and Raza (2016), personal remittances have a positive impact on the economic growth of SAARC countries. Whereas, Roy and Dixon (2016) and Uddin and Murshed (2017) suggest the case of Dutch Disease as far as the impact of personal remittance on the real exchange rate and competitiveness in the tradable sector is concerned. However, in our estimation, we expect the sign of the coefficient to be positive and statistically significant. Additionally, we also employ quasi-money (M2) and domestic credit to the private sector (Private) as bilateral trade-facilitating variable because credit expansion and increase in money supply have a positive effect on productivity and export of every country (see Tsiang, 1961; Oskooee-Bahmani and Shabsigh, 1996; Minetti and ChunZhu, 2011; Manova, 2013).

As aforementioned, SAARC countries do not enjoy good relations with each other due to regional conflict and mistrust. To capture the impact of political risk on the bilateral exports and imports of sample SAARC countries, we rely on the political risk rating from the ICRG. ICRG's political risk database provides the basis to examine the political stability of a country on a relative basis. We rely on ICRG's political risk components, which provide a means of assessing the political stability of the countries on a relative basis. The index has been widely used, e.g., by Diamonte et al., (1996), Erb et al. (1996), Bilson et al. (2002), and Asiedu and Lien (2011) to study foreign direct investment and stock market behaviour. The ICRG political risk index is composed of 12 components which include government stability, external conflicts, internal conflicts, ethnic tensions, military in politics, religious tensions, socioeconomic conditions, investment profile, bureaucracy quality, corruption, law and order, and democratic accountability. The index assigns the value of these components with minimum points being zero and the maximum depending upon the maximum weight that the particular component occupies in the overall index. The higher points imply lower political risk. For our analysis, we have considered only nine components. According to Chou et al. (2015), political risk factors often act as implicit transaction costs to trading nations and can also be called as one of the important impediments of trade expansion. Influential studies in this field of research have also suggested that the absence of democratic set-up also often acts as friction to free flow of goods and services (see Méon and Sekkar, 2004; Giavazzi and Tabellini, 2005; Yu, 2007; Eichengreen and Leblang, 2008; Aidt and Gassebner, 2010; Bekaert et al. 2011a, 2011b; Valentina et al. 2013; Chou et al. 2015). To the best of our knowledge, this is the first study that examines the impact of different components of political risk on bilateral import and export of SAARC countries. Some of the prominent studies have used ICRG data to investigate the impact on foreign direct investment in case of Pakistan (Ahmad and Ahmed, 2014), corruption in SAARC (Kiran et al. 2013) and economic performance of SAARC (see Balach and Law, 2015; Pulok and Ahmeh, 2017) on corruption in Bangladesh. Under even multi-country context, studies are restricted to the effect of institutions and governance on economic growth. For example, Nawaz (2015) analyse the growth effects of institutions on a panel of 56 countries and conclude that improvement in the quality of institutions has a positive effect on economic growth. On trade openness, Marjit et al. (2014) examine the relationship between corruption and trade openness for a group of over 100 countries for the period 1982–1997. They find that the effect of corruption on trade openness depends upon the extent of relative factor abundance.

Results

After accounting spatial interaction, Tables 4.3 and 4.4 highlight the major findings from the gravity model estimation in the context of major SAARC countries. Table 4.3 reports findings from the gravity export model, whereas Table 4.4 illustrates estimates for the import model. Subsequently, we perform a Wald test to determine which spatial econometric model is better suited for modelling the trade flow in the selected SAARC countries. Wald test for the null hypothesis that SDM can be reduced to the spatial lag model is rejected in both the export and import models.[5] In a similar vein, the Wald test for the null hypothesis that SDM can be simplified to SEM is also rejected in both export and import models.[6] In both of the provided tables, we report the direct, indirect and total effects of a covariate on the modelled trade flow. LeSage and Pace (2009) illustrate that the direct effect incorporates direct and feedback effect from a neighbouring trading partner, whereas indirect effect comprises spatial spillover effect. In furtherance, reported total effect augments both direct and indirect effects to present the overall influence of a concerned explanatory variable on the trade flow.

Table 4.3 elicits the findings of modelling export in the selected SAARC countries. RFEs, population, openness, exchange rate and bureaucracy quality pickup statistical significance, and others remain mostly insignificant. Surprisingly, coefficients of GDP and GDP_j come out to be insignificant, which can be attributed to the fact that regional instability in the region hampers overall trade among the member countries. This seems relevant because according to the United Nations Economic and Social Commission for Asia and the Pacific (UNESCAP), the absolute intra-regional trade of South Asia is less than one-third of its trade potential. In 2014, the actual trade figure was about $27 billion compared to its potential at $81.2 billion (see UNESCAP, 2016).[7] The insignificance of coefficients of GDP also highlights the policy weaknesses and the absence of strategic trade policies in harnessing the regional trade potential. However, these findings are in contrast with the existing studies mainly Hassan (2001) and Kumar and Ahmed (2015) who report that GDP plays a vital role in determining the export and import flows. A RFE shows a weaker negative direct effect but strong positive indirect and total effect. In other words, we can say that terms of trade are influencing trade flow positively. In the context of intra-industry trade, it appears that the intra-industry is the mainstay of total SAARC export. This finding is consistent with Kumar and Ahmed (2015) who also find the same. The coefficient of the POP_j variables comes out to be positive and statistically significant across all of the intended effects, whereas POP_j is reported to be mostly insignificant with a weak indirect effect. Moreover, $OPEN_i$ is statistically significant in direct, indirect and total effect, whereas $OPEN_j$ picks up statistical significance with indirect effect positively. Findings on the interaction between openness and trade flow are in line with the prior expectation. $REER_i$ is reported to be insignificant across all effects, whereas $REER_j$ is mentioned to be impacting trade negatively indirect and total effects. Illustratively, we can argue that the depreciating exchange rate of the partner country is influencing overall

Table 4.3 SAARC Export Model

Variables	(1)	(2)	(3)	(4)	(5)
	Main	W*X	Direct	Indirect	Total
ln GDP$_i$	0.731	3.357	1.294	3.212	4.507
	(1.060)	(2.987)	(1.065)	(2.885)	(3.589)
ln GDP$_j$	−0.484	−2.402	−0.783	−2.075	−2.858
	(1.060)	(2.981)	(1.423)	(3.010)	(4.093)
RFE	−1.330***	5.164***	−0.513*	4.471***	3.958***
	(0.278)	(0.744)	(0.274)	(0.631)	(0.679)
ln Remit$_i$	0.145	0.477	0.255	0.614	0.870
	(0.169)	(0.541)	(0.214)	(0.517)	(0.689)
ln Remit$_j$	0.176	−0.300	0.161	−0.291	−0.130
	(0.169)	(0.541)	(0.212)	(0.491)	(0.653)
ln POP$_i$	7.197***	36.81**	14.57***	38.82**	53.39**
	(2.091)	(18.080)	(4.225)	(19.68)	(23.44)
ln POP$_j$	4.944**	−37.87**	−0.674	−33.06*	−33.73
	(2.091)	(18.10)	(4.560)	(19.05)	(23.22)
ln OPEN$_i$	1.365***	3.642***	2.196***	4.321***	6.517***
	(0.513)	(0.892)	(0.635)	(1.096)	(1.633)
ln OPEN$_j$	2.303***	−1.044	2.317***	0.267	2.584
	(0.513)	(0.890)	(0.709)	(1.138)	(1.734)
ln HDI$_i$	−1.241	−4.461	−0.301	11.84	11.54
	(6.813)	(78.30)	(15.57)	(75.97)	(90.23)
ln HDI$_j$	−5.820	−12.33	−12.09	−32.78	−44.86
	(6.813)	(78.30)	(16.25)	(77.15)	(92.02)
ln REER$_i$	0.601	0.691	0.635	0.617	1.251
	(0.551)	(1.425)	(0.713)	(1.482)	(2.087)
ln REER$_j$	−1.399**	−1.978	−1.895**	−2.530	−4.425*
	(0.551)	(1.425)	(0.829)	(1.683)	(2.407)
ln GOVT$_i$	−0.030	0.841	0.079	0.795	0.873
	(0.177)	(0.517)	(0.214)	(0.525)	(0.684)
ln GOVT$_j$	0.070	0.148	0.122	0.232	0.353
	(0.177)	(0.517)	(0.199)	(0.522)	(0.676)
ln SOC$_i$	0.018	−0.178	−0.026	−0.077	−0.103
	(0.162)	(0.696)	(0.235)	(0.748)	(0.925)
ln SOC$_j$	−0.009	−0.513	−0.141	−0.655	−0.796
	(0.162)	(0.696)	(0.261)	(0.759)	(0.981)
ln INV$_i$	−0.284	−0.067	−0.294	−0.156	−0.450
	(0.246)	(0.958)	(0.326)	(0.950)	(1.198)
ln INV$_j$	0.546**	−0.212	0.561*	0.014	0.575
	(0.246)	(0.958)	(0.331)	(0.914)	(1.165)
ln Internal$_i$	0.088	0.727	0.216	0.691	0.907
	(0.070)	(0.699)	(0.151)	(0.697)	(0.834)
ln Internal$_j$	−0.043	−0.134	−0.048	−0.018	−0.065
	(0.070)	(0.699)	(0.143)	(0.695)	(0.823)
ln External$_i$	−0.250	−0.759	−0.388	−0.848	−1.236
	(0.363)	(0.918)	(0.467)	(0.907)	(1.244)
ln External$_j$	−0.809**	0.256	−0.842*	−0.262	−1.104
	(0.363)	(0.917)	(0.489)	(0.916)	(1.315)

(Continued)

Variables	(1)	(2)	(3)	(4)	(5)
	Main	W*X	Direct	Indirect	Total
ln Corruption$_i$	0.066	−0.074	0.065	−0.039	0.025
	(0.066)	(0.343)	(0.097)	(0.363)	(0.443)
ln Corruption$_j$	−0.093	−0.084	−0.123	−0.147	−0.270
	(0.066)	(0.343)	(0.104)	(0.344)	(0.429)
ln Law$_i$	−0.021	−0.941	−0.171	−0.840	−1.011
	(0.083)	(0.585)	(0.149)	(0.626)	(0.757)
ln Law$_j$	0.002	0.615	0.0874	0.472	0.559
	(0.083)	(0.585)	(0.137)	(0.573)	(0.683)
ln Democrat$_i$	0.0003	−0.022	−0.015	−0.027	−0.042
	(0.049)	(0.130)	(0.059)	(0.126)	(0.170)
ln Democrat$_j$	−0.062	−0.130	−0.096	−0.157	−0.253
	(0.049)	(0.130)	(0.066)	(0.145)	(0.199)
ln Burea$_i$	−0.004	0.450*	0.079	0.437*	0.516
	(0.062)	(0.233)	(0.087)	(0.245)	(0.314)
ln Burea$_j$	−0.177***	−0.343	−0.249***	−0.415*	−0.664**
	(0.062)	(0.233)	(0.090)	(0.225)	(0.298)
ln M2$_i$	0.087	−1.246	−0.176	−1.628	−1.804
	(0.469)	(1.886)	(0.675)	(1.931)	(2.446)
ln M2$_j$	−1.106**	1.485	−0.885	1.316	0.431
	(0.469)	(1.885)	(0.680)	(1.755)	(2.291)
ln Private$_i$	−0.137	−0.708	−0.294	−0.801	−1.095
	(0.312)	(1.148)	(0.412)	(1.124)	(1.410)
ln Private$_j$	0.056	−0.230	0.006	−0.315	−0.309
	(0.312)	(1.147)	(0.409)	(1.163)	(1.477)
ρ	0.522***				
	(0.049)				
σ^2	0.193***				
	(0.013)				
Observations	496	496	496	496	496
R^2	0.45	0.45	0.45	0.45	0.45

Source: Authors.
Standard errors in parentheses.
[1] Wald Test for SAR model; χ^2 (35) = 329.99; Prob > χ^2 = 0.0000.
[2] Wald Test for SEM model; χ^2 (35) = 197.00; Prob > χ^2 = 0.0000.
*** $P<0.01$, ** $P<0.05$, * $P<0.1$.

export level. In the proceeding, investment profile and external conflict of the trading partner are showing a positive and negative direct effect on the overall export level, although weakly significant. In the subsequence, bureaucracy quality is highlighted to impact export level negatively in all of the estimated effects, with varying levels of statistical significance. This contradictory behaviour of the bureaucracy in our model can be attributed to the fact the stringent bureaucratic control is hampering trade scenario among the SAARC members. Lastly, positive spatial autocorrelation (ρ)

Table 4.4 SAARC Import Model

Variables	(6)	(7)	(8)	(9)	(10)
	Main	*W*X*	*Direct*	*Indirect*	*Total*
ln GDP$_i$	0.767	−0.751	0.589	−0.866	−0.277
	(0.957)	(2.692)	(1.001)	(2.705)	(3.396)
ln GDP$_j$	0.166	1.725	0.704	2.498	3.202
	(0.957)	(2.695)	(1.315)	(2.891)	(3.910)
RFE	−1.354***	4.803***	−0.540**	4.286***	3.746***
	(0.251)	(0.674)	(0.248)	(0.608)	(0.663)
ln Remit$_i$	0.192	0.417	0.307	0.612	0.919
	(0.153)	(0.489)	(0.202)	(0.498)	(0.664)
ln Remit$_j$	0.189	−0.332	0.163	−0.319	−0.157
	(0.153)	(0.489)	(0.199)	(0.471)	(0.627)
ln POP$_i$	3.191*	−24.35	−1.334	−25.84	−27.17
	(1.888)	(16.32)	(4.277)	(19.34)	(23.25)
ln POP$_j$	9.004***	21.51	15.04***	30.42	45.46*
	(1.888)	(16.31)	(4.768)	(19.12)	(23.57)
ln OPEN$_i$	1.970***	1.455*	2.515***	2.654***	5.169***
	(0.463)	(0.801)	(0.580)	(1.001)	(1.498)
ln OPEN$_j$	1.350***	0.542	1.595**	1.469	3.064*
	(0.463)	(0.801)	(0.666)	(1.145)	(1.714)
ln HDI$_i$	−1.042	16.80	4.250	33.70	37.95
	(6.151)	(70.71)	(15.30)	(72.77)	(86.99)
ln HDI$_j$	−3.104	−29.00	−12.77	−49.52	−62.29
	(6.151)	(70.71)	(15.97)	(74.06)	(88.91)
ln REER$_i$	−0.889*	−2.172*	−1.562**	−3.204**	−4.765**
	(0.497)	(1.288)	(0.683)	(1.492)	(2.086)
ln REER$_j$	0.009	0.856	0.178	1.089	1.268
	(0.497)	(1.287)	(0.756)	(1.583)	(2.242)
ln GOVT$_i$	0.052	0.733	0.166	0.777	0.943
	(0.160)	(0.467)	(0.201)	(0.510)	(0.665)
ln GOVT$_j$	0.007	0.181	0.0611	0.239	0.300
	(0.160)	(0.467)	(0.187)	(0.502)	(0.652)
ln SOC$_i$	−0.033	−1.939***	−0.435*	−1.994***	−2.429**
	(0.147)	(0.631)	(0.233)	(0.774)	(0.960)
ln SOC$_j$	0.088	1.225*	0.306	1.226	1.532
	(0.147)	(0.630)	(0.259)	(0.771)	(0.998)
ln INV$_i$	0.307	−0.371	0.293	−0.159	0.133
	(0.222)	(0.866)	(0.308)	(0.913)	(1.154)
ln INV$_j$	−0.307	−0.005	−0.341	−0.240	−0.581
	(0.222)	(0.865)	(0.311)	(0.873)	(1.116)
ln Internal$_i$	−0.046	0.207	−0.022	0.110	0.088
	(0.063)	(0.631)	(0.146)	(0.663)	(0.798)
ln Internal$_j$	0.123*	0.458	0.252*	0.693	0.945
	(0.063)	(0.631)	(0.142)	(0.667)	(0.796)
ln External$_i$	−0.486	−0.513	−0.621	−0.788	−1.409
	(0.328)	(0.828)	(0.433)	(0.871)	(1.193)
ln External$_j$	−0.204	0.167	−0.197	−0.0308	−0.228
	(0.328)	(0.828)	(0.455)	(0.873)	(1.251)

(Continued)

Variables	(6)	(7)	(8)	(9)	(10)
	Main	W*X	Direct	Indirect	Total
ln Corruption$_i$	-0.049	0.071	-0.034	0.048	0.014
	(0.059)	(0.310)	(0.094)	(0.350)	(0.430)
ln Corruption$_j$	0.046	-0.244	-0.004	-0.246	-0.249
	(0.059)	(0.310)	(0.099)	(0.331)	(0.414)
ln Law$_i$	0.049	-0.272	0.021	-0.150	-0.129
	(0.075)	(0.528)	(0.145)	(0.597)	(0.726)
ln Law$_j$	-0.072	0.082	-0.090	-0.094	-0.183
	(0.075)	(0.528)	(0.130)	(0.541)	(0.649)
ln Democrat$_i$	-0.088**	-0.307***	-0.169***	-0.382***	-0.551***
	(0.045)	(0.118)	(0.057)	(0.128)	(0.173)
ln Democrat$_j$	0.019	0.096	0.036	0.119	0.155
	(0.045)	(0.118)	(0.062)	(0.144)	(0.196)
ln Burea$_i$	-0.164***	-0.027	-0.186**	-0.136	-0.322
	(0.056)	(0.211)	(0.082)	(0.234)	(0.302)
ln Burea$_j$	0.024	0.133	0.059	0.176	0.235
	(0.056)	(0.211)	(0.086)	(0.217)	(0.289)
ln M2$_i$	-1.031**	0.628	-1.066*	-0.335	-1.401
	(0.423)	(1.702)	(0.627)	(1.847)	(2.337)
ln M2$_j$	-0.629	-0.562	-0.752	-0.576	-1.328
	(0.423)	(1.702)	(0.635)	(1.678)	(2.189)
ln Private$_i$	-0.136	-1.218	-0.410	-1.398	-1.808
	(0.282)	(1.037)	(0.385)	(1.090)	(1.367)
ln Private$_j$	0.0730	0.573	0.182	0.544	0.727
	(0.282)	(1.036)	(0.383)	(1.102)	(1.404)
ρ	0.550***				
	(0.046)				
σ^2	0.158***				
	(0.010)				
Observations	496	496	496	496	496
R^2	0.53	0.53	0.53	0.53	0.53

Source: Authors.
Standard errors in parentheses.
[1] Wald test for SAR model; null: SAR is preferable to SDM; χ^2 (35) = 388.22; Prob > χ^2 = 0.0000.
[2] Wald test for SEM model; null: SEM is preferable to SDM; χ^2 (35) = 229.97; Prob > χ^2 = 0.0000.
*** P<0.01, ** P<0.05, * P<0.1.

entails that export between a trading pair is positively influenced by exports to other member countries.

Table 4.4 mentions the result for the spatial econometric model of the import between SAARC members. Here as well, a similar set of variables pick up statistical significance as mentioned in the export model. RFE shows negative (positive) direct (indirect and total) effects. Overall, we can make emphasis that RFE is promoting intra-industry trade between partner countries. It also means that the RFE does not only contribute to the import directly but also through spatial spillover effects. POP_j comes out to be positively significant with indirect as well as total effect, which is in line with the standard gravity model results. This finding is consistent with Moinuddin (2013) and Kumar and Ahmed (2015). $OPEN_i$ is impacting import level positively across all the effects reported, whereas $OPEN_j$ is reported to be having positive direct and total effect although weakly significant. The possible explanation could be because of the underdeveloped legal, institutional and regulatory set-up. In a similar vein, as reported in the export model, $REER_i$ is influencing overall import level negatively. Surprisingly, the coefficient of the SOC_i variable shows negative direct, indirect and total effects on the import. For instance, we can argue that relatively well-off SAARC countries are exporting more and importing less. *Internal$_i$* variable shows positive impact on exports but it is weakly significant. Surprisingly, *Democrat$_i$* variable exhibits negative and appropriate statistical significance across all of the effects modelled. This finding asserts that more democratic countries among the SAARC nations are importing less, which can be attributed to the fact that they might be economically robust to import from other countries in the world, rather trading among them. In the proceeding, $M2_i$ exhibits a negative direct effect on the import but weakly significant. Lastly, as reported in the export model, here also the spatial autocorrelation parameter (ρ) comes out to be positive and statistically significant. Said otherwise, trade between partner country is positively influenced by the trade between another member country.

Conclusion and final remarks

Much of the empirical evidence has been reported on the trading patterns of SAARC countries. Here, in contrast, we provide evidence on the major factors which determine the bilateral trade of SAARC countries, a region characterized by a low level of interregional trade in South Asia and also by lack of economic coordination and mistrust. Therefore, some learnings for countries in South Asia and East Asia, which are also having a huge trade potential, can be derived from our results. Based on the estimated results of the spatial econometric model, we suggest that the bilateral trade policy should give importance to the cross-country trade flows instead of only on inter-industry or intra-industry trading patterns. We find that the RFEs, population, openness, exchange rate and bureaucracy quality have direct and indirect effects on the import and export flows of SAARC countries. However, in contrast to previous studies, we do not find GDP as a significant contributor to the export and import of SAARC. The possible explanation could be because of the limited trade creation opportunities provided by large countries. Another reason could be because of the lack of trade policy coordination and inefficient utilization of resources. This is in contrast with Hassan (2001), Ismail (2012), Moinuddin (2013) and Kumar and Ahmed (2015). The positive and statistically significant population co-efficient suggests that a higher rate of population will help in import and export expansion through economies of scale.

Given the low quality of regulatory institutions, widespread poverty and income inequality within and among SAARC nations, the results of this study suggest that the socioeconomic factors such as socioeconomic conditions, corruption, democratic accountability, human development index do not significantly explain the bilateral export of major SAARC nations. However, in the case of import, we find that socioeconomic conditions and democratic accountability determine the extent of import in these countries. To ensure the better level of trade interaction and to harness the trade potential of SAARC nation, there is an urgent need to revive the SAFTA and SATIS linked to services sector trade facilitation. The infrastructure projects to link major cities and ports across the SAARC region will also help utilize the trade potentials optimally.

As expected, we do not find the significant direct, indirect and total impacts personal remittances have on the bilateral trade (imports and exports) of sample SAARC nations. This finding is in agreement with Ahmad and Sehgal (2017) who also report that the personal remittances have limited impact on the bilateral business and financial cycles interactions.

Overall, the findings of this chapter suggest that the major determinants of trade in case of SAARC countries are population, endowments concerning per-capita income difference, economic openness and real effective exchange rate. The spatial econometric model visibly captures the extent of low economic and financial integration. The findings of this chapter also suggest that the low quality of regulatory and socioeconomic backwardness has limited impact on import and export. The findings of this chapter can also be analysed from the perspective of the relevance of SAARC as a viable economic block. The weak trade integration also opens the door for possible trade expansion through BIMSTEC and BBIN.

Notes

1 BIMSTEC comprises Bangladesh, Bhutan, India, Myanmar, Nepal, Sri Lanka and Thailand. The group is the home of around 21% population with a combined gross domestic product (GDP) of $2.5 trillion and more.
   See for more details: http://www.livemint.com/Politics/4JsOSUC4N-81BK0T7zNYecK/Why-is-Bimstec-so-important-for-India.html (accessed on 18 September 2017).

2 The BBIN connectivity project laid down by India during 18th SAARC Summit in Kathmandu as a symbol to showcase the willingness of four SAARC countries in favour of regional connectivity and sidelining Pakistan as a spoiler in the regional integration faced a setback when Bhutan failed to join the group because of its failure to get the formal approval from the parliament. For further details: http://www.livemint.com/Politics/ol0E49p8V9WqXpJUXBqFPL/

India-to-redraw-BBIN-connectivity-project-as-Bhutan-opts-out.html (accessed on 18 September 2017).

3 Please refer Appendix A for a detailed specification of spatial econometric model used in this chapter.

4 Conventionally, this variable is calculated by taking capital and labour ratios but due to unavailability of data, we take GDP per-capita as a proxy variable.

5 Export Model: χ^2 (35)= 329.99, Prob> χ^2=0.00; Import Model: χ^2 (35)= 388.22, Prob> χ^2=0.00.

6 Export Model: χ^2 (35)= 197.00, Prob> χ^2=0.00; Import Model: χ^2 (35)= 229.97, Prob> χ^2=0.00.

7 See for more detail: http://www.unescap.org/sites/default/files/Unlocking%20 the%20Potential%20of%20RECI%20in%20South%20Asia_0.pdf (accessed on 22 September 2017).

UNDERSTANDING THE BUSINESS AND FINANCIAL CYCLES' INTERDEPENDENCE IN SAARC COUNTRIES[1]

Wasim Ahmad and Sanjay Sehgal

Introduction

After examining the major determinants of economic integration and bi-lateral trade in Chapters 3 and 4, we now turn to examine a new research issue in the context of South Asia and empirically investigate the role of credit expansion within and across SAARC in this chapter. An appraisal of existing literature on the role of credit expansion suggests that the credit expansion has significant implications on the movements of business cycles of an economy (see Bernanke and Gertler, 1989; Bernanke et al. 1996, 1999; Kiyotaki and Moore, 1997; Fostel and Geanakoplos, 2008; Brunnermeier and Pedersen, 2009; Gertler and Kiyotaki, 2010; Jermann and Quadrini, 2012; Taylor and Schularick, 2012). In the case of developed countries, Antonakakis et al. (2015) examine the credit-growth spillover among G7 nations and apply directional spillover technique on a long time-series data spanning from 1957Q1 to 2012Q4. Using quarterly data on real credit growth and real GDP growth, their study finds that among G7, Canada, France, Italy and the UK report a relatively moderate level of interdependence between real credit growth and real GDP growth compared to Germany, Japan and the USA. They also conclude that the extent of directional spillover is the highest from the USA to other G7 countries. However, some studies have also reported that the credit-linked financial disruptions are often connected to the economic crisis, which in turn impacts the economy adversely (see Berger and Udell, 1998; Claessens et al. 2012; Jordà et al. 2013). In the cross-country credit spillover framework, credit-based financial spillovers impact the partner's country financial and business cycles significantly (see Antonakakis et al. 2015).

The main motivation comes from the fact that in the last one decade, South Asia has received considerable attention across the world and academia because of its sustained economic growth and development (see World Bank, 2017). The high growth record of South Asian countries has also re-kindled the interest of researchers to investigate whether its economic interest group, popularly known as the SAARC, could play a decisive role in creating the futuristic growth and development scenarios. On the economic growth front, South Asia has registered an impressive growth of 6.8% in 2015 which is relatively higher than the East Asia and Pacific (6.5%) and substantially better than the negative growths of Latin America and Sub-Saharan African nations. Despite these growth numbers, the factors like cross-border conflict, high incidence of poverty and ethnic conflict, the poor state of infrastructure development, rampant corruption and institutional failures often act as impediments in seeking the investors' attention at the global level and also thwart the possible opportunities of regional economic and financial integration.

The motivation to carry out this analysis also comes from the fact that the research landscape of credit-growth nexus has not paid sufficient attention to South Asia. Considering the possible rise of Bangladesh, India, Pakistan, and Sri Lanka in the international arena and even in South Asia, it is vital that these countries must be mapped on the credit-growth spillover scale and attempt to outline at least the first empirical evidence of such type. To the best of our knowledge, our research to study the linkage between credit growth and economic growth is the first of its kind on SAARC. The findings of this chapter are expected to provide a new roadmap for the success of SAFTA and SAARCFINANCE. The outcome of this chapter will also give a direction to infer upon whether the further development of the financial sector should be promoted. According to Estrada et al. (2010), further development of the financial sector will help in harnessing the better growth and development opportunities in developing Asia.[2]

In the literature, studies have defined financial cycle as the period which takes bullish and bearish periods into account, the same as a conventional business cycle (see Kiyotaki and Moore, 1997; Claessens et al. 2012). The bullish periods are those periods which are linked with the expansion phase of the business cycle, and bearish phases cover the periods of tranquil or contraction phases of the business cycles. From the perspective of policymakers, the analysis of dynamic interdependence between business and financial cycles helps understand whether the economy is ahead of the financial sector of the economy or it is otherwise. At the cross-country level, business-finance interaction facilitates the researchers and investors whether the disturbance in a large country or in a group of countries have positive or negative growth spillovers. In the case of SAARC nations, the outcome of this research will sharpen our understanding of the connection between the business and financial cycles.

The main objective is to examine the dynamic interdependence between financial cycle represented by real credit growth and business cycle shown by real GDP (Gross Domestic Product) of five leading SAARC countries, viz., Bangladesh, India, Nepal, Pakistan and Sri Lanka for the period 1975–2013.[3] We also consider China because of its rising influence in South Asia. After establishing the relationship between business and financial cycles, this research also sheds light on the possible determinants of interdependence and attempts to suggest some of the relevant factors responsible for credit-growth interactions. To do this, we apply the method of directional spillover of Diebold and Yilmaz (2012), henceforth DY. One of the salient features of the DY method is that it helps bifurcate the directional spillover (static and dynamic) into two directions namely *To* and *Fro*. This decomposition helps further in drawing inference about whether the particular variable is a net transmitter or net receiver of shocks. For instance, in our context, the interdependence between the real credit growth and real economic growth may help reveal whether the real credit growth is the net receiver or net transmitter of spillover to real economic growth and vice-versa.[4]

Overview of the financial landscape of SAARC region

Banks cover the financial landscape of SAARC countries with a share of 48% followed by the stock market (32%) and the small percentage of public and private bonds placements. The better economic outlook of Sri Lanka has also contributed to improving the financial outlook of SAARC. As a result, the share of the stock market has gone up significantly (see ADB, 2015).[5] The external sources of financing majorly come in the forms of foreign direct investment, official development assistance and remittances. South Asia is one of the largest recipients of remittances from its migrant population in the world. According to IFAD (2014), the remittances account for 28.5% of GDP in Nepal followed by Bangladesh (11.6%), Sri Lanka (about 10%), Pakistan (6%) and India (4%). On magnitude, India is the largest receiver of remittances in South Asia.

Overall, it is apparent that the banking sector dominates the financial sector of the SAARC region because of the limited availability of other financial services and the widespread poverty and illiteracy. The literature on finance-growth nexus suggests that in case of emerging and less developed economies, banking sector promotes economic growth through its central bank-guided pro- and-countercyclical credit expansion policies, which in turn help expand the financial horizon and reach of the financial services. However, given the critical role played by the banking sector in driving the economic growth, these countries should undertake measures for a well-guided banking sector reform that can help these economies to mobilize savings and ease credit availability, and help in the allocation of the inefficient resources to the productive sector of economies.

Data and methodology

For this chapter, we use the quarterly data from 1975Q4 to 2013Q4, for five SAARC countries, viz., Bangladesh, India, Nepal, Pakistan and Sri Lanka. The unavailability of long time-series data does not allow us to incorporate

Afghanistan, Bhutan and Maldives in our analysis. The credit growth is represented by domestic claims series available on International Financial Statistics (IFS) database of the International Monetary Fund (IMF).

The series of domestic claims on the IFS database include total claims of banks from national residency. The series is available under two different codes, viz., IFS-32 and IFS-FDSAD; we combine both the series to generate longer time-series. Since the data on GDP, GDP deflator and domestic claims are not available quarterly, these annual series are converted into quarterly data by using the interpolation method. The choice of the sample period is based on the availability of data. We have transformed both the series in real terms by deflating it with GDP deflator. Lastly, we calculate log-differenced year-on-year quarterly growth rate of both the series.

The descriptive statistics shown in Table 5.1 provides an overview of the variations in the real credit growth and real GDP growth of sample SAARC countries. India reports the highest mean value of real GDP growth of 5.5% followed by Sri Lanka (5%). Nepal exhibits the lowest real GDP growth during the sample period. The standard deviation of India is also higher compared to SAARC countries. As far as real credit growth is concerned, a comparison suggests that Nepal reports the maximum real credit growth rate (9.4%) followed by Bangladesh (8.2%) and India (8.1%). It appears that the countries reporting higher real GDP growth are low on real credit growth. It means that the financial sector of these economies is dependent on economic growth. To avoid the issue of non-stationarity and the presence of an outlier in the data, we check for stationarity and find that the real GDP growth series of Nepal and Sri Lanka and credit growth of series of Sri Lanka are non-stationary. All other

Table 5.1 Descriptive Statistics

	Mean	Std. Dev.	Skew.	Kurt.	JB	Prob.	ADF	Obs.
Gr_BAN	0.048	0.016	0.376	5.979	60.19**	0.000	−3.968**	153
Gr_IND	0.055	0.025	−1.194	6.520	115.3**	0.000	−3.559**	153
Gr_NEP	0.040	0.023	−0.570	4.322	19.41**	0.000	−1.843	153
Gr_PAK	0.047	0.019	−0.206	2.241	4.75**	0.093	−3.829**	153
Gr_SRI	0.050	0.018	−0.875	4.327	30.74**	0.000	−2.778	153
Cr_BAN	0.082	0.112	0.297	7.189	114.1**	0.000	−4.296**	153
Cr_IND	0.081	0.041	−0.687	3.152	12.18**	0.002	−3.160*	153
Cr_NEP	0.094	0.077	1.007	4.509	40.38**	0.000	−3.975**	153
Cr_PAK	0.054	0.074	−0.385	2.832	3.96**	0.138	−3.101*	153
Cr_SRI	0.070	0.124	−0.212	5.173	31.26**	0.000	−2.572	153

Source: Authors.

Note: Cr_BAN, Cr_IND, Cr_NEP, Cr_PAK, Cr_SRI represent real credit growth in Bangladesh, India, Nepal, Pakistan and Sri Lanka, respectively. Gr_BAN, Gr_IND, Gr_NEP, Gr_PAK and Gr_SRI show real GDP growth in Bangladesh, India, Nepal, Pakistan and Sri Lanka, respectively. * and ** denote the level of significance at 1% and better and 5% and above, respectively.

series achieve stationarity at their growth levels. The non-stationary series are further differenced before VAR-based DY estimation. Refer Appendix B on a detailed exposition on DY methodology.

Empirical results

Directional spillover within SAARC

We report the spillover indices of sample countries in Table 5.2. It appears that the sample SAARC countries exhibit homogenous patterns as far as the spillover between real credit growth and real economic growth is concerned. However, the spillover results are not encouraging as the extent of directional spillover across sample SAARC countries does not exhibit high values, and it hovers around 6%. To shed further light on this, we also calculate and analyse the net directional spillover of each country, the results report the same pattern as above. Based on the magnitude of total spillover index, we can say that among sample SAARC nations, Pakistan, Nepal, and Bangladesh exhibit a relatively higher level of credit-growth interdependence than India and Sri Lanka. The results of Sri Lanka seem to be surprising as it also enjoys the same level of financial development as Bangladesh and Nepal. However, we should not put stress more on the magnitude as all countries reported have their total spillover index less than 10% which can be called as very low.

In the context of financial development and economic growth, the net directional spillover results will have strong implications. It is because the spillover moving from credit to growth implies that the credit channel enforces the expansion of economic growth and vice-versa. The calculated net spillover results suggest that in the case of Bangladesh, economic growth augments the credit cycle of the economy. We find that the forecast error variance (FEV) of real economic growth explains more than the FEV of real credit growth. In terms of numbers, the real credit growth explains the FEV of real economic growth by only 3% compared to real economic growth which explains about 9.34%. The net directional returns spillovers report the same inference as India, Pakistan and weakly in case of Sri Lanka. However, the case of Nepal seems to be different as we find that the real credit growth spillover leads to the real economic growth cycle of the economy. In other words, the business cycle precedes the financial cycle. A close appraisal of existing studies on finance-growth nexus in the case of SAARC countries suggests that the results reported are in line with Ahmed and Ansari (1998), Shahid et al. (2015), Uddin et al. (2012) and Kharel and Pokhrel (2012) in cases of South Asia, Pakistan, Bangladesh and Nepal, respectively. These studies invariably report that the economic growth is contingent upon the financial development except Bangladesh which reports bilateral dependence.

Table 5.2 Spillover Table for Real Credit Growth and Real GDP
Growth within the SAARC

	gr_BAN	cr_BAN	From Others
gr_BAN	97	3	3
cr_BAN	9.34	90.66	9.3
Contri. to other	9.3	3	12.3
Contri. Incl. own	106.3	93.7	6.20%
	gr_IND	cr_IND	From Others
gr_IND	96.78	3.22	3.2
cr_IND	8.54	91.46	8.5
Contri. to other	8.5	3.2	11.8
Contri. Incl. own	105.3	94.7	5.90%
	gr_NEP	cr_NEP	From Others
gr_NEP	89.17	10.83	10.8
cr_NEP	4.27	95.73	4.3
Contri. to other	4.3	10.8	15.1
Contri. Incl. own	93.4	106.6	7.50%
	gr_PAK	cr_PAK	From Others
gr_PAK	95.92	4.08	4.1
cr_PAK	13.69	86.31	13.7
Contri. to other	13.7	4.1	17.8
Contri. Incl. own	109.6	90.4	8.90%
	gr_SRI	cr_SRI	From Others
gr_SRI	99.96	0.04	0.00%
cr_SRI	0.89	99.11	0.9
Contri. to other	0.9	0	0.9
Contri. Incl. own	100.8	99.2	0.50%

Source: Authors.

Note: The DY model is estimated using 10-step ahead VAR procedure.

The plot of the total spillover index of credit- growth shown in Figure 5.1
(a–e) suggests that for Bangladesh, the spillover index reaches its peak and
trough during 2002–2005 and 2008–2009, respectively. The reason for
2008–2009 can be marked as the contagion effect of the second phase of
the global financial crisis discussed in Chapter 3. The total spillover index
of India also reports a similar trend. The index reaches its peak and trough
during 2006–2007 and 2003–2004, respectively. The plots also exhibit the
same pattern in the case of Nepal that shows its peak in 2010. For Pakistan,
the spillover index reaches its maximum during 2005–2007. The index of
Sri Lanka exhibits moderate variation with a significant dip during 2008–
2009, marking the possible impact of the financial crisis. To summarize, it

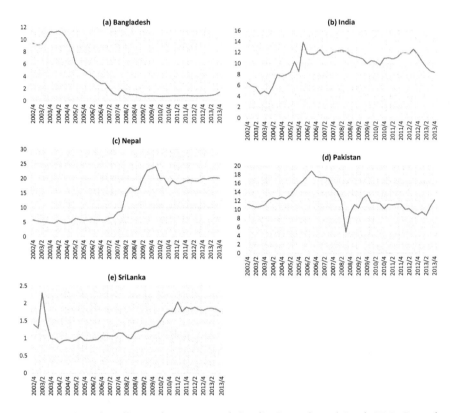

Figure 5.1 Total Spillovers between Real Credit Growth and Real GDP Growth within SAARC Countries.

Source: Authors' Calculations.

Note: Plot is estimated using 100-quarter rolling window.

is apparent that the total spillover index of most of SAARC countries captures the effect of the global financial crisis (2008–2009) and also highlight the periods of economic prosperity. The main reason for high variations in spillover index during a global financial crisis could be because of the massive decline in remittances and export distortions. These spillover trends are in agreement with the study of Antonakakis et al. (2015) who reported similar outcome in the case of G7 countries. The findings also seem relevant to the study of Bhaskaran and Ghosh (2010).

To confirm the direction of interdependence between real credit growth and real economic growth under the dynamic framework, we plot the net spillover series obtained from the DY estimation. These plots are shown in Figure 5.2 (a–e). The findings from this analysis will also validate the results of Table 5.2. The plots of Figure 5.2 (a–e) suggest that real credit is the

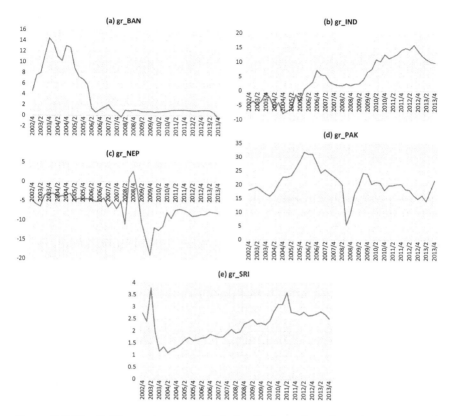

Figure 5.2 Net Spillovers between Real Credit Growth and Real GDP Growth within SAARC Countries.

Source: Authors' Calculations.

Note: (a) BAN, IND, NEP, PAK and SRI denote Bangladesh, India, Nepal, Pakistan and Sri Lanka, respectively. (b) Plots are estimated using 100-quarter rolling window.

net receiver of shocks in most of the cases except Nepal. These results imply that the real credit growth precedes the economic growth, and economic growth seems to be dependent upon the other factors such as remittances, trade and development assistance discussed in Chapter 3. In the case of Nepal, we find the strong case of credit channel linked economic growth, implying that the exogenous shocks on the credit channels of the country may hamper the domestic growth. However, the plots of dynamic net spillovers confirm the results presented in Table 5.2.

Directional spillover across SAARC

In this section, we analyse the process of directional spillover across SAARC countries to take into account the process of directional spillover moving from one country to another. The inference of economic integration presented in Chapter 3 provides the weak empirical evidence, indicating the economic integration as an evolving process. We re-estimate the DY model on credit-growth series of five SAARC countries.[6]

Table 5.3 exhibits the estimated results. We find that the extent of total spillover has gone up substantially and has reached up to 36.70% which is relatively better than the standalone results shown in Table 5.2. However, the magnitude of the total spillover index seems to be significantly lower than the results reported by Antonakakis et al. (2015) in their study on G7 countries. Taking the case of Bangladesh, we find that Bangladesh seems to be more integrated on the credit-growth front with India than any of the SAARC countries. The results of India reciprocate the high interdependence of Bangladesh and India, as the results suggest a relatively higher level of spillover between the credit-growth nexus of India and Bangladesh. However, the results do not report high interdependence between India and Pakistan from credit-growth spillover perspective. Sri Lanka and Pakistan exhibit relatively better level of economic integration via directional spillover. The direction of spillover seems to agree with the extent of bilateral results discussed in Chapter 3. The estimates of directional spillover allow us to conclude that among sample SAARC nations, the credit-growth channel of India seems to be more responsive than other members. India appears to be more integrated with Bangladesh followed by Nepal, Pakistan and Sri Lanka. The possible explanation of such interdependence could be linked with the trade and bilateral linkages that India provides to these nations including Pakistan. The favourable trade relation of India with SAARC countries could be one of the other explanations of such interdependence.

It is apparent that the analysis of credit-growth interdependence substantiates the regression results reported in Chapter 3. Based on the above findings, it can be concluded that the process of economic and financial integration via credit and growth is in an evolving stage and may be more useful for further analysis at a later stage. However, in the light of the socio-economic set-up of SAARC, the results seem appropriate as there is a wide gap among SAARC nations on regional coordination. Another formidable reason could be because of the strong presence of China in the SAARC. And as reported in Chapter 3, the presence of China and the political differences between India and Pakistan have provided enough space for a distraction from the core issues of regional economic integration and development in SAARC.[7]

The results of the net spillover shown in Figure 5.3 indicate that there is a visible impact of major turns in economic and financial cycles of sample SAARC countries during the Asian financial crisis (1997) and the global financial crisis (2008–2009). These turning points are also in line with the studies of Claessens et al. (2012), Jordà et al. (2013) and Antonakakis et al. (2015) in the context of developing and emerging economies. Figures 5.4 and 5.5 exhibit

UNDERSTANDING BUSINESS AND FINANCIAL CYCLES'

Table 5.3 Spillover Table for Real Credit Growth and Real GDP Growth among Sample SAARC Nations

	gr_BAN	gr_IND	gr_NEP	gr_PAK	gr_SRI	Cr_BAN	Cr_IND	Cr_NEP	Cr_PAK	Cr_SRI	From Others	Net Spillover
gr_BAN	50.17	21.51	3.16	0.52	1.47	2.59	11.89	5.36	2.45	0.88	49.8	−20.5
gr_IND	1.28	64.34	1.5	6.63	0.13	11.09	7.69	2.74	4.16	0.45	35.7	19
gr_NEP	1.36	8.1	61.85	4.33	1.34	5.58	2.08	8.26	4.82	2.29	38.2	−21.8
gr_PAK	4.18	7.24	0.42	72.28	2.29	7.18	0.25	0.79	3.76	1.61	27.7	19.8
gr_SRI	1.93	2.82	1.09	1.93	80.93	5.45	1.2	0.86	2.84	0.94	19.1	9.4
Cr_BAN	5.56	2.87	0.71	4.02	11.53	56.09	3.06	5.68	8.69	1.79	43.9	13.5
Cr_IND	4.9	3.9	0.5	0.66	1.94	7.92	73.69	3.95	0.39	2.17	26.3	3.7
Cr_NEP	2.52	4.32	4.3	2.42	2.03	11.65	1.15	51.01	18.87	1.74	49	−10.9
Cr_PAK	4.88	0.84	0.94	21.29	4.46	4.96	0.34	1.31	57.06	3.91	42.9	6
Cr_SRI	2.73	3.12	3.81	5.75	3.28	1.01	2.35	9.17	2.96	65.81	34.2	−18.4
Contri. to other	29.3	54.7	16.4	47.5	28.5	57.4	30	38.1	48.9	15.8	366.8	
Contri. incl. own	79.5	119.1	78.3	119.8	109.4	113.5	103.7	89.2	106	81.6	36.70%	

Source: Authors.

Note: The lags in the VAR model are calculated using appropriate information criteria. The 10-step ahead generalized variance decomposition is based on Diebold and Yilmaz (2012).

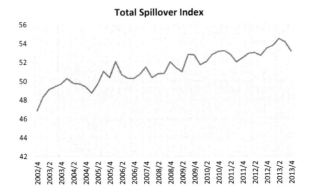

Figure 5.3 Total Spillovers between Real Credit Growth and Real GDP Growth across SAARC Countries.

Source: Authors' Calculations.

Note: Plot is estimated using 100-quarter rolling window.

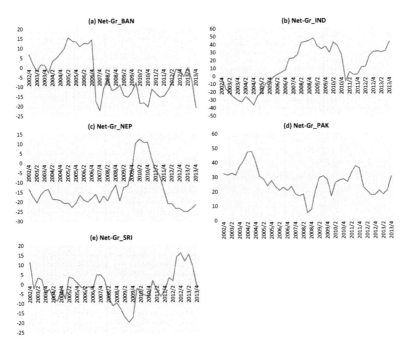

Figure 5.4 Net Spillover between *To* and *Fro* of Real GDP Growth of SAARC Countries.

Source: Authors' Calculations.

Note: Plots are estimated using 100-quarter rolling window.

88

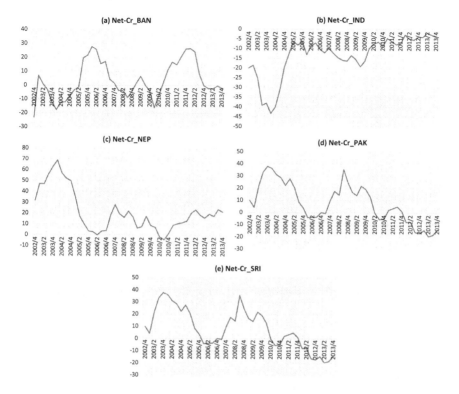

Figure 5.5 Net Spillover between *To* and *Fro* of Real Credit Growth of Sample SAARC Countries.

Source: Authors' Calculations.

Note: Plots are estimated using 100-quarter rolling window.

the net real GDP growth and net real credit growth spillovers among SAARC countries, respectively. The plots of net growth spillovers confirm the trend that we have seen in case of standalone (within) net spillover results of all the sample countries discussed above except Pakistan. Nepal consistently confirms its presence in SAARC as the credit-driven economy as the real credit growth is the net transmitter of growth spillover to the real economic growth even during the financial crisis period (2008–2009).

However, the extent of the impact of the global financial crisis (2008–2009) is not consistent across sample countries as some economies remained resilient during a turbulent period, implying that the heightened risk and uncertainty of US economy during 2008–2009 and its aftermath had variably moderate impact on these economies. These findings are in line with World Bank (2009) and Bhaskaran and Ghosh (2010). The above findings are also in agreement with the regression results of Chapter 3 in which the US-EPU had a mixed impact on the economic integration of SAARC countries including China.

Determinants of directional interdependence

After examining the dynamics of directional spillover under within and across scenarios, the study takes a different perspective and attempts to explore the factors which can explain the movements of directional spillover between real credit growth and real economic growth. To do this, we consider the following economic and investment promoting factors. For economic factors, we include government debt as a percentage of GDP, current account balance-to-GDP, inflation and interest rate as measures of economic and policy competitiveness of SAARC nations.[8] All variables are downloaded from Thomson Datastream. For investment-promoting factors, we consider macroeconomic environment rankings of sample SAARC countries from the Global Competitiveness Report published by the World Economic Forum (WEF). To account the cross-country investment spillover through financial instruments, we include gross portfolio equity assets to GDP.[9] We have also included indicators that can capture the role of financial inclusion in explaining the variations in business and financial cycles interdependence. For this purpose, we include two variables, viz., the number of bank branches per 100,000 adults and mobile cellular subscriptions per 100 people.[10] We have sourced the number of bank branches from the Global Financial Development Database maintained by the World Bank and the mobile subscribers from the World Development Indicators (WDI) maintained by the World Bank. According to World Bank's "The Global Findex Database 2014", owning a bank account is one of the pre-requisites of measuring the progress of financial inclusion of a country.

According to Villasenor et al. (2016), the mobile ecosystem in South Asia is playing a critical role in facilitating the quality financial services even at the grass root level. The recent trend suggests that there has been a spectacular increase in the number of mobile subscribers in the South Asian region.[11] It is likely that the introduction of mobile payment services and the mobile-based transaction system will help banks in providing the banking services at ease and also help them in mobilizing funds to lend it to the firms operating in a different spectrum of the economy. It is also highly likely that certain proportions may also be used for cross-country investment which may in turn help augment the process of credit-growth spillover.

In South Asian economies, remittances are often considered as a backbone as it helps in numerous ways to drive the economy. To incorporate this into our analysis, we include remittance inflows as a percentage of GDP retrieved from the Development and Structure Database maintained by the World Bank.[12] To estimate and identify the significant determinants of credit-growth spillover in SAARC, we form a balanced panel of five sample SAARC countries for the period 2006Q1–2013Q4.[13] We estimate the fixed-effect model by considering the corresponding net pairwise growth spillover series.[14] We also introduce the time-varying dummy covering the global financial crisis period (2008–2009). The dummy takes the value 1 during the crisis period and 0 otherwise.

Table 5.4 reports the results of the fixed-effects model. We find that among economic indicators, government debt/GDP and interest rate impact the net credit-growth spillover positively. The positive effect of government debt/GDP ratio in case of SAARC countries seems appropriate as most countries are heavily dependent on external aid and lines of credits as discussed in Chapter 3. According to the World Bank (2016), the debt to GDP ratio of South Asian economies is around 58%. The coefficient of inflation picks positive sign, implying that the interaction between business and financial cycles augments the inflationary pressure in these economies. The coefficient of investment indicator exhibits a positive sign though not statistically

Table 5.4 Panel Regression Results

	Without Dummy	*With Dummy*
Constant	−50.197 (−3.21)**	−27.846 (−1.73)**
		−2.080 (−3.79)**
Macroeconomic variables		
Government debt/GDP	7.47 (2.32)**	1.618 (0.47)
Current account/GDP	0.122 (1.10)	0.128 (1.21)
Inflation	−0.109 (−1.65) *	−0.116 (−1.84)**
Interest rate	0.327 (2.54)**	0.388 (3.13)**
Proxies for investors' sentiment		
Macroeconomic environment	0.797 (0.53)	0.949 (0.62)
Proxies for cross-country investment and financial inclusion		
Portfolio equity assets	0.012 (0.01)	1.302 (1.05)
Remittances	−0.499 (−0.65)	−0.576 (−0.78)
Mobile subscribers	0.339 (1.79)**	0.280 (1.54)*
Number of bank branches	5.488 (2.87)**	1.770 (0.85)
R^2		
Within	0.165	0.242
Between	0.624	0.104
Overall	0.532	0.048
Observations	155	155

Source: Authors.

Note: Table illustrates panel regression results of determinants of net directional spillovers moving from one to all others. Dependent variable is net spillover index. Values in brackets exhibit *t*-statistics.
** denotes the level of significance at below 5% and below 10%.
* denotes the level of significance between 10% and 15%.

significant, indicating the positive spillover effect on credit-growth nexus in SAARC. However, the variables explaining the phenomena of cross-country investment and financial inclusion report mixed results. The coefficient of portfolio equity asset has a positive impact on the net directional spillover, and it is not statistically significant. However, the coefficient of remittances picks a negative sign, and it is statistically insignificant. It is surprising because it seems intuitionally incorrect as it is supposed to exhibit a positive relationship with cross-country spillover. A close appraisal of existing literature suggests that the remittance inflows have a visible impact more on the real economic activities than the financial sector. In a study at ADB, Ozaki (2012) suggests that remittances inflow in South Asian economies through formal and informal channels have a limited role in the effective capital enhancement mechanism in the financial system. It has been found that due to lack of proper financial infrastructure, remittances are mostly used for the livelihood purposes and physical asset creation such as housing, purchase of land and other durable and non-durable items in these economies.

However, the financial inclusion variables exhibit a positive and significant impact on the credit-growth spillover as the coefficents of the number of mobile subscribers and number of bank branches exhibit positive sign and are statistically significant, stating a direct impact on the credit-growth interdependence. Based on these results, it can be said that the measures of financial inclusion have improved the outreach of financial infrastructure. The coefficient of the dummy variable picks a positive sign and is statistically significant, confirming the impact of the global financial crisis (2008–2009) on these economies. These results are in agreement with Fernández-Rodríguez et al. (2015) who also report similar results in case of EMU bond market. In the context of emerging markets, these results are also in agreement with Ahmad et al. (2013).

Spillover across SAARC countries and China

In Chapter 3, we have highlighted the aggressive expansion through economic and trade linkages of China with most of the SAARC countries. Some of the critical studies dealing with China's dominance in the South Asian region include Malik (2001), Sahoo (2013a, b), Brunjes et al. (2013) and Lamb and Small (2014). To re-confirm this, we have re-estimated the DY model including China.[15] Table 5.5 reports the estimated results.

The results indicate a rise in the magnitude of directional spillover. We find that China seems to be better integrated with Bangladesh from real GDP growth spillover perspective. In line with the findings of Chapter 3, we find that there is a transmission of credit-to-credit spillover moving from China to Bangladesh, India and Nepal. This result implies that the role of

Table 5.5 Spillover Table for Real Credit Growth and Real GDP Growth between SAARC and China

	gr_BAN	gr_IND	gr_NEP	gr_PAK	gr_SRI	gr_CHN	cr_BAN	cr_IND	cr_NEP	cr_PAK	cr_SRI	cr_CHN	From Others	Net
gr_BAN	42.45	8.66	3.8	0.91	0.26	7.49	2.24	19.38	4.54	0.58	1.1	8.58	57.5	–11.6
gr_IND	7.82	50.14	5.82	12.02	3.28	4.04	0.97	4.72	4.19	4.22	0.72	2.07	49.9	12.6
gr_NEP	0.59	7.26	71.76	4.19	1.54	2.25	1.07	1.08	3.2	2.87	4.07	0.1	28.2	0.7
gr_PAK	4.07	17.85	2.14	50.51	0.63	3.76	1.28	1.53	0.66	0.89	15.32	1.36	49.5	–12.7
gr_SRI	1.23	7.99	1.29	3.88	51.44	0.02	4.91	0.54	2.09	0.57	23.66	2.38	48.6	–27.2
gr_CHN	2.63	0.32	1.97	9.38	0.28	70.36	1.35	4.33	0.3	4.34	4.21	0.53	29.6	–8.2
cr_BAN	10.47	1.71	1.29	0.6	8.55	6.45	50.28	0.83	2.48	1.14	5.19	11	49.7	–27.5
cr_IND	2.49	0.91	0.61	0.9	0.75	0.19	3.16	58.42	3.71	2.13	6.55	20.19	41.6	1.7
cr_NEP	5.41	5.47	2.81	1.26	1.16	7.39	2.32	0.73	49.89	15.32	1.61	6.62	50.1	–19.7
cr_PAK	1.6	0.81	3.47	0.45	0.83	3.74	1.67	0.54	4.75	79.94	1.1	1.1	20.1	13.4
cr_SRI	4.9	10.97	5.5	2.74	2.81	1.04	0.19	2.7	4.39	0.95	60.29	3.51	39.7	28.6
cr_CHN	4.65	0.58	0.21	0.5	1.29	3.24	2.97	6.96	0.12	0.45	4.8	74.24	25.8	31.7
Contri. To other	45.9	62.5	28.9	36.8	21.4	39.6	22.2	43.3	30.4	33.5	68.3	57.5	490.3	
Contri. Incl. own	88.3	112.7	100.7	87.3	72.8	110	72.4	101.8	80.3	113.4	128.6	131.7	40.90%	

Source: Authors.

Note: The lags in the VAR model are calculated using appropriate information criteria. The 10-step ahead generalized variance decomposition is based on Diebold and Yilmaz (2012). The sample period of this study is adjusted due to unavailability of data.

China is significant in extending the credit channels in the form of development assistance or foreign direct investment in these countries. However, Pakistan and Sri Lanka exhibit relatively lower levels of interdependence with China as far as credit market spillover is concerned. The results of credit-growth spillover also show high dependence on the economic growth of Bangladesh, Pakistan and India. The results further suggest that the extent of dependence on China and Pakistan seems to be lower than in Bangladesh and India. These results are in agreement with the regression results of Chapter 3. The low relationship between China and Pakistan appears to be contrary to the general perception of "all-weather friendship". The findings seem to be in agreement with Beckley (2012) who also reports on the economic and financial relationship of China with Pakistan. Concerning the credit-growth dynamics of China and Bangladesh, the findings confirm the regression results discussed in Chapter 3. The investment and development assistance provided by China to Bangladesh is one of the most formidable reasons of high interdependence. Figures 5.6 and 5.8 exhibit the total spillover index and the pairwise net spillovers between China and the rest of the economies, respectively. The plots exhibit that the total spillover index captures the contagion effects of the global financial crisis (2008–2009). However, the index shows its peak during 2011–2012. Figure 5.7 (a–f) exhibits the pairwise net spillover plots of India with other sample countries. We find that the credit growth of India has limited spillover on the economies of Bangladesh, Pakistan and Sri Lanka. However, we find that credit growth spillover is stronger from China to SAARC countries than India.

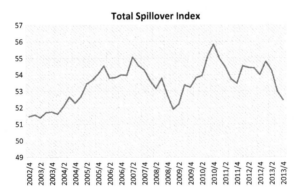

Figure 5.6 Total Spillovers between Real Credit Growth and Real GDP Growth among SAARC Countries and China.

Source: Authors' Calculations.

Note: Plot is estimated using 100-quarter rolling window.

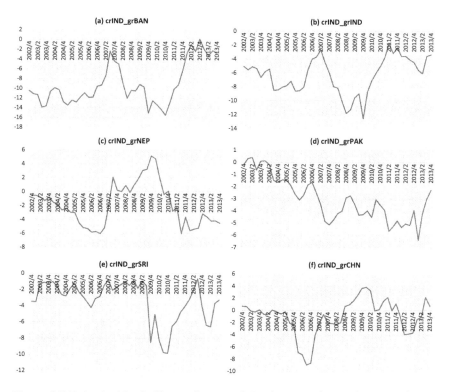

Figure 5.7 Pairwise Net Spillovers from Real Credit Growth in India to Real GDP Growth in SAARC Countries and China.

Source: Authors' Calculations.

Note: (a) BAN, CHN, IND, NEP, PAK and SRI denote Bangladesh, China, India, Nepal, Pakistan and Sri Lanka, respectively. (b) Plots are estimated using 100-quarter rolling window.

Conclusion and final remarks

In continuation with the issue of examining the process of economic integration dealt in Chapters 3 and 4, in this chapter we undertake a new research issue to explore the dynamic interaction between business and financial cycles of SAARC countries and China. We have included China because of its rising influence in the SAARC region. Relying on the estimated results of the DY method, we find that there is a limited interdependence between the real credit growth and real economic growth in the case of sample SAARC countries. The extent of credit-growth interdependence is lower than the study of Antonakakis et al. (2015) in the case of G7 countries. We find the mixed impact of the global financial crisis (2008–2009) on SAARC countries which is consistent with the study of Bhaskaran and

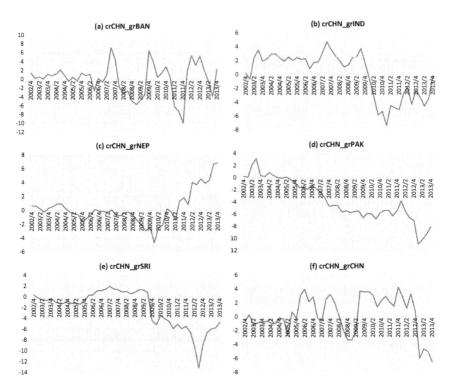

Figure 5.8 Pairwise Net Spillovers from Real Credit Growth in China to Real GDP
Growth in SAARC Countries.

Source: Authors' Calculations.

Note: (a) BAN, CHN, IND, NEP, PAK and SRI denote Bangladesh, China, India, Nepal, Pakistan
and Sri Lanka, respectively. (b) Plots are estimated using 100-quarter rolling window.

Ghosh (2010). One of the most striking findings of this analysis is that the
within SAARC results suggest the presence of business cycle led financial
cycle movement except for Nepal, indicating that the process of financial
development is growth dependent. For Nepal, we find that the business
cycle is a financial cycle dependent, suggesting that the economic growth
precedes financial development. The findings appear to be at variance with
the Ahmed and Ansari (1998), Uddin et al. (2012) and Shahid et al. (2015)
in cases of South Asia, Bangladesh and Pakistan, respectively. However,
the case of Nepal seems to agree with Kharel and Pokhrel (2012) who also
report that the banking sector induces the economic growth more strongly
than the financial market.

Based on our findings, it can be concluded that there is a visible level of
dominance of India in SAARC followed by Bangladesh and Pakistan. Sri

Lanka can be called a latecomer because of its domestic reasons. However, the economy is progressing well, and its data may start showing the dominant regional spillover effect in Sri Lanka's favour. Overall, at the regional level, it appears that the role of India seems to be critical for the survival of SAARC followed by Bangladesh and Pakistan.

The results of SAARC and China reveal an unusual pattern. China appears to be a credit-driven economy which seems to be in agreement with the previous studies of Brunjes et al. (2013) and Sahoo (2013a, b). On credit growth, we find that China is placed better than India.

The results of fixed-effect suggest that the government debt to GDP and interest rate impact the net credit-growth spillover positively, implying that the process of economic integration is highly skewed towards cross-border financial assistance and inter-country borrowing and lending. Among financial indicators, the number of mobile subscribers and the number of branches appear to be the significant determinants of credit-growth spillover. However, the coefficient of remittances picks a negative sign and is not statistically significant, establishing an insignificant relationship with real credit growth and real economic growth interdependence. As above mentioned, it is in line with the Ozaki (2012).

We finally conclude that the process of economic integration is evolving as the limited cross-country interactions are well captured by the results of this study. In cases of most of the sample SAARC countries, financial cycle precedes the business cycle except Nepal. China appears to be relatively better placed in SAARC than India, though, among five SAARC nations, India comes out to be the natural driver of credit-growth spillover. Among determinants, government debt and interest rate play a vital role in augmenting economic integration. The most striking finding of this analysis could be the significant impact of financial inclusion indicators on credit-growth interactions. The major findings of this chapter are in line with Chapter 3.

Notes

1 The earlier version of this paper has appeared in the *Journal of Quantitative Economics*. Complete Citation: Ahmad, W., & Sehgal, S. (2018). Business cycle and financial cycle interdependence and the rising role of China in SAARC. *Journal of Quantitative Economics*, 16 (2), 337–362.

2 For further details on the role of financial sector development, please refer Dabla-Norris et al. (2016), Batten et al. (2015). A brief account is also provided in ADB (2015).

3 The members of SAARC are Afghanistan, Bangladesh, Bhutan, India, the Maldives, Nepal, Pakistan and Sri Lanka.

4 In the literature, a large volume of studies has used this method to analyse the different segments of financial markets and assets (Yilmaz, 2009; Antonakakis et al. 2013; Antonakakis and Vergos, 2013; Cronin, 2014; Sehgal et al. 2014, 2015; Antonakakis et al. 2015; Antonakakis and Kizys, 2015; Ahmad et al. 2017; Ahmad, 2017; Ahmad and Sharma, 2017).

5 The placements of public and private bonds are higher in cases of India and Pakistan compared to other SAARC members. The numbers reported are the averages calculated from the Annex: Financial structure in developing Asia, 2011 (see ADB, 2015).

6 AIC criterion has been used to select the number of lags and estimate the 100-period rolling window.

7 See also https://timesofindia.indiatimes.com/india/If-SAARC-fails-theres-BIMS-TEC-India-warns-Pakistan/articleshow/55545978.cms (accessed on 26 October 2017).

8 In the literature, the studies of Csonto and Ivaschenko (2013), Piljak (2013), Dornbusch et al. (2000), Gómez-Puig et al. (2014) and Fernández-Rodríguez et al. (2015, 2016) have used these economic indicators to examine the possible impact on cross-country and asset spillovers.

9 The variable helps capture the cross-country spillover by taking into account the assets creation through stocks, shares and American Depository Receipt (ADR) and other participatory equity-related instruments.

10 Martin et al. (2012) maintain the Global Financial Development Database on the World Bank website. The database provides the information about the status of financial development in 203 economies since 1960. The database covers the aspects of access, depth, efficiency and stability. The database can be accessed at http://www.worldbank.org/en/publication/gfdr/data/global-financial-development-database (accessed on 26 October 2017).

11 In 2015, the over the counter (OTC) mobile money usage are outsmarted by the annual mobile registered accounts (see Villasenor et al. 2016).

12 The World Bank maintains a database on The Financial Development and Structure Database. The available frequencies are updated by the Beck et al. (2000). The database can be accssed through: http://www.worldbank.org/en/publication/gfdr/data/financial-structure-database (accessed on 24 October 2017).

13 Due to unavailability of historical data, we have excluded the china. In order to satisfy the asymptotic properties, we have interpolated the yearly frequencies into quarterly ones using appropriate method. For series exhibiting rankings, we run the same rank in every quarter in a year.

14 Among 66 pairs, we select only 4 net pairwise spillover series of sample country and exclude the others and spillover series of China.

15 Based on the availability of historical data, we have considered the sample from 1979Q4 to 2013Q4.

6

DYNAMICS OF STOCK MARKET INTEGRATION IN THE SOUTH ASIAN REGION[1]

Sanjay Sehgal and Piyush Pandey

Introduction

Emerging market economies have become much more integrated into world economy mainly because of trade and financial system linkages. Global value chains provided Asia's emerging economies with a fast-paced development. Financial integration followed with a delay, started gaining momentum from the early 1990s. Major improvement in information technology reduced the transaction costs which combined with higher long-term returns for foreign investors helped them to diversify their risk internationally. This combined with the financial reforms and liberalization helped countries attract overseas investors. This surge in capital flows helped fuel the increase in bank credit-financed investment boom. But this "Asian miracle" as it was called then was short-lived as with the devaluation of Thai Bhat in 1997, the region plunged into economic crises (the worst since World War 2) with growth being negative in 1998 for many regional countries. The Asian countries came out of the Asian Financial Crises of 1998 by strengthening their macroeconomic fundamentals, improving their balance sheet, addressing domestic and external financial vulnerabilities thereby facilitating cross-border trade through export-led growth model leading to improved efficiency and higher productivity. The crises created new possibilities for ASEAN,[2] formed as an important economic bloc in 1969 to contribute to the growth and development of member countries, as a regional actor. ASEAN has been in existence for more than 50 years now and aspires to be an instrument of regional governance and political management, and has taken a big step in that direction by formation of ASEAN Economic Community in 2015 which would help realize the dream of the Asian century.

South Asian countries were following restrictive state policies by having license raj regimes with heavy state presence, exchange rate controls, non-outward looking external trade policies which led to tepid investments from foreign investors and contraction in their growth. Post the 1990s, the South Asian countries have embraced upon outward-oriented pro-liberalization strategies and have increasingly acknowledged that regional approaches are quintessential to accomplish their developmental challenges. Linking small and large economies can help in tapping the economies of scale, upgrading of infrastructure and multiplying investment prospects thereby leading to equitable growth.

Trade integration even after the ratification of SAFTA agreement in 2004 has been moving at a lumbering pace and is far from reaching its full potential to leverage on the concept of trans-Himalayan growth axis on which SAARC was formed. But as critical as trade integration is, policymakers of the region are convinced that capital markets are a key component of national development, improving the mobilization of savings by providing alternative sources of financing for productive investments and supporting the development of long-term savings channels. An underdeveloped and rigidly fragmented financial markets will be countercyclical for effective mobilization of financial resources within the region. Financial integration shall provide benefit through more efficient allocation of capital, greater opportunities for risk diversification, better inter-temporal consumption smoothing, a lower probability of asymmetric shocks and a more robust market framework (Pauer, 2005). Moreover, financial integration may also lead to financial development thereby contributing to economic growth in the region. Against this backdrop, we provide a comprehensive analysis of the extent of equity market linkages of the South Asian countries and also identify some key determinants of equity market integration, wherein concerted efforts of policy realignment from SAARC members are quintessential for harmonization and progressive integration of the region's capital markets as a worthy aim and part of a wider commitment to greater economic and financial integration

Equity market integration in South Asia

Data

Daily data in local currency units for stock market benchmark index closing prices was retrieved from Bloomberg for South Asian countries for the period January 2004 (date when SAFTA agreement was reached) to December 2015. The following benchmark indices have been selected for the empirical analysis – Bangladesh (DSEX Broad Index), India (NIFTY Index), Nepal (NEPSE Index), Maldives (MASIX Index), Pakistan (KSE100 Index), Sri Lanka (Sri Lanka 20 Index). No data was available for Afghanistan and Bhutan. The MSCI USA is included as a proxy for global factor as in prior research (Baele et al. 2004; Bartram, et al. 2007, and Sehgal et al. 2016a).

Further, portfolio equity inflows for each SAARC member country from the SAARC region as well as larger ASEAN+6[3] regions for the period 2004 to 2017 are constructed. Similarly, portfolio outflows from each SAARC member country to the SAARC and the ASEAN+6 regions. The portfolio flow data was sourced from IMF-CPIS (International Monetary Fund-Coordinated Portfolio Investment Survey) database.

Empirical methods

Empirical research on financial integration has used two broad measures: price-based and quantity-based measures.[4] On the price-based measures, empirical research started with using beta and sigma convergence (Adam et al. 2002; ECB, 2004; Rizavi et al. 2011). Early investigations into the linkages between the two markets used the Value at Risk models to study co-movement of stock market returns. Modern literature has moved on to modern time series approaches such as dynamic co-integration (Mylonidis and Kollias, 2010) and MGARCH models (BEKK model, DCC models and its extensions mainly Asymmetric DCC-GARCH of Cappiello et al. 2006 and Threshold DCC-GARCH of Pesaran and Pesaran, 2007) to study the dynamic process of integration.[5] Recently, copula-based models have been used to study the asymmetric nature of dependence between financial market returns (Patton, 2006; Rodriguez, 2007). The quantity- or flow-based measures assess the level of linkages based on cross-country equity portfolio holding of assets and securities.

Price-based approach

We examine the level of equity market linkages amongst the South Asian countries by employing the copula GARCH models (refer Appendix C for detailed description of Copula methodology). Copula model helps us to empirically determine the dependence structure by providing estimates of conditional correlations. To describe the symmetric and asymmetric dependence structure between the uniform distributions of each sample country returns with that of the other, we use two Elliptical (Gaussian and Student t) and two Archimedean's (Clayton and Gumbel) family of copula models. Because the nature of copulas can be either time-invariant or time-variant, we include both for our empirical analysis. The time-invariant copula measure provides a static level of dependency between the equity markets while the time-varying measure shows its evolution over time.

Additionally, we examine South Asian equity market integration by quantifying the contribution of shocks from each member country to other member countries at different points in time. The daily data of equity returns have been used to examine the connectedness of the stock markets of the region so as to provide support to the copula results. Diebold and

Yilmaz (2009, 2012) methodology is based on dynamic variance decompositions from vector autoregression (VAR). While copulas provide only the estimates of conditional correlation, Diebold and Yilmaz methodology allows us to quantify the cross-market directional returns spillovers (pairwise spillovers) thereby providing further insights into the equity market linkages for the member countries. Refer Appendix B for detailed description of Diebold and Yilmaz spillover index methodology.

Quantity-based measures

Quantity-based measures supplement the price-based measures for assessing and monitoring the changes and trends in the equity market integration. Thus, we examine the cross-border equity holdings of the sample countries to assess whether there is a shift to investment within/from SAARC region or the broad ASEAN+6 region. ASEAN group is selected as it is the neighbouring regional economic bloc in Asia with a much longer history (created in 1967) and having a wider membership base (ten members ASEAN which extends to ASEAN+3/ASEAN+6).

South Asian stock market integration

There seems to be a low level of equity market linkages amongst the sample South Asian countries as can be seen from the time-invariant dependence parameter values computed from copula models (refer Table 6.1) of these countries which are hovering in and around 0 implying almost no association between equity returns of sample countries. The largest economy of the region i.e. India has the highest association with Nepal while the lowest association with Sri Lanka.

The low values of equity markets association in the SAARC region can be attributed to its poor regional trade intensity (total trade within SAARC members/total trade with the world). It can be clearly seen from Figure 2.7 that the regional trade intensity is the lowest for SAARC member group compared to other regional economic blocs. In this regards, the levels of dependences are around 0 even for time-varying integration charts (see Figure 6.1) for all the pair of sample countries implying little or no integration between them. This indicates that equity markets in this region are not fairly mature and well developed in comparison with their other Asian counterparts (refer Sehgal et al. 2018b) with the exception of India. Also corroborating these low dependences is the graph of financial development index[6] (see Figure 6.2) of this region which shows that besides India, the other SAARC member countries are very low on the financial development index.

The time aggregated equity returns spillover matrix for six South Asian countries, obtained from Diebold and Yilmaz spillover index approach, is

Table 6.1 Dependencies amongst Equity Markets of South Asian Countries

		Gaussian		Student t		Clayton		Gumbel	
		Value	LL	Value	LL	Value	LL	Value	LL
BANG	IND	**0.00**	**0.00**	0.00	0.08	0.00	0.01	1.11	0.81
BANG	MALD	0.02	−0.26	**0.02**	**−0.63**	0.01	−0.04	1.13	1.51
BANG	NEP	0.00	−0.01	**0.01**	**−3.45**	0.04	−0.92	1.14	1.69
BANG	PAK	−0.05	−1.38	**−0.04**	**−2.62**	0.00	0.01	1.10	2.48
BANG	SRI	0.02	−0.21	**0.02**	**−0.79**	0.03	−0.52	1.09	1.23
IND	MALD	0.02	−0.17	**0.01**	**−1.66**	0.02	−0.60	1.11	3.17
IND	NEP	**0.03**	**−0.66**	0.03	−0.19	0.00	0.00	1.12	1.79
IND	PAK	**0.00**	**−0.02**	0.00	0.07	0.01	−0.04	1.11	6.39
IND	SRI	**−0.02**	**−0.53**	−0.02	−0.47	0.00	0.01	1.11	2.88
MALD	NEP	−0.04	−1.43	**−0.04**	**−3.12**	0.00	0.01	1.19	2.60
MALD	PAK	0.02	−0.53	**0.02**	**−12.59**	0.05	−2.78	1.19	2.69
MALD	SRI	−0.01	−0.17	**−0.01**	**−0.32**	0.01	−0.06	1.16	3.12
NEP	PAK	−0.01	−0.10	**−0.01**	**−0.40**	0.00	0.00	1.14	1.09
NEP	SRI	0.00	0.00	0.00	−0.12	**0.04**	**−0.15**	1.15	1.92
PAK	SRI	0.08	−6.34	**0.08**	**−7.94**	*0.09*	*−7.27*	*1.13*	5.38

Source: Authors.

Notes: The table summarizes time-invariant copula estimation results for South Asian equity markets.

a Value denotes pairwise dependence parameter between equity return series of the South Asian countries using different copula models.

b LL denotes the log likelihood value of dependence parameter between equity return series of the South Asian countries using different copula models.

c Value in bold denotes the lowest negative log likelihood thereby providing the best fit copula model amongst the family of models under study.

d BANG, IND, MALD, NEP, PAK and SRI denote Bangladesh, India, Maldives, Nepal, Pakistan and Sri Lanka, respectively.

presented in Table 6.2. The last column of the matrix ("from others") highlights the gross directional volatility spillovers to the country from rest of the countries. The second last row ("to others") indicates the gross directional spillover from a country to rest of the countries. It can be clearly seen from the table that for each of the South Asian country, much of the contribution to its forecast error variance is coming from shocks given to its own equity returns, and the cross-market spillovers (off diagonal elements of the table) are very small. The Indian equity market dominates the equity markets of South Asia region as can be seen from the result of net directional returns spillover, where the largest spillover transfers are from India to others (6.6–5.70 = 0.9%), whereas the other countries in the study (with the exception of Nepal and Sri Lanka) are net receiver of returns spillovers. The total returns spillover which appears in the lower right corner of Table 6.2 indicates that on the average 3.1% of the forecast error variance in all the six markets comes from spillovers which confirm that connectedness of the regional equity markets is low. The reasons for the lack of

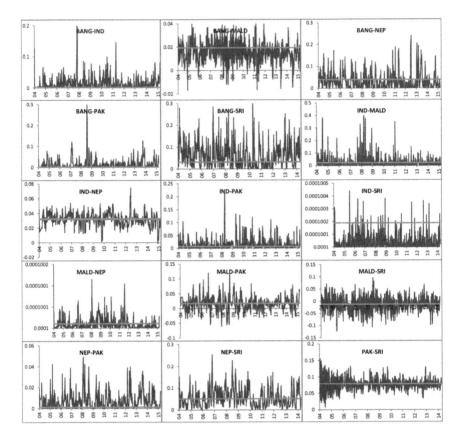

Figure 6.1 Dynamic Dependencies between South Asian Equity Markets.
Source: Authors' Calculations.

Notes: (a) The best fit time-varying copula model selected by the goodness of fit test for different family of copula models plotted is along with its corresponding time-invariant dependency measure (in horizontal line). (b) BANG, IND, MALD, NEP, PAK and SRI denote Bangladesh, India, Maldives, Nepal, Pakistan and Sri Lanka, respectively.

capital market integration are many and varied, but what stands out is the lack of information and involvement in other SAARC markets combined with a lack of opportunities and structures through which the different markets can learn from each other's experience.

Figure 6.3 shows the annual values of portfolio equity inflows from the SAARC and ASEAN+6 member groups into the sample countries. The portfolio equity inflows are predominantly into India not from SAARC but other larger ASEAN+6 regions reinforcing the confidence in the strength of the Indian economy. India seems to be predominantly the only source of

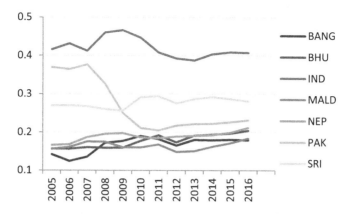

Figure 6.2 Financial Development Index.
Source: IMF, Authors Calculations.

Notes: (a) All figures in units. (b) BANG, IND, MALD, NEP, PAK and SRI denote Bangladesh, India, Maldives, Nepal, Pakistan and Sri Lanka, respectively.

Table 6.2 Return Spillovers across South Asian Equity Markets

	BANG	*IND*	*MALD*	*NEP*	*PAK*	*SRI*	*From Others*
BANG	98.74	0.51	0.05	0.07	0.43	0.20	1.30
IND	0.18	94.26	0.19	1.22	1.14	3.02	5.70
MALD	0.26	0.12	98.52	0.50	0.34	0.26	1.50
NEP	0.13	0.73	0.25	98.30	0.07	0.51	1.70
PAK	0.17	2.20	0.29	0.32	96.26	0.75	3.70
SRI	0.50	3.01	0.19	0.12	0.68	95.50	4.50
Contribution to others	1.20	6.60	1.00	2.20	2.70	4.80	18.40
Contribution including own	100.00	100.80	99.50	100.50	98.90	100.30	3.10%

Source: Authors.

Notes: The table presents Diebold and Yilmaz (2012) spillover table summary for equity markets of the South Asian countries.

a The diagonal entries of the matrix represent the own variance share of the sample countries, and the off-diagonal elements show the cross-market spillovers.

b The last column of the matrix ("from others") highlights the gross directional return spillovers to the country from rest of the countries.

c The second last row ("to others") indicates the gross directional spillover from a country to rest of the countries.

d BANG, IND, MALD, NEP, PAK and SRI denote Bangladesh, India, Maldives, Nepal, Pakistan and Sri Lanka, respectively.

equity portfolio inflows into Nepal and Maldives even when we consider the bigger ASEAN+6 region.

Figure 6.4 shows the annual values of portfolio equity outflows from sample countries to the SAARC and ASEAN+6 member groups. Regarding the portfolio equity outflows, there are no outflows from Sri Lanka,

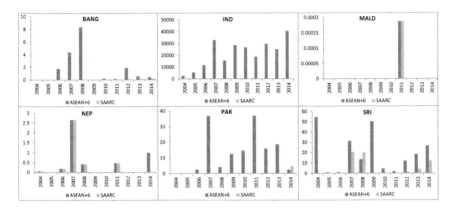

Figure 6.3 Portfolio Equity Inflows into SAARC Countries from SAARC and ASEAN+6 Groups.

Source: IMF CPIS, Authors Calculations.

Notes: (a) All figures are end of the period and in USD millions. (b) BANG, IND, MALD, NEP, PAK and SRI denote Bangladesh, India, Maldives, Nepal, Pakistan and Sri Lanka, respectively.

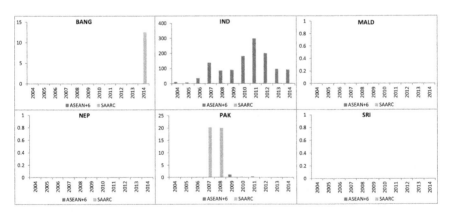

Figure 6.4 Portfolio Equity Outflows from SAARC Countries to SAARC and ASEAN+6 Groups.

Source: IMF CPIS, Authors Calculations.

Notes: (a) All figures are end of the period and in USD millions. (b) BANG, IND, MALD, NEP, PAK and SRI denote Bangladesh, India, Maldives, Nepal, Pakistan and Sri Lanka, respectively.

Maldives and Nepal to the SAARC or the larger ASEAN+6 regions which can be attributed to the internal instability in these countries which lead to their slow economic growth and development. Pakistan seems to be heavily invested in SAARC region (though only in Sri Lanka) before the global crises of 2008 but has shifted its investments though at much lower levels to larger ASEAN+6 region for few years after the crises. Bangladesh seems to be the latest member to invest in the SAARC region. Though the portfolio equity outflows from India are considerably higher to larger ASEAN+6 group region, India also seems to be invested in SAARC in predominantly all members' countries except Pakistan across the study period which can be attributed to its political standoffs with Pakistan.

SAARC equity markets are varied and India being the biggest and most sophisticated market of the region but the results from the price-based analysis on the basis of time-invariant copula models show that albeit after decades of its formation, the SAARC regional bloc has not come out of its political standoffs and embraced regionalism to bring dynamism into this region. The SAARC region has a relatively low level of equity market linkages. The levels of associations between the South Asian countries are virtually 0 confirming little equity market integration in the region. Even after operationalization of SAFTA agreement in 2006, regional trade intensity is the lowest for SAARC group compared to major regional economic blocs of the world for the period under study.

Determinants of equity market integration

We consider the exhaustive list of potential determinants of equity market integration that have been considered by various studies in the literature and have been summarized in Table 6.3. We analyse the trends of these variables for the SAARC countries individually and compare the same with the member countries comprising the larger ASEAN group i.e. ASEAN+6. ASEAN group is selected as it is the neighbouring regional economic bloc in Asia with a much longer history (created in 1967) and having a wider membership base (ten members ASEAN which extends to ASEAN+3/ ASEAN+6). Sehgal et al. (2016) observe dependencies of the ASEAN+6 bloc members with the Asian benchmark thereby confirming varying degree of equity market integration of the sample countries. Thus, analysing and comparing the trends in these fundamental determinants for the two regional blocs will help to show how important these variables are for SAARC.

For majority of these determinants, the values are not much different for the SAARC and ASEAN+6 member nations. Trend of only those variables for which we find an observable difference between the two groups are presented. The governance indicators (refer Figure 6.5) are all in negative for the SAARC member countries (except Bhutan) but the same for ASEAN+6

Table 6.3 Fundamental Determinants of Equity Market Integration

Category	Variable	Measurement	Reference Studies	Data Source
Macro	GDP growth rate	Annual real GDP growth rate (%)	Vo and Daly (2007), Guesmi et al. (2013), Ng et al. (2013)	World Bank
	GDP per capita	Real GDP per capita	Vo and Daly (2007), Ng et al. (2013)	World Bank
	Index of industrial production	Log (IIP)	Büttner and Hayo (2011), Guesmi et al. (2013)	CEIC Asia Database
	Current account balance	Current account as % of GDP	Guesmi et al. (2013)	World Bank
	Inflation rate	Annual growth rate of GDP deflator (%)	Vo and Daly (2007), Hooy and Goh (2007)	World Bank
	Short-term interest rate	Repo rate (%)	Hooy and Goh (2007), Guesmi et al. (2013)	CEIC Asia Database
	Budget balance	Budget balance/surplus as % of GDP	Arfaoui and Abaoub (2010)	World Bank
	Govt. debt	Gross public debt as % of GDP	Gill et al. (2014)	World Bank
	Govt. tax revenues	Tax revenue as % of GDP	Vo and Daly (2007)	World Bank
	Foreign direct investment	Net FDI as % of GDP	Ng et al. (2013)	World Bank
	Foreign indirect investment	Net FII as % of GDP	Ng et al. (2013)	World Bank
	Governance index	Arithmetic mean of six broad dimensions of governance	Vo and Daly (2007), Ng et al. (2013)	World Governance Indicators, Authors Calculation
	Volatility of forex rate	EGARCH(1,1)-based conditional volatility estimate of FX rate	Hooy and Goh (2007), Guesmi et al. (2013)	Bloomberg, Authors calculations
	Liquidity risk	Money supply (M2) to total reserves	Brunnermeier et al. (2008)	World Bank

Category	Variable	Measurement	Reference Studies	Data Source
Trade	Trade tariff	Trade tariff as % of Duty	Hooy and Goh (2007), Guesmi et al. (2013)	WEF Global Competitive Index
	Total trade	Total trade as % of GDP	Vo and Daly (2007), Guesmi et al. (2013)	World Bank
	Trade intensity	Total trade of country i with India/total trade of India	Hooy and Goh (2007)	World Bank, Authors calculation
Market	Market size	Market capitalization as % of GDP	Vo and Daly (2007), Arfaoui and Abaoub (2010)	World Bank
	Stock market efficiency	Stock market turnover ratio	Vo and Daly (2007), Narayan et al. (2014)	World Bank
	Volatility of market return	EGARCH(1,1)-based conditional volatility estimate of market return	Abad et al. (2014)	Bloomberg, Authors calculations
	Domestic growth opportunities	PE ratio of the sample market index	Bekaert et al. (2005)	Bloomberg
	Local stock market conditions	Dividend yield of the sample market index	Hooy and Goh (2007), Guesmi et al. (2013)	Bloomberg

Source: Authors.

members (Singapore, Malaysia, Japan, Brunei) which have high integration with the Asian benchmark (Sehgal et al. 2016a, b) is positive. We all know that governance factor reflected by the sound institutional, legal and investment environment is very important for international capital flows driving equity market linkages.

Linkages in equity markets is likely to be driven by increase in physical trade The trend analysis for the total trade as a % of GDP variable (refer Figure 6.6) shows that except for Maldives and Bhutan, all South Asian countries have the value less than 100% in comparison with many ASEAN+6 countries which have a large total trade position (Singapore, Malaysia, Thailand, Vietnam).

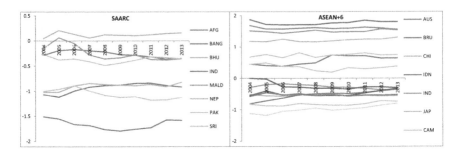

Figure 6.5 Trends in Governance Indicators of SAARC and ASEAN+6 Countries.

Source: World Governance Indicators, Authors Calculations.

Notes: (a) AFG, BANG, BHU, IND, MALD, NEP, PAK and SRI denote Afghanistan, Bangladesh, Bhutan, India, Maldives, Nepal, Pakistan and Sri Lanka, respectively. These countries are members of SAARC. (b) AUS, BRU, CAM, CHI, IND, IDN, JAP, KOR, LAO, MYS, MMR, NZ, PHLP, SING, THAI and VIET denote Australia, Brunei, Cambodia, China, India, Indonesia, Japan, Korea, Lao, Malaysia, Myanmar, New Zealand, the Philippines, Singapore, Thailand and Vietnam, respectively. These countries are part of larger ASEAN+6 group.

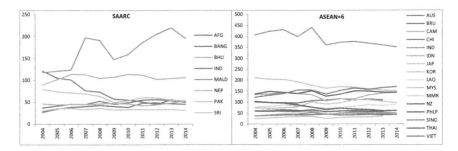

Figure 6.6 Trends in Total Trade (as percentage of GDP) of SAARC and ASEAN+6 Countries.

Source: World Bank, Authors Calculations.

Notes: (a) AFG, BANG, BHU, IND, MALD, NEP, PAK and SRI denote Afghanistan, Bangladesh, Bhutan, India, Maldives, Nepal, Pakistan and Sri Lanka, respectively. These countries are members of SAARC. (b) AUS, BRU, CAM, CHI, IND, IDN, JAP, KOR, LAO, MYS, MMR, NZ, PHLP, SING, THAI and VIET denote Australia, Brunei, Cambodia, China, India, Indonesia, Japan, Korea, Lao, Malaysia, Myanmar, New Zealand, Philippines, Singapore, Thailand and Vietnam, respectively. These countries are part of larger ASEAN+6 group.

For the trade tariff variable (refer Figure 6.7), except for the concerted trade policy commitment and contingency measures undertaken by World Trade organization (WTO) in 2009 to arrest the contraction in total trade due to great economic recession of 2008, the level of trade tariffs (as % of duty) is around 10–20% for SAARC member nations. In contrast, low

110

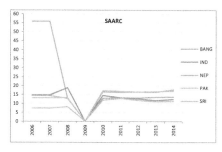

Figure 6.7 Trends in Trade Tariff (as percentage of duty) of SAARC and ASEAN+6 Countries.

Source: World Economic Forum (WEF), Global Competitiveness Index.

Notes: (a) AFG, BANG, BHU, IND, MALD, NEP, PAK and SRI denote Afghanistan, Bangladesh, Bhutan, India, Maldives, Nepal, Pakistan and Sri Lanka, respectively. These countries are members of SAARC. (b) AUS, BRU, CAM, CHI, IND, IDN, JAP, KOR, LAO, MYS, MMR, NZ, PHLP, SING, THAI and VIET denote Australia, Brunei, Cambodia, China, India, Indonesia, Japan, Korea, Lao, Malaysia, Myanmar, New Zealand, the Philippines, Singapore, Thailand and Vietnam, respectively. These countries are part of larger ASEAN+6 group.

tariff rates (less than 10%) are prevalent amongst majority of the ASEAN+6 countries which help in facilitating intra-regional trade thereby promoting integration.

The trend analysis for market capitalization as a % of GDP (refer Figure 6.8) shows that except for India, sample SAARC countries have values less than 50% while majority of ASEAN+6 member countries have corresponding values close to 100%. This shows that the SAARC member states have to work on their governance parameters, improve on their trade linkages and trade tariffs and develop their equity market infrastructure to achieve higher levels of equity market integration.

India enjoys a prominent place in the South Asian region as its GDP is eight times the size of Pakistan[7] (which is the second biggest economy in South Asia) and the only country in the region which shares common borders with all other nations except Afghanistan. Hence, the regional cooperation in South Asia will not succeed without the active participation and sincere commitment of India. Figure 6.9 shows the trade intensity of India with respect to other regions (total trade of region *i* with India/total trade of India) for the SAARC, ASEAN and ASEAN+3 countries. It clearly brings about the fact that India trades higher with the ASEAN+3 members and even ASEAN members than the SAARC members. This is counterintuitive as India provides overland transit to Bangladesh, Nepal and Bhutan for their bilateral trade and maritime transit to Nepal and Bhutan for its international trade.

111

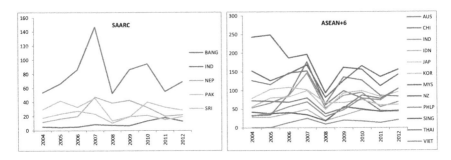

Figure 6.8 Trends in Market Capitalization (as percentage of GDP) of SAARC and ASEAN+6 Countries.

Source: Federal Reserve Bank of St. Louis, Economic Research.

Notes: (a) AFG, BANG, BHU, IND, MALD, NEP, PAK and SRI denote Afghanistan, Bangladesh, Bhutan, India, Maldives, Nepal, Pakistan and Sri Lanka, respectively. These countries are members of SAARC. (b) AUS, BRU, CAM, CHI, IND, IDN, JAP, KOR, LAO, MYS, MMR, NZ, PHLP, SING, THAI and VIET denote Australia, Brunei, Cambodia, China, India, Indonesia, Japan, Korea, Lao, Malaysia, Myanmar, New Zealand, the Philippines, Singapore, Thailand and Vietnam, respectively. These countries are part of larger ASEAN+6 group.

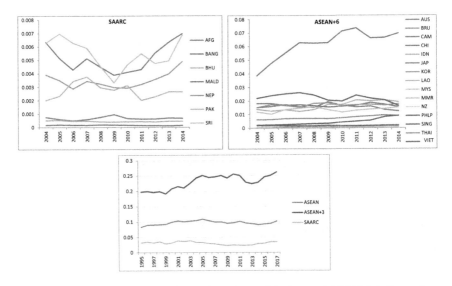

Figure 6.9 Trade Intensity of India with SAARC, ASEAN and ASEAN+3 Countries.

Source: World Bank, Authors Calculations.

Notes: (a) Trade intensity of India with country *i* is the ratio of total trade of India with country *i* to total trade of India with the world.

Summary and policy suggestions

In this chapter, stock market linkages of the South Asian countries were examined and empirical analysis is based on copula GARCH approach to capture the dynamic process of dependencies of the sample country's equity index with each other. The results indicate dependencies between the equity markets of SAARC member countries are close to 0 indicating very low level of equity market integration in the region. This can be attributed to the low regional trade intensity in the South Asian region which is in fact the lowest amongst all the major regional economic blocs of the world. Results obtained from Diebold and Yilmaz methodology confirmed low connectedness between equity markets of member countries and thereby are in support of the copula-based findings. Flow-based indicators reconfirm that the quantum of equity portfolio inflows for individual SAARC members is much greater from ASEAN+6 group than from the SAARC group. However, India seems to receive equity portfolio flows only from the larger ASEAN+6 group and none whatsoever from the SAARC region but it is itself invested in the SAARC group members. This can be attributed to the fact that contrary to groupings in other regional blocs, India is the largest country in the region, not only in terms of geographical territory and population, but also in terms of size of the economy (third largest economy in terms of Purchasing Power Parity in the world[8]). From a comparative analysis, one could see that the equity market integration in the SAARC members lagged their ASEAN+6 counterparts owing to poor governance quality, lower trade linkages, higher trade tariffs and less sophisticated equity markets with relatively weaker institutional and regulatory architecture.

SAARC countries may be expected to foster a stable political environment giving importance to each other security concerns. People to people contact must be facilitated to develop social cohesion and imbibe shared cultural ethos which is unique to this region. While most of the countries in the SAARC region have considerable similarities, not least in their legal systems, there is currently very little intra-regional trade which is the least for any region in the world. The obstacle within SAARC is that members do not see their own region as an attractive investment destination. With regard to the equity markets development, the members can coordinate to subsequently formulate a SAARC Disclosure Standards Scheme and a SAARC Corporate Governance Scorecard to further enhance cooperation in the integration of equity market segments. The former would help in the cross-border offerings of securities, while the later would ensure better transparency. SAARC members can come up with an Integrated Equity Markets Platform where companies of the member countries could list their shares. India, which has the most sophisticated, regulated and compliant equity market, can provide its financial support and technical expertise for building and operating equity market infrastructure in other SAARC member countries. A federation of market intermediaries (brokers of member countries bourses) association, South Asian Securities Association, could be set up to help formalize and institutionalize a process of interaction amongst members to know each other and share best practices.

Notes

1 An earlier version of this chapter has been published in *Cogent Economics & Finance*, an open access journal of Taylor & Francis. Citation: Sehgal et al. (2018c).
2 ASEAN was created with the signing of Bangkok Declaration in 1967 by Indonesia, Malaysia, the Philippines, Singapore and Thailand. Subsequently, the ASEAN bloc grew with the addition of Brunei, Vietnam, Laos, Myanmar and Cambodia (in the order of their entry).
3 ASEAN+6 is an economic partnership of ten ASEAN members plus Australia, China, India, Japan, New Zealand and South Korea. Japan regards this ASEAN+6 (EAS group) as an appropriate group for East Asia's trade and investment cooperation.
4 For a survey of the literatures and various indicators (see Cavoli et al. 2004; Baele et al. 2004; Poonpatpibul et al. 2006).
5 For survey of literature using these indicators (see Yu et al. 2010; Gupta et al. 2015).
6 The World Economic Forum publishes a Financial Development Index annually, which measures and analyses the factors enabling the development of financial systems amongst different economies. It provides a comprehensive means for economies to benchmark various aspects of their financial systems.
7 Source: IMF.
8 Source: World Bank.

7

INTERDEPENDENCIES AMONGST SHORT- AND LONG-TERM DEBT MARKETS OF SOUTH ASIA[1]

Sanjay Sehgal, Sakshi Saini and Piyush Pandey

Introduction

For inclusive economic development of Asia, it is important to develop an Asian financial system for efficient and safe financial intermediation. The onset of Asian crises of 1997 showed the over-reliance on foreign debt borrowed for short intervals of time. Before the crises, Asian companies were overly dependent on bank loans from inside and outside the country which exposed them to currency and maturity mis-matches. The financial system of the Asian economies was also plagued by excessive reliance on the banking sector without institutional safeguards at place. The need was increasingly felt in the aftermath of the Asian crises to develop the regional bond markets as they provide long-term financial intermediation and the interest rate structure that is established by the bonds markets is indispensible for risk management. Bond issuance supports infrastructure development, activates capital investment and provides a channel for mobilization of abundant savings. Having realized the weaknesses of a bank-centred financial system, East Asian economies began efforts in the aftermath of crisis to develop efficient and liquid debt market that manifested into the Asian Bond Market Initiative (ABMI)[2] to foster high degree of development and integration of the bond markets of the region. With the formation of ASEAN Economic Community (AEC) in 2015, deepening regional financial integration has become a policy goal besides developing the bond markets of each country.

There was no fallout of the Asian crises of 1997 for the South Asian countries due to their isolated and underdeveloped financial markets. The tepid rate of growth of South Asian countries in the 1990s compelled them to change their economic paradigm and move towards liberalization and privatization. With the gradual reforms in financial markets, these countries have largely become bank-centric and equity-oriented, but development of active and liquid fixed income market has not been emphasized yet. This is reflected in the size of South Asian banking system (measured as amount of deposits) being equivalent on an average to 57% of GDP and stock market capitalization 60.3% of GDP, while the public debt outstanding is only worth 27% of GDP (Burger et al. 2015). Financial system in this region is banking centric which is unable to meet the needs of commerce and industry and also remain fragile posing a systemic risk in the region. South Asian economies share common characteristics – high GDP growth, high savings and investment rates, and persistent budget deficits. The structures of their financial markets reveal common patterns yet the development of the debt markets has varied substantially across the SAARC member countries with India being the most advanced but even its market is small relative to its GDP. As on 2017 according to respective central banks, it is Sri Lanka (76.9%) which has the largest outstanding government bond market relative to that of its economy followed by India (68.7%), Pakistan (67%) and Bangladesh (27%). The Indian debt market being the biggest in terms of size in South Asia while composed of bonds, both government and corporate, is dominated by the government bonds. The central government bonds are the predominant and most liquid component of the bond market. Debt markets in rest of the South Asian countries are at nascent stages and are reflected in the level of short- and long-term debt inflows into the SAARC region (that too predominantly in India) amounting to USD 10 billion and 78 billion, respectively, in 2017 (Figure 7.1).

Developing liquid, deep and functioning bond markets can help countries generate long-term financing needed for sustainable economic growth. India's experience along with those of South Asian economies suggests much potential remains for developing South Asian bond markets thereby contributing to its growth and development.

Debt market linkages in South Asia

Data and methodology

Monthly data for 91-day Treasury bill yield (short-term) and 10-year Government Securities (long-term) yield are retrieved for five South Asian countries: Bangladesh, India, Nepal, Pakistan and Sri Lanka. Data however was not available for Afghanistan, Bhutan and Maldives. The data for short-term debt of Bangladesh, Pakistan and Sri Lanka is retrieved from CEIC, whereas those of India and Nepal are obtained from their respective central bank's database. Data for long-term debt for all countries is obtained from Bloomberg. We obtain debt yields from January 2004 to May 2016 for all sample countries. Short- and long-term debt returns for the sample

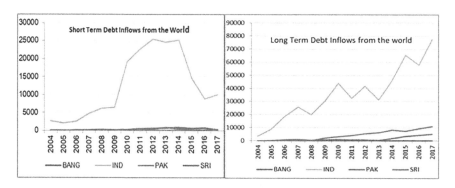

Figure 7.1 Short- and Long-Term Debt Inflows into South Asian Countries from the World.

Source: IMF CPIS, Authors' Calculations.

Notes: (a) All figures are end of the period and in USD millions. (b) BANG, IND, PAK and SRI denote Bangladesh, India, Pakistan and Sri Lanka, respectively. Flows into Nepal and Maldives were negligible hence not included.

countries are computed on the basis of formula used by Abad et al. (2010) in calculating bond returns for a sample of European countries, and are used for subsequent analysis. The returns are defined as $R_{it} = n(y_{it-1} - y_{it})$, where R_{it} denotes returns on bonds, n denotes the maturity of bonds and y_{it} is the natural logarithm of gross yield to maturity i.e. $y_{it} = \ln(1 + Y_{it})$, Y_{it} denotes the bond yields.

We examine the level of short-term as well as long-term debt market integration amongst five South Asian countries (Bangladesh, India, Nepal, Pakistan and Sri Lanka). Further, the level of association amongst the short- and long-term debt markets within each sample country is assessed. We employ copula models (refer Appendix C for detailed description of Copula methodology) to empirically determine dynamic interdependencies of short- and long-term debt markets across and within these economies. Copula functions help us ascertain dependence structure between debt markets by providing their estimates of conditional correlations. To describe the symmetric and asymmetric dependence structure between the currency markets, two Elliptical (Gaussian and Student *t*) and two Archimedean's (Clayton and Gumbel) family of copula models are used. Time-invariant and time-varying copula models are estimated to examine both linkages amongst the debt markets of the South Asian region.

We supplement our analysis using Diebold and Yilmaz (2012) spillover index methodology (Refer Appendix B for detailed description) to examine the level of transmission of shocks across the debt markets. This methodology allows us to quantify the cross-market directional spillovers thereby giving further insights into the connectedness of financial linkages across the debt markets.

Short-term debt market integration

Results of time-invariant copula models are presented in Table 7.1. We find that the short-term debt markets of South Asia exhibit weak dependencies amongst them as is indicated by low value of dependence parameter for all country pairs. Trade integration, which is regarded as an important factor reinforcing cross-country linkages in capital markets (see Kumar and Okimoto, 2011), is poor amongst the South Asian countries; hence, it can plausibly be the reason for low level of debt market linkages in the region. Also South Asia bond market development is plagued by supply- and demand-side bottlenecks, absence of market infrastructure and lack of adequate legal and regulatory framework.

Results also suggest that short-term debt markets of Nepal and Pakistan have the highest interdependence. The degree of integration at the short

Table 7.1 Dependencies amongst Short-Term Debt Markets of South Asian Countries

		Normal		Clayton		Gumbel		Student t	
		Value	LL	Value	LL	Value	LL	Value	LL
BANG	IND	0.11	−0.65	0.04	−0.04	1.10	−0.51	0.11	−0.61
BANG	NEP	0.10	−0.64	0.10	−0.35	1.10	−1.90	**0.08**	**−2.75**
BANG	PAK	0.03	−0.04	0.06	−0.15	1.10	0.79	**0.02**	**−0.43**
BANG	SRI	**0.01**	**−0.01**	0.00	0.00	1.10	1.08	0.02	0.03
IND	NEP	**−0.05**	**−0.20**	0.00	0.00	1.10	3.00	−0.05	−0.16
IND	PAK	0.09	−0.58	**0.19**	**−1.79**	1.10	0.88	0.09	−0.86
IND	SRI	0.07	**−0.40**	0.03	−0.03	1.10	0.38	0.08	−0.29
NEP	PAK	0.21	−3.27	0.19	−1.56	**1.16**	**−4.05**	0.21	−3.39
NEP	SRI	0.03	−0.05	0.12	−0.89	1.10	1.71	−0.03	**−1.13**
PAK	SRI	0.14	−1.48	**0.18**	**−1.49**	1.10	−0.32	0.15	−1.34

Source: Authors.

Notes: The table summarizes time-invariant copula estimation results for short-term debt markets of the South Asian countries.

a Value denotes pairwise dependence parameter between short-term debt return series of South Asian countries using different copula models.

b LL denotes the log likelihood value of dependence parameter between short-term debt return series of South Asian countries using different copula models.

c Value in bold denotes the lowest negative log likelihood thereby providing the best fit copula model amongst the family of models under study.

d BANG, IND, NEP, PAK and SRI denote Bangladesh, India, Nepal, Pakistan and Sri Lanka, respectively.

end is dictated by business cycle synchronization across the countries (see Kumar and Okimoto, 2011; Yang and Hamori, 2014; Sowmya et al. 2016). Thus, the level of GDP growth of the two countries can possibly be the determining factor as the two countries have been, on an average, growing at a similar rate of 4.1% over the last 10 years (from 2005 to 2015).[3]

Further, we find that short-term debt market of India is found to have relatively strong association with that of Bangladesh as compared to other South Asian debt markets. This is probably due to the development assistance extended by India to Bangladesh in form of line of credit worth USD 1 billion in 2010 which has boosted bilateral relations between the countries and has provided impetus to trade and financial integration between the countries.

Now looking at the pairwise dynamic evolution of dependencies of the short-term debt markets of South Asia (Figure 7.2), we see that the

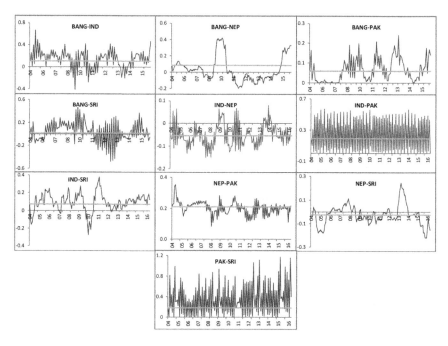

Figure 7.2 Dynamic Dependencies between Short-Term Debt Markets of South Asian Countries.

Source: Authors' Calculations.

Notes: (a) The best fit time-varying copula model selected by the goodness of fit test for different family of copula models is plotted along with its corresponding time-invariant dependency measure (in horizontal line). (b) BANG, IND, NEP, PAK and SRI denote Bangladesh, India, Nepal, Pakistan and Sri Lanka, respectively.

dependencies amongst them remain volatile for majority of the sample period. There are, in fact, no visible divergences in the pattern of dependencies during and post the crisis period. This shows that bond markets of South Asian countries are weakly integrated not just with each other but relatively insulated from the global shocks of the economic crises of 2008 and afterwards.

Financial integration of the short-term debt markets of the South Asian countries is also analysed using Diebold and Yilmaz (2012) spillover index methodology. This helps us gain further insights into the level of bond market linkages amongst them. Spillovers across the short-term debt markets of South Asian countries are reported in Table 7.2.

The total return spillover (bottom right corner of the matrix) across the short-term debt markets of South Asian countries is on an average 11.9%, indicating that the debt markets of these countries are not much influential in transmitting shocks within the region. This might be because of the small size of bond markets in the region and also due to limited cross-border trade and investment in the South Asian countries as spillovers are mainly propagated through trade and financial channels. Low return spillover across short-term debt markets of the region corroborates copula results which demonstrate low level of pairwise dependencies amongst the short-term debt markets of the region, thereby implying low level of debt market linkages of the short end of the yield curve in the South Asian region.

Table 7.2 Return Spillovers across Short-Term Debt Markets of South Asian Countries

	BANG	IND	NEP	PAK	SRI	From Others
BANG	83.07	7.88	0.52	5.28	3.25	16.90
IND	2.69	92.99	1.37	0.88	2.08	7.00
NEP	2.10	3.51	86.86	6.89	0.63	13.10
PAK	0.96	2.39	5.92	89.81	0.93	10.20
SRI	4.30	5.19	1.13	1.69	87.69	12.30
Contribution to others	10.10	19.00	8.90	14.70	6.90	59.60
Contribution including own	93.10	111.90	95.80	104.50	94.60	11.90%

Source: Authors.

Notes: The table presents Diebold and Yilmaz (2012) spillover table summary for short-term debt markets of South Asian countries.
a The diagonal entries of the matrix represent the own variance share of the sample countries, and the off-diagonal elements show the cross-market spillovers.
b The last column of the matrix ("from others") highlights the gross directional return spillovers to the country from rest of the countries.
c The second last row ("to others") indicates the gross directional spillover from a country to rest of the countries.
d BANG, IND, NEP, PAK and SRI denote Bangladesh, India, Nepal, Pakistan and Sri Lanka, respectively.

Amongst all South Asian short-term debt markets, Nepal and Pakistan exhibit the highest integration. Relatively strong connectedness of the short-term debt markets of the two countries is reflected in the pairwise directional spillover index, with Nepal contributing 5.92% to forecast error variance of Pakistan and receiving 6.89% spillovers from it. This strengthens copula results that also revealed strong dependences between the short-term debt markets of the two countries.

The level of connectedness of short-term debt market of India, as reflected by the pairwise gross directional spillovers (to and from), is the highest with that of Bangladesh as compared to the short-term debt market of any other South Asian economy. This implies that the short-term debt markets of these two countries are strongly linked with each other, with India being the net transmitter of information. This is predominantly due to the large size of the bond markets in India w.r.t Bangladesh and also probably due to increased trade between India and Bangladesh. With additional line of credit extended recently by India to Bangladesh worth USD 2 billion that is so far the highest credit extended by India, the bilateral trade and financial links between the two countries is expected to take a leap in future which might be reflected in enhanced linkages in their debt markets. It is noteworthy to point here that India is the chief net transmitter of spillovers in the entire region. This can be attributed to the size and depth of the Indian debt market that is the third largest in Asia after China and Korea and has grown at a compounded annual (outstanding local currency bonds) growth rate of 10.6% between 2005 and 2015 (see Park, 2016).

Long-term debt market integration

Like short-term debt markets of South Asian countries, long-term debt markets are also weakly linked with each other. This is reflected in the low value of dependence parameter for majority of the country pairs (Table 7.3). As highlighted in the previous section, trade integration plays a key role in strengthening cross-country linkages in capital markets. Hence, weak linkages amongst the long-term debt markets can be attributed to poor trade linkages of the countries and also lack of infrastructure for development of local bond markets. Also long end of the yield curve is susceptible to long-term investors' appetite for these papers. This investor's appetite to invest in long-term bonds depends upon the macroeconomic and political strengths of the member countries. SAARC members with the exception of India are in the same homogenous characteristic group when it comes to macroeconomic strengths to resuscitate the bond markets.

An interesting characteristic of the long-term debt markets of the region, as revealed by our empirical results, is that the level of dependency of India with other South Asian members is relatively low than that of other countries amongst themselves. Dependency is found to be particularly high

Table 7.3 Dependencies amongst Long-Term Debt Markets of South Asian
Countries

		Normal		Clayton		Gumbel		Student t	
		Value	LL	Value	LL	Value	LL	Value	LL
BANG	IND	−0.10	−0.63	0.00	0.00	1.10	2.54	−0.11	−0.49
BANG	NEPAL	−0.26	−4.04	0.00	0.00	1.10	4.47	**−0.30**	**−4.45**
BANG	PAK	0.15	**−1.31**	0.11	−0.36	1.10	−1.11	0.16	−1.23
BANG	SRI	0.19	−2.05	**0.32**	**−3.19**	1.12	−1.53	0.18	−2.91
IND	NEPAL	0.05	**−0.16**	0.03	−0.05	1.10	0.25	0.05	−0.16
IND	PAK	0.08	−0.47	**0.20**	**−1.81**	1.10	0.83	0.08	−0.84
IND	SRI	0.00	0.00	0.00	0.00	1.10	0.00	**0.02**	**−0.59**
NEPAL	PAK	−0.24	−4.37	0.00	0.01	1.10	5.07	**−0.32**	**−7.10**
NEPAL	SRI	0.05	−0.17	0.09	−0.33	1.10	0.52	**0.09**	**−0.90**
PAK	SRI	**0.01**	**0.00**	0.00	0.00	1.10	1.02	0.01	0.04

Source: Authors.

Notes: The table summarizes time-invariant copula estimation results for long-term debt
markets of the South Asian countries.
a Value denotes pairwise dependence parameter between long-term debt return series of
South Asian countries using different copula models.
b LL denotes the log likelihood value of dependence parameter between long-term debt
return series of South Asian countries using different copula models.
c Value in bold denotes the lowest negative log likelihood thereby providing the best fit
copula model amongst the family of models under study.
d BANG, IND, NEP, PAK and SRI denote Bangladesh, India, Nepal, Pakistan and Sri
Lanka, respectively.

between Bangladesh-Nepal and Nepal-Pakistan. This might be attributed
to China's growing presence in the South Asian region, transcending India
as the major player in the region in terms of trade and investment links with
other South Asian countries. China has surpassed India as the largest FDI
contributor to Nepal with several infrastructure and energy projects being
financed by it in Nepal. Trade and financial investments have increased
in Bangladesh from China, wherein China has even signed USD 24 billion credit agreement with Bangladesh recently. China-Pakistan Economic
Corridor is an ambitious project of China and Pakistan that will boost
investment links between the countries. Further, China has taken lead in
investing in Sri Lanka by providing financial assistance in infrastructure
projects like building highways, ports and airport. Thus, relatively high
association amongst the long-term debt markets of the South Asian countries (except India) seems to be reflected in China's massive trading and
investment in these countries. Since infrastructure and financial assistance
of China in member countries of SAARC are predominantly for long-term
basis in accordance with the long gestation period of these projects, this may
be of particular interest to long-term investors as Chinese investments will
act as safety valve to signal long-term prospects in these member countries.

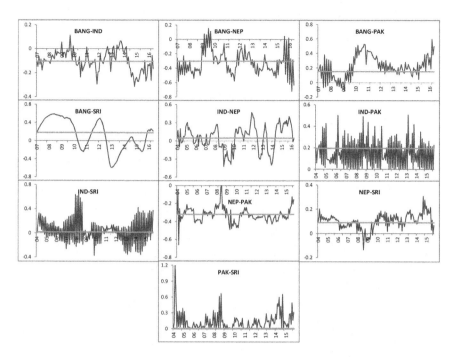

Figure 7.3 Dynamic Dependences between Long-Term Debt Markets of South Asian Countries.

Source: Authors' Calculations.

Notes: (a) The best fit time-varying copula model selected by the goodness of fit test for different family of copula models is plotted along with its corresponding time invariant dependency measure (in horizontal line). (b) BANG, IND, NEP, PAK and SRI denote Bangladesh, India, Nepal, Pakistan and Sri Lanka, respectively.

Dynamic evolution of long-term debt market dependencies of South Asia (Figure 7.3) suggests persistent volatility in the dependencies of majority of the country pairs. No specific trend during and post the Global Financial Crisis is observed so as to say that long-term debt markets of South Asia are impacted by the turmoil period. This points to the global segmentation of the South Asian debt markets as they are unsusceptible to the global shocks.

Results from Diebold and Yilmaz (2012) spillover index methodology (Table 7.4) indicate weak integration of the long-term debt markets of South Asia. This is clearly reflected in the low level of total return spillover across debt markets, which is on an average 11.10%. This strengthens copula results of low level of long-term debt market dependencies amongst majority of the South Asian country pairs. As highlighted before, this is probably due to limited trade and investment in the South Asian region as spillovers are mainly

Table 7.4 Return Spillovers across Long-Term Debt Markets of South Asian
Countries

	BANG	IND	PAK	SRI	From others
BANG	94.26	0.58	4.94	0.22	5.70
IND	0.71	90.71	4.95	3.62	9.30
PAK	9.10	7.59	78.21	5.10	21.80
SRI	3.49	1.71	2.47	92.33	7.70
Contribution to others	13.30	9.90	12.40	8.90	44.50
Contribution including own	107.60	100.60	90.60	101.30	11.10%

Source: Authors.

Notes: The table presents Diebold and Yilmaz (2012) spillover table summary for long-term debt markets of South Asian countries.
a The diagonal entries of the matrix represent the own variance share of the sample countries, and the off-diagonal elements show the cross-market spillovers.
b The last column of the matrix ("from others") highlights the gross directional return spillovers to the country from rest of the countries.
c The second last row ("to others") indicates the gross directional spillover from a country to rest of the countries.
d BANG, IND, PAK and SRI denote Bangladesh, India, Pakistan and Sri Lanka, respectively.

propagated through trade and financial channels. Regional segmentation of the long-term debt markets of South Asia as member country's bond markets is predominantly affected by shocks to their own bond markets with the exception of Pakistan. It can be seen that the debt market of Pakistan is a net receiver of shocks from other South Asian markets as it is relatively more receptive to the shocks originating in other markets. Hence, the long-term debt market of Pakistan is comparatively more interlinked to other South Asian debt markets. Amongst all South Asian markets, Bangladesh long-term bond markets are financially more interlinked with Pakistan as the pairwise gross spillover across the countries is the highest. Linkages between the debt markets of the two countries are probably an outcome of rising Chinese influence in their economies especially through its long-term investment. High interconnectedness is also observable between India and Pakistan possibly due to their relatively developed debt markets with public bonds outstanding close to 30% of their GDP (see Burger et al. 2015).

Empirical results confirm the assertion that bond markets are far from developed in the region. The SAARC region has a relatively low level of integration, both in terms of physical trade and capital markets particularly in bond markets. The heterogeneity in the level of bond market development is also huge in SAARC, wherein India's market is the most developed. Its experience along with those of East Asian economies suggests much potential for developing bond market infrastructure in other member countries of SAARC. Greater regional integration of South Asian bond market could add to the benefits as there is massive infrastructure needs to be met in these regions and bank-centric model of financing is prone to systemic shocks for the financial system and asset liability mis-management for the banks themselves.

Summary and policy suggestions

This chapter studies linkages amongst the short- and long-term debt markets of the South Asian countries. Bond markets gained prominence after the Asian crises of 1997. Bank-centric financial system of East Asian countries after the crises created awareness for a need to supplement bank finance with better diversified debt securities markets within the region and particularly medium- to long-term debt to cater to the maturity and currency mismatch which came into forefront in the Asian crises of 1997. Post the Asian crises, economies of the region have strived to have a diversified financial systems having well-regulated banks and functioning equity and bond markets. It further helps to promote financial stability and helps in efficient resource allocation thereby ensuring medium- to long-term economic growth. SAARC nations can learn from their eastern counterparts and strive to realize these benefits which require developing their debt securities markets. Hence, we examine the current level of integration across the short-term as well as long-term debt markets of South Asian countries. Our results demonstrate low level of financial integration in both short- and long-term debt markets of the South Asian region. However, measures are needed to enhance both the depth and breadth of the South Asian bond markets. Low level of debt market linkages can be ascribed to limited cross-border trade and investment, lack of infrastructure to develop functioning bond markets and absence of adequate regulation. In case of long-term debt markets, we find that the level of dependency of India with other South Asian members is relatively lower than that of other countries amongst themselves. Time-varying results seem to suggest, first, low inter-temporal linkages of bond markets between member nations and, second, global insulation of the South Asian debt markets as the dependencies amongst them remain immune to the volatility unleashed by Global Financial Crisis of 2008 which might be because their size of bond markets itself is low.

Low level of debt market integration amongst the South Asian countries indicates potential diversification opportunities for global fixed income funds. Given the size and attractiveness of Indian bond markets, long-term debt securities inflows by global fixed income investors in the region are predominantly directed towards India. Global bond investors, therefore, can reap diversification benefits by mobilizing their investments across the region and not particularly aligning it in one country.

South Asia bond markets, though relatively small, can nevertheless be expected to grow at a fast pace in line with the high GDP growth of the region. This growth will reinvigorate firms seeking financing and an immense pool of savings asking for new investment opportunities. But all this requires sound well-functioning bond markets which will require supply- and demand-side bottlenecks to be addressed, market infrastructure to be created and providing for a legal and regulatory framework. For this respective local government's sound debt management strategy is the key to kick-start its development. On the demand side, a large and diversified investor base ensure strong and stable demand for bonds under broad market conditions. Market infrastructure speaks about the presence of primary dealer system, electronic trading platform, clearing and settlement system and credit rating agencies in which India has competence with the best in the world. Further, countries need to work on strengthening macroeconomic fundamentals and improving on governance and transparency to gain investors' confidence. South Asian countries can concentrate on the development of Government Securities markets, and it is here wherein they can take domain expertise from India which has a well-regulated and functional government securities market. India, being the biggest country in terms of debt markets in the region, can come up with local currency debt issuance which must be accessible to other South Asian members to increase regional debt market integration. Unleashing the full potential of domestic debt markets will require concerted efforts by policymakers across the region. The developmental finance needs of the member countries of the SAARC can be easily met with the coming of age of its bond markets as they help mobilize long-term funding required for massive infrastructure projects which can then contribute to growth and development of the region.

Notes

1 An earlier version of this chapter has been published in *Theoretical Economics Letters*, an open access journal of Scientific Research Publishing (SCIRP). Citation: Sehgal et al. (2018d).
2 Asian Bond Market Initiative (ABMI) is an initiative of Association of South East Asian Nations Plus Three (ASEAN+3) that includes ten members of ASEAN plus the People's Republic of China, Japan and South Korea. This initiative was put in place in 2003.
3 Source: WDI.

8

CURRENCY LINKAGES ACROSS THE SOUTH ASIAN ECONOMIES[1]

Sanjay Sehgal and Piyush Pandey

Introduction

The collapse of Bretton Woods System of pegged exchange rates and strict capital controls in the early 1990s ushered in an era of financial liberalization and globalization. Financial linkages between the economies started to gather pace with the adoption of flexible or floating exchange rate regimes, removal of strict capital controls and deregulation of financial markets after the abandonment of Bretton Woods. It also coincided with deepening financial linkages due to information, communication and technological advancements. This regime shift led to unexpected changes in the international market environment like dramatic increase in capital movements across markets and extreme exchange rate fluctuations, which posed significant challenges to the world economies. The Asian currency crisis of 1997 demonstrated how uncertainty in one currency may spread to other currencies and eventually cause a chain reaction of interdependence/contagion throughout the global financial markets (Forbes and Rigobon, 1999). The Asian crises of 1997 didn't seem to have much effect on South Asia partly because of low capital flows into this region which prevented any outflows of capital. Government-controlled economic activities including exchange control, restrictive trade policies and weak governance practices insulated the South Asian economies from the ramifications of the crisis. However, with the increasing integration of global capital markets, South Asian countries are now susceptible to similar external shocks in the form of volatile capital flows. Also, these countries have large immigrant population around the world that is a source of remittances (117.9 billion USD in 2015[2]) which have implications for the balance of payments.

Currency market clearly dominates other asset classes as it is one of the largest[3] and most liquid markets in the world. Its attractiveness stems from the fact that it can be traded 24 hours a day. The analysis of currency co-movements is of great importance for central bank interventions, international trade, risk management and portfolio diversification (Antonakakis, 2012). The presence of co-movement of exchange rates would suggest that news originating in a specific market is not country-specific and idiosyncratic, but efficiently transmitted to other foreign markets (Bekiros and Marcellino, 2013). The interdependence of exchange rates may also be relevant for monetary policymakers, because it implies that exchange rates are influenced by common global/regional factors, which cannot be controlled only by local monetary policies (Ciner, 2011).

Exchange rate coordination amongst members of any regional group reduces exchange rate mis-alignments thereby preventing loss of competitiveness for a country. Also it would facilitate greater stability in exchange rates which could further support investment by increasing price transparency and reducing currency-related hedging cost. Also sharp exchange rate movements in one currency could affect another country's ability to maintain a particular exchange rate regime. Exchange rate coordination by limiting exchange rate volatility is expected to lend support to intra-regional trade. This coordination in exchange rate also stems from the fact that South Asian member countries are susceptible to symmetric or similar external shock i.e. volatile capital flows. Despite the benefits of exchange rate coordination, such coordination is a result of long-drawn discussions and policy formulation in this regards. Given the heterogeneity of South Asian member countries in terms of their institutional capability and policy frameworks, any success in this regards for South Asia is long and arduous task. Given the increasing emphasis on closer regional economic coordination in Asia to realize what is termed as the "Asian century" and realization that one needs greater monetary policy cooperation to support the economic growth, this chapter attempts to empirically assess financial integration of the South Asian countries by examining their exchange rate linkages.

Linkages amongst South Asian currency markets

Data and empirical approach

Daily currency data (with the exception of Afghanistan) measured in national currency per USD has been retrieved from Bloomberg for all South Asian countries for the period 6 January 2004 to 31 March 2016. We transform the data by defining exchange rate returns as $R_t = \ln{(s_t/s_{t-1})}$, where s_t is (spot) exchange rate at date t, and s_{t-1} is the exchange rate at date $t-1$.

We investigate the linkages of South Asian currency markets by employing copula functions. Copula functions provide us the degree of pairwise dependence structure between the financial assets. To describe the symmetric and asymmetric dependence structure between the currency markets, we use two Elliptical (Gaussian and Student t) and two Archimedean's (Clayton and

Gumbel) family of copula models. Time-invariant and time-variant copula models are estimated to examine both time static and time-varying nature of dependencies amongst the currency markets of the South Asian region. Refer Appendix C for detailed description of Copula methodology.

We supplement our analysis using Diebold and Yilmaz (2012) spillover index methodology to examine the level of transmission of shocks across the currency markets. This methodology allows us to quantify the cross-market directional spillovers thereby giving further insights into the level of currency market linkages. Refer Appendix B for detailed exposition of Diebold and Yilmaz (2012) spillover index methodology.

South Asian currency market linkages

Results from the time-invariant copula models (refer Table 8.1) suggest that the dependence parameter between foreign exchange (FX) returns of the South Asian countries is very low (almost close to 0) implying little or no association. Pandey and Sehgal (2018) confirmed trade linkages as one of the factors explaining exchange rate co-movements between select Asian currencies. The low values of the dependence parameters in the SAARC region can be attributed to its poor regional trade intensity (total trade within SAARC members/total trade with the world) and low intra-regional equity portfolio flows (as shown in Chapter 6). It can be clearly seen that the regional trade intensity (refer Figure 2.7) is the lowest for SAARC member group compared to other regional economic blocs and has rather remained stagnant over time.

Bhutanese Ngultrum has been pegged against Indian currency and trades at par with Indian rupee, and hence, they both show perfect positive association (0.99). In terms of circulation, the Indian currency can be called a subsidiary currency in Bhutan as the Ngultrum does not exchange independently with anyother nations' currencies but is interchangeable with the Indian rupee. Since the time series of India and Bhutan currencies are both perfectly collinear, going forward we only take Indian currency for our pairwise analysis with other South Asian countries.

Indian currency returns also show high linkages with Nepal currency. India has historical, economic and social ties with Nepal, and Nepalese currency is also pegged to Indian currency. Both the Nepali and Indian rupees were legal tender in Nepal till 1956 but after the formation of Nepal central bank in 1956, existing dual currency system was changed in favour of single currency and Nepalese rupee was the sole legal tender. The primary reason why Nepal pegs its currency to India to Indian rupee is because three-fifth of Nepal's trade deficit is accounted for by India. Since the close association between FX returns of India and Bhutan, Nepal could also be attributed to close trade linkages between them (India provides overland transit route to

Table 8.1 Dependencies amongst Currency Markets of South Asian Countries

		Normal		Clayton		Gumbel		Student t	
		Value	LL	Value	LL	Value	LL	Value	LL
BANG	IND	0.02	−0.56	**0.03**	**−1.33**	1.11	42.56	0.02	0.12
BANG	MALD	−0.06	−4.79	0.00	0.01	1.12	70.32	**−0.06**	**−8.22**
BANG	NEP	0.03	−1.57	**0.04**	**−1.92**	1.13	36.11	0.03	−1.18
BANG	PAK	0.06	−4.74	**0.07**	**−6.93**	1.11	28.12	0.06	−4.03
BANG	SRI	−0.01	−0.18	0.01	−0.20	1.16	51.88	**−0.01**	**−2.56**
IND	MALD	0.02	−0.37	**0.02**	**−0.60**	1.12	39.59	0.02	−0.23
IND	NEP	0.37	−219.87	0.58	−244.57	1.29	−196.99	**0.39**	**−265.42**
IND	PAK	**0.06**	**−4.83**	0.05	−3.34	1.11	20.21	0.06	−4.52
IND	SRI	0.07	−7.59	**0.08**	**−8.25**	1.13	11.36	0.07	−8.03
MALD	NEP	0.04	−2.09	**0.06**	**−4.86**	1.14	32.10	0.04	−3.62
MALD	PAK	−0.02	−0.38	0.00	0.00	1.13	56.21	**−0.01**	**−0.43**
MALD	SRI	**0.02**	**−0.91**	0.01	−0.20	1.12	31.84	0.02	−0.58
NEP	PAK	0.05	−4.05	0.06	−4.88	1.11	18.95	**0.05**	**−6.06**
NEP	SRI	**0.06**	**−5.97**	0.06	−5.46	1.11	19.33	0.06	−5.81
PAK	SRI	**0.04**	**−2.11**	0.04	−1.77	1.11	32.61	0.04	−1.15

Notes: The table summarizes time-invariant copula estimation results for South Asian currency markets.

a Value denotes pairwise dependence parameter between FX return series of South Asian countries using different copula models.

b LL denotes the log likelihood value of the dependence parameter FX return series of South Asian countries using different copula models.

c Value in bold denotes the lowest negative LL values thereby providing the best fit copula model amongst the family of models under study.

d BANG, IND, MALD, NEP, PAK and SRI denote Bangladesh, India, Maldives, Nepal, Pakistan and Sri Lanka, respectively.

Bhutan and Nepal for their bilateral trade and maritime transit to Bhutan and Nepal for their international trade). Bhutan and Nepal have access to direct invoicing and settlement of their trade in Indian rupees.

Figure 8.1 depicts the results relating to the dynamic copula models which show inter-temporal dependence measure between each country's currency index returns with the other. Within the SAARC region, the highest time-varying dependence amongst the country pairs is shown by currency market indices of India and Nepal. There seems to be slight increase in linkages for India and Nepal currency pair from 2009 to 2011 which might be attributed to the revised India Nepal treaty of trade which was signed in 2009. This treaty helped to further expand the trade between the two countries (total trade of Nepal with India as a % of its total trade increased from 58% in 2009 to 65% in 2011[4]). The copula models confirm that level of dependencies is around 0 for all the other pair of sample countries implying little currency market linkages or idiosyncratic factors affecting individual currency movements.

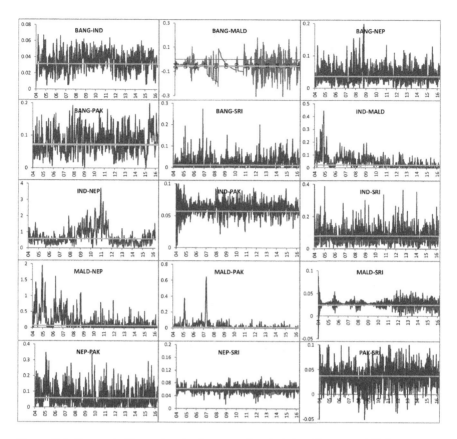

Figure 8.1 Dynamic Dependencies between South Asian Currency Markets.
Source: Authors' Calculations.

Notes: (a) The dynamic linkage of the best fit copula model selected by the goodness of fit test (which predominantly selects Clayton family for most of the currency pairs) for different family of copula models is plotted along with its corresponding time-invariant dependency measure (in horizontal line). (b) BANG, IND, MALD, NEP, PAK and SRI denote Bangladesh, India, Maldives, Nepal, Pakistan and Sri Lanka, respectively.

Table 8.2 presents the time-aggregated currency returns spillover matrix for four South Asian countries[5] (India, Nepal, Pakistan and Sri Lanka).

In the "Contribution to others" row, we see that gross directional return spillover was the highest from India (20.7%) and subsequently from Nepal (15.3%). Of the gross directional return spillover from India to others, 92.8% (19.2/20.7) is for explaining the forecast error variance of Nepal, whereas in case of Nepal, 93% (14.23/15.3) is for explaining the forecast error variance of India. Also we can see from the "From others" column that gross directional return spillovers were the highest to Nepal (19.5%) followed by India (15%). Of

Table 8.2 Returns Spillovers across South Asian Currency Markets

	IND	NEP	PAK	SRI	From Others
IND	85.04	14.23	0.2	0.53	15
NEP	19.2	80.49	0.08	0.23	19.5
PAK	0.55	0.48	98.93	0.04	1.1
SRI	0.96	0.61	0.05	98.37	1.6
Contribution to others	20.7	15.3	0.3	0.8	37.2
Contribution including own	105.8	95.8	99.3	99.2	9.30%

Notes: The table presents Diebold and Yilmaz (2012) spillover table summary for South Asian currency markets.

a   The diagonal entries of the matrix represent the own variance share of the sample countries, and the off-diagonal elements show the cross-market spillovers.

b   The last column of the matrix ("from others") highlights the gross directional return spillovers to the country from rest of the countries.

c   The second last row ("to others") indicates the gross directional spillover from a country to rest of the countries.

d   IND, NEP, PAK and SRI denote India, Nepal, Pakistan and Sri Lanka, respectively

the gross directional return spillover to Nepal from others, 98.4% (19.2/19.5) is from India for explaining the forecast error variance of Nepal, whereas in case of India, 95% (14.23/15) is from Nepal to explain its forecast error variance. This confirms strong linkages between Indian and Nepalese currency which could be explained by close trade and financial linkages between the two countries. India accounts significantly for both exports and imports for Nepal (refer Figure 8.2). Also, the remittance outflows from Nepal to India as a % of total remittances from Nepal have been above 90% from 2010 to 2014 (94.17% as of 2014[6]). Except this pair, there are no spillovers of any other

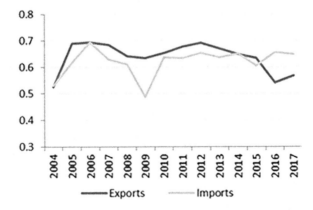

Figure 8.2 Trade Linkages between Nepal and India.
Source: UNCTAD Stat, Authors' Calculations.

Notes: Exports here mean total exports of Nepal to India as a % of its total exports. Imports here mean total imports of Nepal from India as a % of its total imports.

currency pair. The Indian currency dominates the currency market of South Asia region as can be seen from the result of net directional returns spillover, where the largest spillover transfer is from India to others (20.7–15 = 5.7%), whereas other South Asian countries are net receiver of returns spillovers. The total returns spillover which appears in the lower right corner of Table 8.2 indicates that on the average 9.3% of the forecast error variance in all the four markets comes from spillovers which confirm that connectedness of the regional currency markets is low.

The dominant role played by Indian currency in the region can be seen from Figure 8.3 which charts out net return spillovers for each South Asian country from all other countries. The figure clearly depicts that India has always been a net transmitter of returns spillovers, while Nepal, Pakistan and Sri Lanka have majorly been the net receivers of the same.

We also note from Figure 8.3 that net returns spillover graph for India is the mirror image of that of Nepal which indicates the strong linkages of information flow between these two countries. These linkages (initially reported in the high co-movements between Indian and Nepal currency returns from copula models) are confirmed when we look at Figure 8.4 which shows dynamic net pairwise return spillover between sample countries.

Thus, we can conclude that South Asian region currency market linkages are weak with the exception of currency linkages between India-Nepal and India-Bhutan. This could be due to the fact that Bhutan and Nepal being landlocked countries are dependent on India to provide them access to international trade and commerce. They have also pegged their local currencies

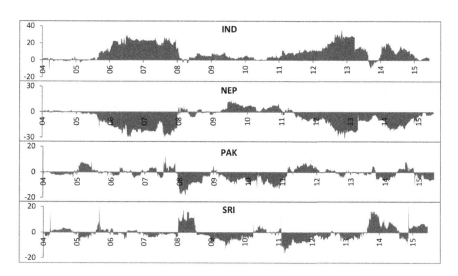

Figure 8.3 Net Return Spillovers across South Asian Currency Markets.
Source: Authors' Calculations.

133

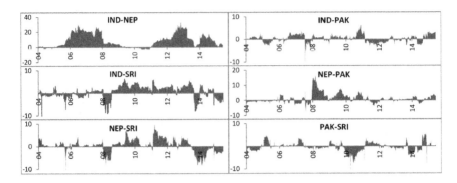

Figure 8.4 Net Pairwise Return Spillovers amongst South Asian Currency Markets.
Source: Authors' Calculations.

to the Indian rupee. The near-perfect level of association between India and Bhutan stems from the fact that Indian currency is accepted as legal tender in Bhutan. The Bhutanese currency in addition to being pegged also trades at par with the Indian currency. Overall, linkages amongst the currency markets of South Asian region are low. This can be attributed to the low regional trade intensity in this region which is the lowest amongst all the major regional economic blocs of the world and also due to low intra-regional equity portfolio flows.

Summary and policy suggestions

In this chapter, we examine the extent of currency market linkages amongst the SAARC member countries. We find little dependence between currency market returns of any pair of South Asian countries except that of India-Bhutan, India-Nepal and Nepal-Bhutan. The high association can be attributed to the fact that Bhutanese and Nepalese currency is pegged to the Indian currency. Further, Bhutanese currency trades at par with Indian currency (equal in value with Indian Rupee). The Bhutanese Ngultrum also does not exchange independently with other nations' currencies but is interchangeable with the Indian rupee. Bhutan and Nepal have access to direct invoicing and settlement of their trade in Indian rupees. The currency market linkages of South Asia, with the exception of India and Nepal, are close to 0 indicating very little level of currency market linkages in the region. This can be attributed to the low regional trade intensity in the region which is in fact the lowest amongst all the major regional economic blocs of the world and also due to low intra-regional portfolio flows. The currency market linkages are found to be quite high between India and Nepal which can be possibly due to close trade and financial linkages, wherein India accounts significantly for both exports and imports for Nepal and strong remittance flows from Nepal to India. A major reason for the limited convergence of nominal exchange rate is the different exchange rate regimes followed in these economies, which signals difference in the priorities of the monetary and exchange rate policy. There seems to be lower levels of trade, investment and connectivity amongst the countries of the region. It seems regionalism in the SAARC member countries is still underdeveloped as perhaps the economic and financial motivation for interaction seems to be over shadowed by political mistrust and outstanding border and other security issues. Thus, it is evident that the South Asian economies have a long way to go to achieve greater degree of exchange rate coordination.

South Asia has emerged as one of the fastest growing regions in the world, and has substantially raised its trade integration with the world but is characterized by very low levels of intra-regional trade integration. Further, the economies of the region have also witnessed significant integration with global capital markets, thereby making it susceptible to the vagaries of global capital flows. Thus, there is a need for greater exchange rate cooperation amongst the economies of the region, while retaining the flexibility to adjust to external currencies. Currency is medium of exchange in international trade and commerce, and a currency shock in one market can lead to a contagion in different markets around the world as was evident from the Asian currency crises of 1998. Exchange rate coordination, by mitigating exchange rate volatility, is likely to improve intra-regional trade. High tariffs are an obstacle for South Asian intra-regional trade, and good payment systems amongst others would go a long way to boost this trade. Countries of the region are expected to foster a stable political environment to ensure clean and transparent governance while taking due consideration for each other's security concerns to increase mutual trust. India, being the largest country of the region, having a robust currency market infrastructure in the region can provide its financial support and technical expertise for building and operating currency market infrastructure in other South Asian countries. South Asia tourism shall help promote acceptance of regional countries' currencies in each other.

The dynamics of exchange rates are crucial for monetary policy decision-making as it is one of the important mandates of any central bank. While making market interventions; policymakers need to lay emphasis on the influence of FX movements on prevailing interest rates and aggregate prices in the economy which are critical for the financial stability for any country. Given the global nature of risks, FX linkages are important for policy-makers to understand the dynamics of currency contagion. Understanding exchange rate dynamics is important for business corporates operating in the region to administer the terms of the trade and better manage their exposure management to currency fluctuations.

Notes

1 An earlier version of this chapter has been published in *Research in International Business and Finance*, an Elsevier journal. Citation: Sehgal et al. (2018a).
2 Source: World Bank.
3 According to the 2013 Triennial Survey of the Bank for International Settlements, the global FX market activity in 2013 reached $5.3 trillion per day, up from $4.0 trillion in 2010 (Rime and Schrimpf, 2013).
4 Source: UNCTAD, Authors' Calculations.
5 Bangladesh and Maldives could not be included in estimating return spillovers as much of the observations for currency returns were 0. Further, we do not include Bhutan for analysis as currency returns of India and Bhutan have near-perfect association (0.99).
6 Source: UNCTAD, Authors' Calculations.

9

BANKING SYSTEM INTEGRATION IN SOUTH ASIA[1]

Piyush Pandey, Sanjay Sehgal and Wasim Ahmad

Introduction

South Asian economies have always been bank-dependent economies with many of the big banks in the region to date their inception during the British India times. Banks have been seen as custodians of the trust in the financial system. After the independence of these countries in South Asia, banks were the fulcrum of economic growth and mainstay of developmental finance, working capital and directional credit. Many of these banks were government-run banks. South Asian countries during their early years of independence suffered from low growth rates and productivity, and were closed economies for foreign capital thereby breeding inefficiency. South Asian countries began introducing far-reaching reforms to their financial sector of their respective economies from the early 1980s. These slew of reforms spanning different areas promoted competition in financial sector, strengthening regulatory supervision, loosening license raj regime, improving transparency and strengthening the legal framework. These measures helped these countries to attract foreign capital, raise domestic savings, improve exports, increase FX reserves and improve economic growth rates. The opening of banking sector of member countries for domestic and private competition brought in much needed operating efficiencies in credit delivery mechanism, product diversification and technological innovations. With the reforms in member countries progressing at their own pace, these economies have largely become more bank-centric which can be reflected in the size of South Asian banking system (measured as amount of deposits) stood on an average to 57% of GDP. Banking sector has always been the primary financial intermediary in this region (commercial banks along with cooperative banks constitute 70% of total assets with financial institutions for the largest economy of the region i.e. India (Arora and Ratnasiri, 2014) with other financial institutions playing a minor role). Figures 9.1 and 9.2 show the importance of banking systems to the overall financial system of the SAARC nation and thereby size of their respective economies.

137

A financial crisis often calls for introspection and further reforms. The Asian crises of 1998 and Global financial crises of 2008 presented a case for strengthening financial system by addressing regulatory and supervisory frameworks. Although in case of South Asia, the financial sector

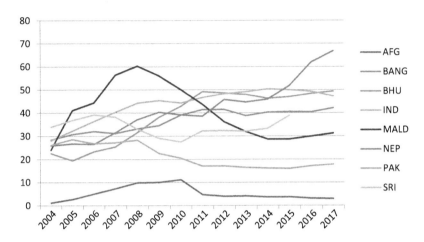

Figure 9.1 Outstanding Loans from Commercial Banks (% of GDP).
Source: IMF.

Notes: AFG,BANG, BHU, IND, MALD, NEP, PAK and SRI denote Afghanistan, Bangladesh, Bhutan, India, Maldives, Nepal, Pakistan and Sri Lanka, respectively.

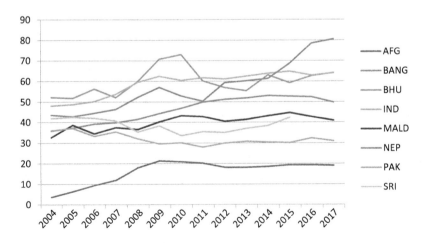

Figure 9.2 Outstanding Deposits with Commercial Banks (% of GDP).
Source: IMF.

Notes: AFG, BANG, BHU, IND, MALD, NEP, PAK and SRI denote Afghanistan, Bangladesh, Bhutan, India, Maldives, Nepal, Pakistan and Sri Lanka, respectively.

138

didn't have direct exposure to the complex financial products but the inter-connectedness of the financial sector led to contagious effects through other alternative channels – capital, remittances and international trade. Although macro- and micro-prudential norms are being promulgated globally, domestically still there are many weaknesses in the current banking architecture for South Asian countries like low financial deepening, high intermediation costs and a low level of access to finance. The financial crisis has highlighted the importance of systemic risk, and hence, a careful reassessment of the banking sector is the bedrock of financial system of South Asian members since an efficient, competitive and resilient financial sector is the key determinant of the ability of South Asian economies to move to a sustainable high growth path.

Given that 2010–2020 has been termed by SAARC as the decade for intraregional connectivity, it is important to examine the banking sector linkages in the region as they are the biggest source of developmental credit besides multilateral institutions. The global financial crises had exposed the vulnerabilities of the financial system architecture, and hence, assessment of the banking linkages in the region would help central banks of the region to manage the systemic risks in moving away from compliance-based supervision to risk-focused supervision. Also the nature of banking sector co-movements has important implications for monetary policy, optimal asset allocation and capital adequacy.

Hence, in this chapter, we investigate the linkages between deposits and lending rates individually for the banks of the South Asian countries. Additionally, we examine the banking linkages of the deposits and lending rates for this region to assess the degree of connectedness of these markets.

Banking sector linkages in South Asia

Data and methodology

We use monthly lending and deposit rates, respectively, for the South Asian countries from Bloomberg for the period 6 January 2004 to 31 March 2016. The starting date has been selected keeping in mind the date when the SAFTA agreement (6 January 2004) was reached which was a landmark event in the process of regional cooperation in South Asia. The data for monthly International Monetary Fund (IMF) deposit rate series for Bangladesh, Bhutan, Maldives, Pakistan and Sri Lanka is available for the study period, while the IMF deposit rate series is not available for India, and hence, alternatively, we selected the monthly deposit rates of the biggest bank in India i.e. State Bank of India. The data for monthly IMF deposit rates for Bangladesh, Bhutan, India, Maldives, Pakistan and Sri Lanka is available for the study period. Thus, we have covered six South Asian countries out of the total eight who constitute the SAARC as no data was available for Afghanistan and data for Nepal ended in 2011.

We investigate the linkages of the savings rate and lending rates, respectively, of the South Asian countries by employing copula functions. Copula functions provide us the degree of pairwise dependence structure between the financial assets. To describe the symmetric and asymmetric dependence structure between the currency markets, we use two Elliptical (Gaussian and Student t) and two Archimedean's (Clayton and Gumbel) family of copula models. Gaussian copula is symmetric and has no tail dependence, whereas Student t copula can capture extreme dependence between variables. The Gumbel copula exhibits greater dependence in the upper tail than in the lower, whereas the Clayton copula exhibits greater dependence in the negative tail than in the positive tail. Time-invariant and time-variant copula models are estimated to examine the nature of dependencies among the savings and deposit rate series of the South Asian region.

We supplement our analysis using Diebold and Yilmaz (2012) spillover index methodology to examine the level of transmission of shocks across the banking sector. This methodology allows us to quantify the cross-market directional spillovers thereby giving further insights into the level of financial linkages. Cross-variance share or cross-market directional spillovers measure the forecast error variance of a variable that is attributable to shocks from another variable(s). The fraction of forecast error variance of variable i due to shocks from variable i represents the own variance share. Total spillover index is the average of spillovers from shocks to all other variables to the total forecast error variance. The difference between directional spillovers transmitted by variable i and directional spillovers received by variable i provides the net spillovers of variable i. Refer Appendix B and C for a detailed exposition of the two methodologies.

Banking sector linkages

Estimation results of time-invariant copula models are reported in Table 9.1. Panel A results report the time-invariant copula results of the lending rate series between the sample countries. It can be clearly seen that the dependency parameter is around 0 for the sample countries which indicates that the lending rates are not harmonized but seem to be catering to the idiosyncratic credit needs for the various countries. This is expected since the developmental needs of these countries are quite distinct and so are the transmissions pass through for the monetary policy to arrive at the lending rates. Panel B results report the time-invariant copula results of the deposit rate series between the sample countries. The linkages for the same are again around 0 which can be attributed to the fact that the deposit rates for

140

Table 9.1 Dependencies amongst Banking Systems of South Asian Countries

Panel A: LENDING

		Normal		Clayton		Gumbel		Student t	
		LL	Value	LL	Value	LL	Value	LL	
BANG	BHU	0.10	−0.74	0.12	−0.47	1.10	−0.47	0.11	−0.70
BANG	IND	0.04	−0.15	0.00	0.00	1.10	−0.11	0.05	−0.11
BANG	MALD	0.06	−0.32	0.09	−0.30	1.10	−0.29	0.07	−0.30
BANG	PAK	0.05	−0.21	0.11	−0.62	1.10	−0.62	**0.07**	**−1.33**
BANG	SRI	−0.10	−0.78	0.00	0.00	1.10	−0.71	−0.11	−0.73
BHU	IND	−0.04	−0.11	0.02	−0.01	1.09	−0.02	−0.04	−0.05
BHU	MALD	0.01	0.00	0.00	0.00	1.11	−0.58	−0.02	−1.20
BHU	PAK	−0.03	−0.09	0.00	0.00	1.10	−0.03	−0.04	−0.04
BHU	SRI	−0.12	−1.00	0.00	0.00	1.11	−0.60	−0.12	−0.89
IND	MALD	−0.04	−0.14	0.00	0.00	1.10	−0.01	−0.05	−0.02
IND	PAK	0.02	−0.02	0.00	0.00	1.11	−0.04	**0.02**	**−0.04**
IND	SRI	−0.03	−0.08	0.00	0.00	1.10	−0.04	−0.04	−0.01
MALD	PAK	−0.02	−0.03	0.03	−0.03	1.10	−0.01	−0.02	−0.02
MALD	SRI	−0.07	−0.41	0.00	0.00	1.10	−0.34	−0.08	−0.30
PAK	SRI	−0.16	−1.89	0.00	0.00	1.10	−0.65	**−0.17**	**−1.96**

Panel B: DEPOSIT

		Normal		Clayton		Gumbel		Student t	
		Value	LL	Value	LL	Value	LL	Value	LL
BANG	BHU	−0.02	−0.04	0.00	0.00	1.10	−0.03	−0.03	−0.03
BANG	IND	−0.06	−0.32	0.00	0.00	1.09	−0.03	−0.07	−0.31
BANG	MALD	0.04	−0.14	0.05	−0.09	1.11	−0.14	**0.05**	**−0.20**
BANG	PAK	0.08	−0.50	0.10	−0.47	1.10	−0.48	0.09	−0.48
BANG	SRI	0.13	−1.36	0.06	−0.15	1.10	−0.70	0.14	−1.19
BHU	IND	−0.19	−2.60	0.00	0.00	1.12	−0.96	−0.20	−2.52
BHU	MALD	−0.39	−11.93	0.00	−0.06	1.12	−10.14	−0.41	−11.85
BHU	PAK	−0.19	−2.80	0.00	0.00	1.10	−0.70	**−0.22**	**−3.22**
BHU	SRI	−0.06	−0.30	0.03	−0.04	1.11	−0.18	−0.06	−1.53
IND	MALD	−0.02	−0.02	0.00	−0.01	1.09	0.00	−0.02	−0.40
IND	PAK	−0.22	−3.79	0.00	0.00	1.11	−0.65	−0.23	−3.75
IND	SRI	0.05	−1.22	0.18	−0.92	1.11	−0.67	0.05	−0.28
MALD	PAK	0.08	−0.44	0.12	−0.65	1.12	−0.18	**0.12**	**−2.03**
MALD	SRI	−0.09	−0.58	0.00	0.00	1.11	−0.23	**−0.12**	**−1.67**
PAK	SRI	0.01	0.00	0.00	0.00	1.11	−0.58	**−0.02**	**−1.20**

Notes: Panels A and B of the table summarizes the time-invariant copula estimation results for lending and deposit rates of South Asian banking systems, respectively.
a Value denotes pairwise dependence parameter between lending/deposit return series of the South Asian banking systems using different copula models.
b LL denotes the log likelihood value of the dependence parameter between lending/deposit return series of the South Asian banking systems using different copula models.
c Value in bold denotes the lowest negative LL values thereby providing the best fit copula model amongst the family of models under study.
d BANG, BHU, IND, MALD, PAK and SRI denote Bangladesh, Bhutan, India, Maldives, Pakistan and Sri Lanka, respectively.

these countries are priced taking into consideration their unique macroeconomic environment (inflation, growth rate, external position, etc.), monetary policy pass through and asset liability considerations. The linkages for both lending and deposit rates, respectively, for majority of sample countries are negative which indicates that despite increasing regional integration in the world, banking sector of SAARC member countries has shown no co-movements. The plausible reason for absence of linkages amongst the banking sector can be the predominance of state presence in the idiosyncratic banking system requirements of these countries, non-synchronized monetary policy followed by central bank, limited exposure to systemic risk factors (i.e. toxic assets), negligible banking activity in the region and poor regional payment system.

Panels A and B of Figure 9.3 show the results relating to the dynamic dependence measure between the sample countries for the lending series and deposit series, respectively. The linkages over time were charted across the study period, and it was found to be around 0 for the pair of sample countries for lending and deposit series implying little or no integration between the banking systems. There also seems to be huge volatility in the dependence parameters for both lending and deposit rates for the sample countries which indicates that the degree of banking integration in the region is rather weak as is found to be true for other asset classes segment (equity, bonds and currency).

Table 9.2 (Panels A and B) presents the time-aggregated lending and deposit returns spillover matrix for six South Asian countries. It can be clearly seen from panel A/B results that for each of the South Asian country, much of the contribution to its forecast error variance is coming from shocks given to its own lending/deposit series and the cross-market spillovers (off-diagonal elements of the table) are very small. The total lending/deposit returns spillover (total connectedness) which appears in the lower right corner of Table 9.2 (Panel A/B) indicates that on the average 9.4%/8.3% of the forecast error variance in all the six markets comes from spillovers which confirm that connectedness of the regional banking sector with respect to lending and deposit rates is low.

The results from the copula models both time invariant and time varying and Diebold and Yilmaz method confirm very little banking sector integration in the region. The dependence parameter between the lending and deposit rate series for SAARC member nations is virtually 0 ruling out interdependence between the banking sectors. Thus, we confirm that the contribution of the banking system in the regional economic integration is limited for the South Asian region. The poor banking linkages in the region can be predominantly attributed to lack of harmonization of banking sector in the region, no cross-border banking activity by banks of regional members, lack of monetary policy synchronization and the lack

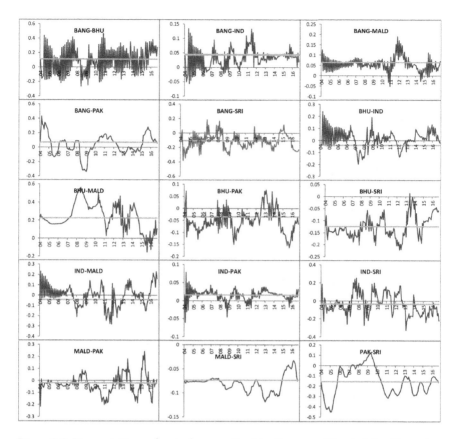

Figure 9.3 Dynamic Dependencies between Banking Systems of South Asian Countries.
Source: Authors' Calculations.

Notes: (a) Panels A and B of the figure present pairwise dynamic dependencies amongst lending and deposit returns of South Asian countries, respectively. (b) The best fit time-varying copula model selected by the goodness of fit test for different family of copula models is plotted along with its corresponding time-invariant dependency measure (in horizontal line). (c) BANG, BHU, IND, MALD, PAK and SRI denote Bangladesh, Bhutan, India, Maldives, Pakistan and Sri Lanka, respectively.

of availability of financial infrastructures such as payments and settlement system. Economic theory suggests that for emerging and low-developed economy, banking sector promotes economic growth through the credit-rationing policy by allocating credit efficiently to the productive sectors of the economy. This obviously is carried out by banks under the supervision of central banks pro-cyclical monetary policy.

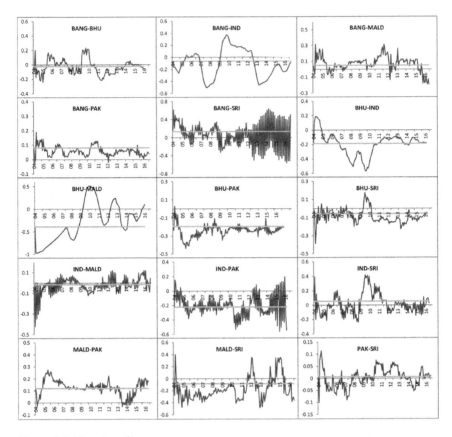

Figure 9.3 (Continued)

Summary and policy suggestions

In this chapter, the extent of banking sector linkages for both the lending and deposit rates for the South Asian countries was investigated. Monthly data for time series of lending and deposit rates, respectively, for the South Asian countries (Bangladesh, Bhutan, India, Maldives, Pakistan and Sri Lanka) was studied from Bloomberg for the period 2004–2016. Copula models both time invariant and time varying were utilized to study the static and dynamic inter-linkages between the lending and borrowing series, respectively. Henceforth, Diebold and Yilmaz methodology was utilized to study the connectedness of banking sector of the region by separately studying the lending and deposit series. Our results

Table 9.2 Return Spillovers across South Asian Banking Systems

Panel A: LENDING	BANG	BHU	IND	MALD	PAK	SRI	From Others
BANG	96.67	0.03	1.22	0.69	1.13	0.27	3.3
BHU	1.96	93.56	3.03	0.03	0.6	0.83	6.4
IND	2.4	2.44	76.55	13.5	3.55	1.56	23.5
MALD	2.1	0.17	4	91.03	1.39	1.32	9
PAK	5.12	0.07	0.88	0.81	90.23	2.88	9.8
SRI	0.12	0.71	0.14	0.92	2.64	95.47	4.5
Contribution to others	11.7	3.4	9.3	16	9.3	6.8	56.5
Contribution including own	108.4	97	85.8	107	99.5	102.3	9.40%

Panel B: DEPOSIT	BANG	BHU	IND	MALD	PAK	SRI	From Others
BANG	94.43	1.47	1.15	0.28	1.76	0.9	5.6
BHU	0.66	96.11	1.07	0.29	0.2	1.67	3.9
IND	1.55	0.48	86.41	2.03	5.35	4.19	13.6
MALD	0.06	0.05	2.2	88.31	0.41	8.97	11.7
PAK	0.52	0.15	1.54	0.14	96.61	1.04	3.4
SRI	1.17	1.49	0.46	7.88	0.67	88.33	11.7
Contribution to others	3.9	3.6	6.4	10.6	8.4	16.8	49.8
Contribution including own	98.4	99.8	92.8	98.9	105	105.1	8.30%

Notes: Panels A and B of the table present Diebold and Yilmaz (2012) spillover table summary for lending and deposit return series of South Asian banking systems, respectively.

a The diagonal entries of the matrix represent the own variance share of the sample countries, and the off-diagonal elements show the cross-market spillovers.

b The last column of the matrix ("from others") highlights the gross directional return spillovers to the country from rest of the countries.

c The second last row ("to others") indicates the gross directional spillover from a country to rest of the countries.

d BANG, BHU, IND, MALD, PAK and SRI denote Bangladesh, Bhutan, India, Maldives, Pakistan and Sri Lanka, respectively.

indicate poor levels of banking linkages in the region as the dependence parameter for both deposits and lending rates was around 0 for the sample countries thereby confirming poor banking sector integration in the region. Further, we confirm that the degree of connectedness for the banking sector for the region with respect to deposit and lending rates is low. The banking sector of South Asia being the biggest intermediary of financial system currently has no role to play in the regional integration in the region.

The presence of a sound and stable financial system is crucial for achieving sustained economic growth and prosperity. Given the global nature of risks, ever-changing financial landscape and global integration of financial markets, it is of utmost importance that financial sector reforms are undertaken to increase efficiency, competition and stability to take South Asian countries to higher growth path. With the opening up of South Asian economies to global risk capital could lead to an asset-pricing bubble, and hence, prudent monetary policy cooperation is essential not just for containing inflationary expectations but for providing conducive environment for promoting financial sector stability. The South Asian region is one of the most dynamic regions of the world and home to the largest number of poor people where financial sector development is predominantly bank-centric. However, banking system harmonization in the region is limited which may be attributed to virtually absent cross-banking activity, non-synchronous monetary policy coordination and unavailability of robust payments and settlement system. Given the homogenous developmental needs of the South Asian nations and the over-reliance on the banks to achieve the same, SAARCFINANCE platform can thereby provide a platform for member countries to jointly coordinate with each other and share best practices related to the banking sector. As these economies carry out more reforms and open up the financial sector, global network linkages will make them vulnerable to global risks, and hence, an efficient micro-prudential regulatory overview is as important as macro-prudential regulatory cooperation which again is possible under the umbrella of SAARCFI-NANCE. There is a need for regulators in the region to form regional alliances under SAARCFINANCE to establish effective mechanism to monitor cross-border financial activities that could threaten financial stability. Consolidation of financial information of the banks operating in various member countries of the region should be made mandatory so that cross-border risks are fully understood. Under the SAARC Payment Network, payments and settlement system should be linked in order to expedite transfer of payments across the borders in the region. Governments of member countries may take upon themselves to increase transparency and improve governance.

Regional policymakers are interested to study banking linkages to better understand the transmission of the monetary policy which can be better anticipated when considering the potential common reactions of credit institutions. Co-movements of interest rates are also important to understand the systemic risk pressures. The banking rate linkages are important for corporate as well as they wish to lower their cost of capital and borrow at the lowest rate not just domestically but from anywhere at the cheapest cost.

Note

1 An earlier version of this chapter has been accepted in *Indian Growth and Development Review*, an Emerald journal. Complete Citation: Pandey, P.; Sehgal, S; & Ahmad, W. (2019). Dynamics of Banking Sector Integration in South Asia: An Empirical Study, Indian Growth and Development Review (Forthcoming) https://doi.org/10.1108/IGDR-07-2018-0079.

10

ROLE OF CHINA IN SOUTH ASIAN FINANCIAL INTEGRATION

Sanjay Sehgal, Sakshi Saini and Piyush Pandey

Introduction

Albeit having an institutional standing of three decades in form of SAARC to promote cooperation and integration amongst the member countries, South Asian region has remained one of the least integrated regions of the world. India, with its large territorial size, huge population and rapid pace of economic growth amongst the South Asian countries, has been regarded as the dominant player of the region that can potentially spearhead the development and integration of the region. However, constrained relationship of India with some of the South Asian countries due to political conflicts and security issues, especially with Pakistan, has culminated in weak integration amongst them. To foster regional integration, some of the SAARC members (particularly Nepal, Pakistan and Sri Lanka) have argued that China, which is currently an observer nation, should be made full member of SAARC because of its growing influence in the region. China's membership is also seen by them as a potential countervailing force to mediate dominance of India, which is often perceived to be a hegemonic power of the region. On the other hand, India is largely circumspect of China's inclusion as it can possibly reduce its leverage in the region. Interests of SAARC member countries, predominantly guided by political motives, are therefore conflicting. But what is more relevant is to analyse whether China's entry into the SAARC is in the economic interest of the region as a whole. In this light, China's economic and geopolitical significance in anchoring integration of the region and its possible entry in SAARC as a full-time member has recently been debated widely amongst academic and policy circles.

It is argued that China's entry will not help regional process, rather will further complicate the efforts of South Asian countries towards regional integration which is already languishing due to their persisting internal conflicts. Authoritarian and non-market-based economy of China can challenge the democratic order in the region, and its active territorial claims in India and Bhutan can pose serious political, economic and security threats to the region.[1] India-China border standoff in Doklam is a recent example that led to heightened tensions between the two countries. If China happens to become a full-time member of SAARC then its economic and strategic presence will instil regional discord which will not be conducive to growth and integration of the region.[2] Contrary to these arguments, there is also a belief that China's membership will bring peace and stability in the neighbourhood through a regional platform and will promote economic prosperity in the region.[3] It is also asserted that inclusion of China in SAARC will strengthen the power of the organization in global landscape that will constitute the world's two fastest growing economies, most populous countries and significant players in strategic affairs of the largest continent of the world.[4]

Empirical evidence, however, is important to analyse China's linkages with the region and objectively approach its case for inclusion in SAARC. China is vigorously undertaking heavy overseas investment projects to deepen its economic and diplomatic ties with countries around the world. This has helped in integrating its economy regionally as well as globally. Das (2014) argues that China's rapid economic growth has been influential in integrating real economies of Asia, with trade, foreign direct investment (FDI) and production connections being the principal channels of market-led integration.

South Asian region entails tremendous benefits to China and is an important region for its strategic ambit.[5] Favourable relations of China with South Asia can provide it access to international sea lanes of the India Ocean thereby helping it boost its trade with the world. Large consumer base in South Asia given its rising population can serve as a huge market for Chinese goods with further potential to increase trade. Thus, China has been actively pursuing its foreign policy strategy of closer integration with South Asia. It is noticeably engaged in expanding its footprint in the South Asian region through improved trade and infrastructural investment. China's exports to South Asia has increased almost sixfolds over the last decade, expanding from USD 15.96 billion in 2005 to USD 94.33 billion in 2015.[6] It has even emerged as the largest trading partner of Bangladesh, India and Pakistan. Also, the trade intensity of the South Asian countries with China[7] has been accelerating over the years for majority of the countries (Figure 10.1). Trade intensity of Pakistan with China has particularly intensified over the years rising from 5.7% in 2004 to 21.2% in 2017.

China is also developing stronghold in the region through expanding investment as is evident from the major infrastructural projects it is undertaking in the region like Bangladesh-China-India-Myanmar (BCIM) Economic Corridor, Maritime Silk Road (MSR) initiative and China-Pakistan Economic Corridor (CPEC). In 2015, China's FDI in the subcontinent is reported to be USD 12.29 billion and South Asia's investment

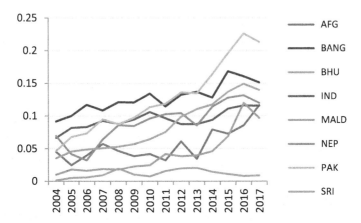

Figure 10.1 Trade Intensity of China with South Asian Countries.
Source: UNCTAD Stat, Authors' Calculations.

Notes: (a) Trade intensity of China with country *i* is the ratio of China's total trade with country *i* to China's total trade with the world. (b) AFG, BANG, BHU, IND, MALD, NEP, PAK and SRI denote Afghanistan, Bangladesh, Bhutan, India, Maldives, Nepal, Pakistan and Sri Lanka, respectively.

is approximately USD 890 million. Increased FDI from China is particularly witnessed by Pakistan in form of CPEC, associated investment in infrastructure and manufacturing in implementing "One Belt One Road" strategy and investments in electricity and transport infrastructure, and Sri Lanka in form of infrastructure projects including highways, port and airport.[8] China is also boosting its investments with Bangladesh and has given a line of credit worth about USD 24 billion to support power plants, seaport and railway project in the country.

Though China's linkages with the South Asian region are apparent on the real side of the economies, its integration with the region on the financial side is largely obscure and unexplored in the empirical literature. Thus, investigation of the extent of financial integration of China with the South Asian countries is warranted to understand its role in inducing integration in the region, based upon which its entry into SAARC as a full-time member can be inferred.

An overview of China's financial system

China's financial system has expanded massively over the last few decades keeping pace with its strong economic growth. With the continuing efforts towards financial liberalization, China's financial markets are gradually getting linked with the foreign markets and gaining pre-eminence globally.

The absolute size of China's financial system is now the fourth largest in the world, only after the USA, the combined euro-financial systems and Japan.[9] It has the world's largest emerging securities market, and its capital markets architecture is fast approaching international standards. The equity market capitalization of China is the third largest in the world and bond markets with fifth largest balance globally.[10] Chinese stock markets value (USD 3697 billion) and share turnover value (USD 4968 billion) both rank second amongst the world's major equity markets (as of December 2012).[11] In the new issues market, China saw maximum number of new listings (55) in 2012 in the world for which the total proceeds raised (USD 16.4 billion) were second globally (as of December 2012).[12] Also, Chinese Renminbi (RMB) has become the fifth reserve currency of the world after USD, Euro, Pound and Yen which shows its importance in international trade and commerce. The efforts to internationalize its currency coupled with foreign exchange reforms since the late 2000s have led to its increasing role on the global platform. China has rapidly developed its offshore bond market that issues RMB-denominated bonds, also called Dim Sum bonds, to foreign investors. Further, it has been actively promoting the use of RMB by signing a series of bilateral currency swap agreements with numerous countries across the globe like South Korea, Iceland, Hong Kong, Indonesia, Singapore, Thailand, Argentina, Brazil, Canada and the United Kingdom. China's banking system has also experienced dramatic growth over the years and has now surpassed Eurozone by becoming the world's biggest banking system. The size of its banking system as measured by its bank assets is approximately USD 33 trillion as of December 2016, which is almost three times the size of its annual economic output.

Given the trajectory of China's financial market development coupled with its remarkable economic growth, its financial linkages with the global economy and particularly with its neighbouring countries are quite likely. Hence, it would be interesting to analyse the role of China in financial integration of South Asia which is its neighbouring region and is important from its geopolitical strategy perspective.

China's financial integration with South Asia

Data and methodology

Financial integration of China with the South Asian economies is examined by focusing on three critical segments of financial markets: equity, bond and currency, as well as the banking system. The magnitude of integration of China and the South Asian countries is investigated over the period January 2004 to March 2016. The dataset for the analysis is comprised of the following:

a   daily stock market benchmark index closing prices of six South Asian countries (namely, Bangladesh, India, Maldives, Nepal, Pakistan and Sri Lanka) as well as China and the USA.[13]

b   monthly 10-year government securities yield of five South Asian countries (Bangladesh, India, Nepal, Pakistan and Sri Lanka) as well as China and the USA.[14]

c   daily foreign exchange rate prices per USD of seven South Asian countries (Bangladesh, Bhutan, India, Maldives, Nepal, Pakistan and Sri Lanka) and China.

d   monthly International Monetary Fund (IMF) deposit rate series for Bangladesh, Bhutan, China, Maldives, Pakistan and Sri Lanka was available for the study period, while the IMF deposit rate series was not available for India, and hence, alternatively, we selected the monthly deposit rates of the biggest bank in India i.e. State Bank of India. The data for monthly IMF deposit rates for Bangladesh, Bhutan, China, India, Maldives, Pakistan and Sri Lanka were available for the study period. Thus, we have covered six South Asian countries out of the total eight who constitute the SAARC as no data was available for Afghanistan and data for Nepal ended in 2011.

The data of the sample countries chosen for analysis is retrieved from Bloomberg. Uniform sample countries for the four financial segments could not be used owing to non-availability of data. Equity price, foreign exchange rate, lending rate and deposit rate series of the sample countries are transformed into returns by taking the natural logarithm of the series and then computing the first difference of the log-transformed series. The bond returns of the sample countries are computed on the basis of formula used by Abad et al. (2010) in calculating bond returns (refer Chapter 7), and are used for subsequent analysis.

We employ copula functions and Diebold and Yilmaz (2012) spillover index methodology to analyse financial integration of China with South Asia. Copula functions help us ascertain dependence structure between financial segments of China and South Asian countries by providing their estimates of conditional correlations. To describe the symmetric and asymmetric dependence structure between the markets, two Elliptical (Gaussian and Student t) and two Archimedean's (Clayton and Gumbel) family of copula models are used. Gaussian copula is symmetric and has no tail dependence, whereas Student t copula can capture extreme dependence between variables. The Gumbel copula exhibits greater dependence in the upper tail than in the lower, whereas the Clayton copula exhibits greater dependence in the negative tail than in the positive tail. We estimate time-invariant and time-variant copula models to examine both static and time-varying nature of dependencies of financial returns of China with that of South Asian countries.

We supplement our analysis using Diebold and Yilmaz (2012) spillover index methodology to examine the level of transmission of shocks across China and the South Asian countries. This methodology allows us to quantify the cross-market directional spillovers thereby giving further insights into the level of financial linkages across markets. Cross-variance share or cross-market directional spillovers measure the forecast error variance of a variable that is attributable to shocks from another variable(s). The fraction of forecast error variance of variable i due to shocks from variable i represents the own variance share. Total spillover index is the average of spillovers from shocks to all other variables to the total forecast error variance. The difference between directional spillovers transmitted by variable i and directional spillovers received by variable i provides the net spillovers of variable i. Refer Chapter 6 for detailed exposition of the two methodologies.

Equity market integration

China is found to have low level of equity market linkages with the South Asian countries. This is indicated by low value of dependence parameter of equity returns of China with South Asian countries (refer Table 10.1).

Table 10.1 Dependencies between Equity Markets of China and South Asian Countries

		Normal		Clayton		Gumbel		Student t	
		Value	LL	Value	LL	Value	LL	Value	LL
BANG	CHI	−0.01	−0.15	0.00	0.00	1.11	22.41	−0.01	−1.03
IND	CHI	0.20	−52.73	0.22	−45.06	1.12	−42.84	0.20	−54.41
MALD	CHI	−0.02	−0.71	0.00	0.00	1.11	37.21	−0.02	−5.11
NEP	CHI	0.07	−3.13	0.07	−2.60	1.11	7.95	0.07	−3.02
PAK	CHI	0.05	−3.56	0.06	−3.74	1.11	14.22	0.05	−6.06
SRI	CHI	0.06	−3.75	0.04	−2.08	1.11	9.10	0.06	−4.70

Notes: The table summarizes the time-invariant copula estimation results for the equity markets of China and the South Asian countries.
a Value denotes the dependence parameter between equity returns of China and sample South Asian equity markets using different copula models.
b LL denotes the log likelihood value of dependence parameter between equity returns of China and sample South Asian countries using different copula models.
c Value in bold denotes the lowest negative log likelihood thereby providing the best fit copula model amongst the family of models under study.
d BANG, CHI, IND, MALD, NEP, PAK and SRI denote Bangladesh, China, India, Maldives, Nepal, Pakistan and Sri Lanka, respectively.

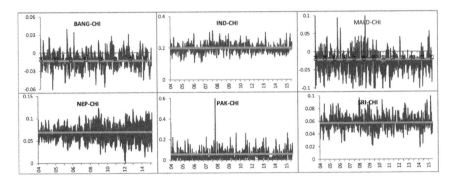

Figure 10.2 Dynamic Dependencies between Equity Markets of China and South Asian Countries.

Source: Authors' Calculations.

Notes: (a) The best fit time-varying copula model selected by the goodness of fit test for different family of copula models is plotted along with its corresponding time-invariant dependency measure (in horizontal line). (b) BANG, CHI, IND, MALD, NEP, PAK and SRI denote Bangladesh, China, India, Maldives, Nepal, Pakistan and Sri Lanka, respectively.

China has the highest equity market linkage with India amongst all South Asian countries. The high time-varying integration is also observed between China and India (refer Figure 10.2) indicating that the equity market of these two countries has the highest linkages amongst all South Asian countries over the entire sample period. Strong linkages between them can be ascribed to their booming economies and financial sector development. Equity markets of China and India have expanded from an average of 11% of their financial system in 1990–1994 to an average of 53% in 2005–2010 (World Bank, 2014a).

Now, comparing the linkages amongst South Asian equity markets (see Chapter 6) and linkages of these countries with respect to China, it can be observed that majority of the countries (particularly India) have relatively high association with China than with other South Asian countries. In other words, South Asian equity markets are relatively more integrated with equity market of China than amongst themselves. This can be attributed to rising economic engagement of China in the region, with its trade climbing to USD 111 billion and investment to USD 12.29 billion in the South Asian countries in 2016.[15] Besides growing trade and investment links, relatively strong equity market linkages between China and India, the two emerging giants of the globalized world, are probably driven by their unprecedented economic growth and rapid financial sector development. The capital market of the two countries has expanded and deepened since the 1990s, and their financial systems are becoming similar to that of developed countries with capital markets gaining huge

Table 10.2 Return Spillovers across Equity Markets of China and South Asian Countries

	BANG	CHI	IND	MALD	NEP	PAK	SRI	From Others
BANG	98.31	0.41	0.51	0.05	0.07	0.44	0.21	1.7
CHI	0.2	92.02	5.34	0.61	0.54	0.47	0.84	8
IND	0.17	4.3	90.24	0.18	1.17	1.06	2.88	9.8
MALD	0.27	0.43	0.12	98.05	0.53	0.34	0.26	1.9
NEP	0.13	0.85	0.72	0.27	97.41	0.08	0.54	2.6
PAK	0.18	0.46	2.17	0.31	0.32	95.82	0.74	4.2
SRI	0.5	0.62	2.98	0.18	0.13	0.68	94.9	5.1
Contribution to others	1.4	7.1	11.8	1.6	2.8	3.1	5.5	33.2
Contribution including own	99.8	99.1	102.1	99.7	100.2	98.9	100.4	4.70%

Notes: The table presents Diebold and Yilmaz (2012) spillover table summary for equity markets of China and the South Asian countries.

a The diagonal entries of the matrix represent the own variance share of the sample countries, and the off-diagonal elements show the cross-market spillovers.

b The last column of the matrix ("from others") highlights the gross directional return spillovers to the country from rest of the countries.

c The second last row ("to others") indicates the gross directional spillover from a country to rest of the countries.

d BANG, CHI, IND, MALD, NEP, PAK and SRI denote Bangladesh, China, India, Maldives, Nepal, Pakistan and Sri Lanka, respectively.

share in the financial sector (Didier and Schmukler, 2013), thereby providing impetus to financial linkages between them.

Table 10.2 presents the time-aggregated equity return spillovers amongst China and the South Asian countries computed from Diebold and Yilmaz (2012) spillover index methodology. The diagonal entries of the matrix represent the own variance share of the sample countries, and the off-diagonal elements show the cross-market spillovers i.e. contribution to the forecast error variance of country i coming from shocks to country j. The last column of the matrix ("from others") highlights the gross directional return spillovers to the country from rest of the countries. The second last row ("to others") indicates the gross directional spillover from a country to rest of the countries.

Results indicate that majorly the degree of equity market interaction of China is with that of India as almost 44% of India's forecast error variance from others is attributable to China. Also, India explains a tremendous amount of China's forecast error variance from others (around 67%). On the other hand, the gross directional return spillovers to/from China as well as India from/to other South Asian countries are low. This suggests that the equity markets of China and India are by and large interdependent of each other, while their linkages with the South Asian equity markets are weak. This supports our copula results of low level of equity market linkages of China with the South Asian countries, except India. As noted above, relatively high equity market integration of China with India can be attributed to their rapid pace of economic growth and financial sector development.

Overall, the equity market integration amongst the South Asian countries and China is extremely low as revealed by the total spillover index of 4.7%. Comparing it with the total spillovers across the sample South Asian equity returns (refer Chapter 6), there is a slight increase in the total spillover index from 3.1% to 4.7% as we include equity returns of China. This implies that the linkages of the equity markets increase, albeit marginally, with the inclusion of China in the South Asian region.

Bond market integration

Like equity market, integration of the bond markets of China with the South Asian countries is found to be low (refer Table 10.3), the only exception being India with the degree of integration higher as compared to other South Asian countries. The highest time-varying dependence is observed for bond market of China and India (refer Figure 10.3), as was found in case of equity market. China's heavy investments in the

Table 10.3 Dependencies between Bond Markets of China and South Asian Countries

		Normal		Clayton		Gumbel		Student t	
		Value	LL	Value	LL	Value	LL	Value	LL
BANG	CHI	**0.04**	−0.08	0.00	0.00	1.10	0.19	0.04	−0.06
IND	CHI	0.23	−3.11	0.21	−1.41	**1.19**	**−4.05**	0.25	−3.12
NEP	CHI	0.06	−0.20	0.05	−0.08	1.10	0.06	**0.06**	−0.28
PAK	CHI	−0.05	−0.16	0.00	0.00	1.10	1.39	**−0.04**	−0.67
SRI	CHI	−0.07	−0.30	0.05	−0.13	1.10	1.99	**−0.13**	−2.98

Notes: The table summarizes the time-invariant copula estimation results for bond markets of China and the South Asian countries.
a Value denotes the dependence parameter between bond returns of China and sample South Asian countries using different copula models.
b LL denotes the log likelihood value of dependence parameter between bond returns of China and sample South Asian countries using different copula models.
c Value in bold denotes lowest negative log likelihood thereby providing the best fit copula model amongst the family of models under study.
d BANG, CHI, IND, NEP, PAK and SRI denote Bangladesh, China, India, Nepal, Pakistan and Sri Lanka, respectively.

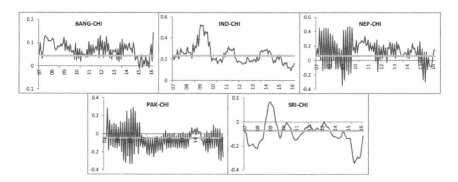

Figure 10.3 Dynamic Dependencies between Bond Markets of China and South
Asian Countries.

Source: Authors' Calculations.

Notes: (a) The best fit time-varying copula model selected by the goodness of fit test for
different family of copula models is plotted along with its corresponding time-invariant dependency measure (in horizontal line). (b) BANG, CHI, IND, NEP, PAK and SRI denote
Bangladesh, China, India, Nepal, Pakistan and Sri Lanka, respectively.

South Asian region, taking over India as a key player in the region, have
possibly strengthened bond market integration amongst the relatively
small South Asian countries having underdeveloped bond markets. On
the other hand, bond market integration is comparatively high between
China and India that have well-developed bond markets coupled with
growing trade and investment linkages. Therefore, China's influential
role in the region can be discerned from its contribution in inducing
bond market integration amongst the South Asian countries, and these
countries may subsequently integrate with China as well as India as they
deepen their bond markets.

Bond return spillovers across the South Asian countries and China (refer Table 10.4) reveal that China's spillovers to South Asian bond markets
are high. India, in particular, receives the highest proportion of bond return spillovers from China. China's massive trade and investment in the
region can be the possible explanation. China is engaging with the region
by carrying out several major infrastructural investment projects like
Bangladesh-China-India-Myanmar (BCIM) Economic Corridor, "One Belt
One Road" Initiative and China-Pakistan Economic Corridor, and also is
currently the largest trading partner of Bangladesh, India and Pakistan.
The influential role of China in the region is clearly reflected from the pairwise comparison of directional spillover which shows that the magnitude
of spillovers from China to the South Asian countries is greater than what
it receives from these countries.

Table 10.4 Return Spillovers across Bond Markets of China and South Asian Countries

	BANG	CHI	IND	PAK	SRI	From Others
BANG	93.77	0.67	0.55	4.85	0.16	6.2
CHI	1.25	87.91	8.13	0.34	2.37	12.1
IND	0.58	19.13	75.72	2.92	1.65	24.3
PAK	10.14	2.47	5.82	76.54	5.03	23.5
SRI	4.89	4.44	0.36	1.61	88.69	11.3
Contribution to others	16.9	26.7	14.9	9.7	9.2	77.4
Contribution including own	110.6	114.6	90.6	86.3	97.9	15.50%

Notes: The table presents Diebold and Yilmaz (2012) spillover table summary for bond markets of China and the South Asian countries.

a The diagonal entries of the matrix represent the own variance share of the sample countries, and the off-diagonal elements show the cross-market spillovers.

b The last column of the matrix ("from others") highlights the gross directional return spillovers to the country from rest of the countries.

c The second last row ("to others") indicates the gross directional spillover from a country to rest of the countries.

d BANG, CHI, IND, NEP, PAK and SRI denote Bangladesh, China, India, Nepal, Pakistan and Sri Lanka, respectively.

Comparison of the total return spillover amongst the South Asian bond markets (refer Chapter 7) and bond markets of South Asia along with China reveals substantive increase in the total spillover from 11.90% to 15.50%. With the inclusion of China in the South Asia, integration amongst the bond markets increases. This is indicative of sizable contribution of China in generating interdependencies in the bond markets of the region.

Currency market linkages

Currency linkages of the South Asian countries with respect to China are also weak as indicated by the low value of dependence parameter (refer Table 10.5). Cross-border trade and investment can act as an important factor in strengthening currency linkages between the countries. Weak currency linkages of the sample South Asian countries with China therefore can be explained by the stringent restrictions kept by the countries on their currency convertibility especially for capital transactions by foreign investors. Also, bilateral trade between China and the South Asian countries is predominantly settled in the global reserve currencies like USD, the euro, British Pound and Japanese Yen instead of their national currencies. Though the currencies of China and India are fully convertible on current account, they are not used for trade settlements as USD largely remains the intermediary currency with 79.9% of the payments settled in it.[16]

Table 10.5 Dependencies between Currency Markets of China and South Asian Countries

		Normal		Clayton		Gumbel		Student t	
		Value	LL	Value	LL	Value	LL	Value	LL
BANG	CHI	0.01	−0.06	0.00	0.00	1.11	41.28	**0.01**	**−0.23**
BHU	CHI	0.13	−25.22	**0.17**	**−30.09**	1.11	−3.89	0.13	−24.78
IND	CHI	0.13	−25.22	**0.17**	**−30.09**	1.11	−3.89	0.13	−24.78
MALD	CHI	0.03	−1.57	0.03	−1.65	1.11	25.40	**0.04**	**−4.38**
NEP	CHI	0.13	−26.59	**0.16**	**−28.29**	1.11	−11.31	0.13	−27.90
PAK	CHI	−0.01	−0.24	0.00	−0.01	1.11	52.10	**−0.01**	**−0.80**
SRI	CHI	**0.06**	**−5.24**	0.06	−5.12	1.11	22.48	0.06	−5.05

Notes: The table summarizes the time-invariant copula estimation results for FX market of China and the South Asian countries.

a Value denotes the dependence parameter between FX returns of China and sample South Asian countries using different copula models.

b LL denotes the log likelihood value of the dependence parameter between FX returns of China and sample South Asian countries using different copula models.

c Value in bold denotes the lowest negative log likelihood thereby providing the best fit copula model amongst the family of models under study.

d BANG, BHU, CHI, IND, MALD, NEP, PAK and SRI denote Bangladesh, Bhutan, China, India, Maldives, Nepal, Pakistan and Sri Lanka, respectively.

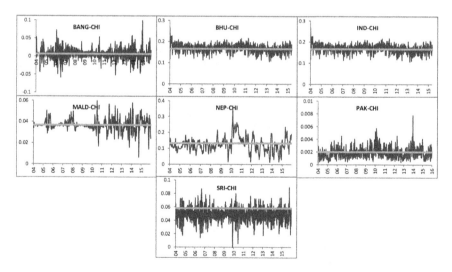

Figure 10.4 Dynamic Dependencies between Currency Markets of China and South Asian Countries.

Source: Authors' Calculations.

Notes: (a) The best fit time-varying copula model selected by the goodness of fit test for different family of copula models is plotted along with its corresponding time-invariant dependency measure (in horizontal line). (b) BANG, BHU, CHI, IND, MALD, NEP, PAK and SRI denote Bangladesh, Bhutan, China, India, Maldives, Nepal, Pakistan and Sri Lanka, respectively.

Like in case of equity and bond market, the highest time-varying dependence is observed between the currency markets of China and India (refer Figure 10.4). The Foreign Exchange (FX) returns of China exhibit the highest and almost similar time-varying dependence (on an average 0.16) with that of India and Bhutan amongst the sample South Asian countries. Relatively high linkages between China and India can be explained by the increasing use of domestic currencies for making payments between the two countries. India's use of Chinese RMB is gradually gaining traction, rising from 0.2% in 2014 to 3.8% in 2016. Also, INR has evolved as the second largest currency used for making payments between the two countries with 7.2% of the payments made in it, overtaking euro in 2016 (see SWIFT, 2016). High FX returns dependence of China-Bhutan which is almost similar to that of China-India is probably due to the nexus fostered by Indian currency between that of China and Bhutan as there is near-perfect level of association between the currency of India and Bhutan with Bhutanese Ngultrum being pegged and traded at par with Indian rupee (refer Chapter 8).

Table 10.6 Return Spillovers across Currency Markets of China and South Asian Countries

	BANG	CHI	IND	MALD	NEP	PAK	SRI	From Others
BANG	98.19	0.02	0.21	0.07	0.21	1.22	0.09	1.8
CHI	0.14	97.22	1.84	0.08	0.51	0.19	0.03	2.8
IND	0.04	1.21	82.09	0.01	16.04	0.13	0.49	17.9
MALD	0.01	0.03	0.02	99.85	0.06	0.01	0.01	0.1
NEP	0.14	0.44	21.55	0.05	77.46	0.15	0.21	22.5
PAK	0.31	0.11	0.21	0.03	0.18	99.1	0.05	0.9
SRI	0.39	0.04	1.01	0.04	0.56	0.16	97.82	2.2
Contribution to others	1	1.8	24.8	0.3	17.6	1.9	0.9	48.3
Contribution including own	99.2	99.1	106.9	100.1	95	101	98.7	6.90%

Notes: The table presents Diebold and Yilmaz (2012) spillover table summary for FX market of China and the South Asian countries.
a The diagonal entries of the matrix represent the own variance share of the sample countries, and the off-diagonal elements show the cross-market spillovers.
b The last column of the matrix ("from others") highlights the gross directional return spillovers to the country from rest of the countries.
c The second last row ("to others") indicates the gross directional spillover from a country to rest of the countries.
d BANG, CHI, IND, MALD, NEP, PAK and SRI denote Bangladesh, China, India, Maldives, Nepal, Pakistan and Sri Lanka, respectively.

Diebold and Yilmaz (2012) spillover index results also indicate that currency market linkages of China with the South Asian countries are almost negligible (refer Table 10.6). As can be clearly seen that the own-variance share of Chinese FX market is extremely high (97.22%) indicating that its forecast error variance is primarily explained by shocks originating in the own market than from shocks in the other markets. Chinese FX market is neither influenced by shocks from the South Asian FX markets nor is influential in transmission of shocks to them, corroborating copula results of weak currency linkages of China with South Asian countries. As highlighted above, heavy restrictions on capital account convertibility have led to low level of integration amongst the countries. Further, use of global reserve currencies to settle transactions instead of national currencies is probably the cause of weak linkages amongst them.

In addition, there is evidence of segmentation of Chinese foreign exchange market with that of South Asian countries. The total foreign exchange return spillover across currency market of South Asian countries and China decreases marginally to 6.90% when compared with the total spillover of 7.30% obtained for the South Asian currency markets (refer Chapter 8). This indicates that inclusion of China in South Asia has no role to play in integrating the foreign exchange markets of South Asia.

Banking system integration

In Table 10.7, Panel A/B results report the association results of the lending/deposit rate series between the South Asian countries and China. For the lending rates, with the exception of India & China and Pakistan & China, the associations are generally weak for other countries. The case seems to be similar in deposit rates where the pair of India & China and Pakistan & China has strong linkages with each other while the dependences are low for other country pairs with China. The associations of lending and deposit rates of China with India & Pakistan, the two biggest country of South Asian region, can be explained by harmonization of theses banking rates which seem to be catering to the idiosyncratic credit needs of these countries which are relatively similar in nature and where the ownership structure is predominantly public. The financial system of these countries is bank centric, and banks are used to act as intermediaries of development credit. The banking association of other SAARC countries with China seems to be low which can be due to their unique macroeconomic environment (inflation, growth rate, external position, etc.), negligible banking activity in the region and poor regional payment system.

Table 10.7 Dependencies between Banking Systems of China and South Asian Countries

		Panel A: LENDING							
		Normal		*Clayton*		*Gumbel*		*Student t*	
		Value	*LL*	*Value*	*LL*	*Value*	*LL*	*Value*	*LL*
BANG	CHI	**0.121**	**−1.1738**	0.0823	−0.299	1.1002	−1.1693	0.1293	−1.1029
BHU	CHI	−0.0404	−0.1167	0.0339	−0.0604	1.109	−0.0337	−0.0416	−0.0317
IND	CHI	0.1832	−2.5536	0.2057	−2.1631	1.2025	−6.1948	**0.1993**	**−7.4053**
MALD	CHI	0.0102	−0.0077	0.0937	−0.0661	1.11	−0.0806	**0.0112**	**−0.0909**
PAK	CHI	0.1823	−2.9525	0.2618	−2.865	1.1003	−0.6379	**0.1932**	−2.4824
SRI	CHI	−0.0582	−0.2562	0.0003	−0.0042	1.12	−0.2243	**−0.0575**	−0.316

		Panel B: DEPOSIT							
		Normal		*Clayton*		*Gumbel*		*Student t*	
		Value	*LL*	*Value*	*LL*	*Value*	*LL*	*Value*	*LL*
BANG	CHI	**0.057**	**−0.2586**	0.0751	−0.2452	1.11	−0.2115	0.0588	−0.1587
BHU	CHI	−0.3587	−10.053	1.31E−04	−1.6081	1.09	−6.4875	**−0.4375**	**−13.1835**
IND	CHI	0.2436	−4.6806	0.4396	−5.2018	1.1601	−3.5019	**0.2659**	**−6.0274**
MALD	CHI	**0.0561**	**−0.2393**	0.0519	−0.1251	1.09	−0.0805	0.0609	−0.1106
PAK	CHI	0.1235	−1.1686	0.148	−0.882	1.1102	−0.5887	**0.1408**	**−1.227**
SRI	CHI	−0.0913	−0.6398	0.0001	0.0006	1.1	−0.5144	**−0.1017**	**−0.7021**

Notes: Panel A of the table summarizes the time-invariant copula estimation results for lending rates of banking systems of China and the South Asian countries, while Panel B summarizes the same for deposit rates.
a   Value denotes the dependence parameter between lending/deposit return series of China and the South Asian countries using different copula models.
b   LL denotes the log likelihood value of the dependence parameter between lending/deposit return series of China and the South Asian countries using different copula models.
c   Value in bold denotes the lowest negative LL values thereby providing the best fit copula model amongst the family of models under study.
d   BANG, BHU, CHI, IND, MALD, NEP, PAK and SRI denote Bangladesh, Bhutan, China, India, Maldives, Nepal, Pakistan and Sri Lanka, respectively.

Figure 10.5 shows time-varying associations of lending and deposit rate series for SAARC member countries with China. The graphs indicate that the associations are largely volatile and their interest rate policies seem to be driven by local macroeconomic conditions as well as financing needs. Though the general magnitude of association seems to be higher for China-India & China-Pakistan for both the lending and deposit rate series. High volatility in the dependence parameters for both lending and deposit rates for the sample countries indicates that the degree of banking integration in the region is rather weak as was found to be true for other asset classes segment (equity, bonds and currency).

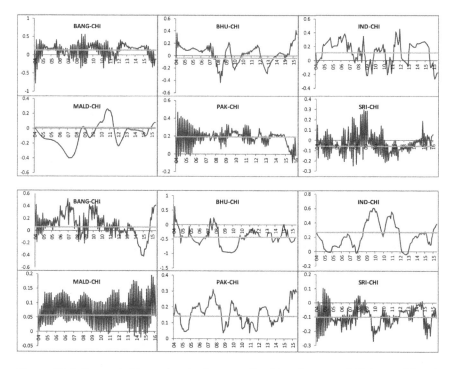

Figure 10.5 Dynamic Dependencies between Banking Systems of China and South Asian Countries.

Source: Authors' Calculations.

Notes: a) Panel A of the figure presents dynamic dependencies between lending return series of China and the South Asian countries, while Panel B of the figure presents the same for deposit return series. b) The best fit time-varying copula model selected by the goodness of fit test for different family of copula models is plotted along with its corresponding time-invariant dependency measure (in horizontal line). c) BANG, BHU, CHI, IND, MALD, PAK and SRI denote Bangladesh, Bhutan, China, India, Maldives, Pakistan and Sri Lanka, respectively.

Diebold and Yilmaz (2012) spillover index results also indicate that aggregated banking sector linkages of the South Asian countries though increase gradually with respect to both lending and deposit series when China is included in the sample than without China (refer Table 10.8 Panel A and B). As can be clearly seen from Table 10.8, Panel A, the aggregated spillover for the lending series increases from 9.4% to 16.9% when China is included in the sample. This can be due to the sheer size of the Chinese banks (four Chinese banks in global top 100). Table 10.8, Panel B, shows the aggregated spillover index for the deposit series also increased from

Table 10.8 Return Spillovers across Banking Systems of China and South Asian Countries

Panel A: LENDING	BANG	BHU	CHI	IND	MALD	PAK	SRI	From Others
BANG	95.4	0.02	1.61	0.67	0.95	1.2	0.14	4.6
BHU	1.57	81.96	9.09	5.46	0.31	0.36	1.24	18
CHI	13.23	4.23	68.04	7.06	2.5	3.3	1.65	32
IND	3.28	4.23	5.5	71.21	11.82	2.97	1	28.8
MALD	3.87	0.17	2.17	2.62	86.29	2.43	2.46	13.7
PAK	3.92	0.44	3.2	1.47	0.88	86.97	3.13	13
SRI	0.72	0.9	0.45	0.68	2.79	2.93	91.54	8.5
Contribution to others	26.6	10	22	18	19.3	13.2	9.6	118.6
Contribution including own	122	91.9	90.1	89.2	105.5	100.2	101.2	16.90%

Panel B: DEPOSIT	BANG	BHU	CHI	IND	MALD	PAK	SRI	From Others
BANG	93.03	1.3	1.4	1.05	0.32	1.86	1.04	7
BHU	0.55	91.56	5.11	0.88	0.28	0.16	1.45	8.4
CHI	0.59	1.71	89.1	6.61	0.43	0.21	1.34	10.9
IND	1.41	0.47	3.65	83.88	2.08	4.96	3.56	16.1
MALD	0.07	0.08	0.19	2.27	87.98	0.4	9.01	12
PAK	0.63	0.12	0.53	1.36	0.14	96.35	0.87	3.6
SRI	1.32	1.56	0.78	0.42	7.92	0.61	87.38	12.6
Contribution to others	4.6	5.2	11.7	12.6	11.2	8.2	17.3	70.7
Contribution including own	97.6	96.8	100.8	96.5	99.2	104.6	104.6	10.10%

Notes: Panel A of the table presents Diebold and Yilmaz (2012) spillover index summary for lending rates of banking systems of China and the South Asian countries, while Panel B presents the same for deposit rates.

a The diagonal entries of the matrix represent the own variance share of the sample countries and the off-diagonal elements show the cross-market spillovers.

b The last column of the matrix ("from others") highlights the gross directional return spillovers to the country from rest of the countries.

c The second last row ("to others") indicates the gross directional spillover from a country to rest of the countries.

d BANG, BHU, CHI, IND, MALD, NEP, PAK and SRI denote Bangladesh, Bhutan, China, India, Maldives, Nepal, Pakistan and Sri Lanka, respectively.

8.3% to 10.1% when China got included in the sample. It thus indicates that though the banking sector connectedness has increased when China is included in the sample the volatility of the associations found out by the time-varying graphs shows that degree of banking integration in the region is rather weak.

Summary and policy suggestions

In the recent years, economic engagement of China in South Asia has been on the rise. China has been actively pursuing its foreign policy strategy of closer integration with South Asia. It is intensifying its bilateral links with the countries of South Asia through increased trade and investment. South Asia indeed confers strategic and economic gains to China, and hence, China has expressed its desire to join SAARC as a full-fledged member to foster closer linkages with the region at multilateral level. Some of the SAARC member countries also support inclusion of China in SAARC given its increasing economic role in the region. Wary of India's dominance in the region, these countries view China's membership as a potential countervailing force to mediate regional supremacy of India. India, on the other hand, is trying to block its entry in SAARC as it is circumspect that it may reduce its leverage in the region.

China's inclusion in SAARC as a full-time member therefore has become a contentious topic of debate amongst academic as well as policy circles. Several arguments have been put forth for and against of China's membership in SAARC. Empirical evidence, however, is important to analyse China's linkages with the region and objectively approach its case for inclusion in SAARC. Though China's linkages with the South Asian region are apparent on the real side of the economies, its integration with the region on the financial side is largely obscure and unexplored in the empirical literature. In this light, we investigate financial market integration of China with the South Asian countries.

Empirical analysis reveals that the level of financial integration of China with the South Asian countries is low in all four segments: equity, bond, currency and banking. Amongst all the South Asian countries, India has the highest level of financial linkages with China. Indeed, the degree of financial integration of China with the South Asian economies is low; its financial linkages with these countries are relatively better in bond markets as compared to equity or currency market. Further, China plays significant role in strengthening bond market integration amongst the countries. Though the banking sector connectedness with respect to lending and deposit rates seems to have increased when China is included in the SAARC the volatility of the associations found out by the time-varying graphs shows that degree of banking integration in the region is rather weak.

It is important to understand why China's financial linkages with India are particularly high but low with other South Asian countries. China and India are the two emerging giants of the globalized world. Relatively strong financial linkages between them are driven by their unprecedented economic growth and rapid pace of financial sector development. In addition, these countries have witnessed increasing growth in trade and investment links which has led to their substantial financial market linkages. On the other hand, rest of the South Asian countries have relatively underdeveloped financial markets which is an impediment in their process of developing strong financial linkages with other markets. China's massive trade and investment in the region is reflected in relatively strong linkages of the bond markets of China with these countries.

Given the substantial role that China plays in the region which is reflected in significant bond market linkages with the South Asian countries, China's inclusion as a full-time member in SAARC can be envisaged in future as it strengthens its financial ties with the South Asian countries. However, China's membership in SAARC presently would be pre-mature. Prior to considering its full-fledged membership, it is pertinent for the member countries to resolve their political differences that create obstacles in achieving closer cooperation and integration amongst them. Regional integration in SAARC has been languishing due to internal political differences amongst the member countries. Expansion of the region will therefore not help, rather may lead to power tussle between China and India.

South Asian countries also need to facilitate trade by removal of trade barriers, building connectivity and developing payment clearance and settlement system. Capital markets of China and India have grown rapidly with gradual adoption of market-oriented policies to liberalize their financial sector. Therefore, both China and India can act as drivers of capital market integration in the region by providing assistance to the neighbouring economies having underdeveloped markets by extending financial support and technological expertise to build and operate market infrastructure. It is imperative for the countries to further liberalize capital controls and harmonize accounting standards, financial regulations and trading practices to expedite equity market integration amongst them. Additionally, development of bond market infrastructure by liberalizing listing requirements and simplification of procedures and processes is required for boosting bond market linkages amongst the countries. Here again, China and India can play a critical role in providing domain expertise to the countries in formation of a well-functioning bond market and also work towards developing a cooperative framework for synchronizing monetary and credit policy. Considering extremely weak currency linkages of China with the South Asian countries, use of national currencies in trade settlement should be promoted. Currency swap agreements can also be extended to address liquidity shocks and further currency market linkages amongst the countries. For banking sector to lend its support to the financial integration between China and South Asia, countries should cooperate amongst themselves to begin the process of harmonization of banking system and regulation. They could start with arriving at a consensus on definition of financial soundness indicator and uniformity in prudential regulation. Consolidation of financial information of the banks operating China and South Asian countries should be made mandatory so that cross-border risks are fully understood.

Notes

1 See Dutta (2011).
2 See Muni (2011).
3 Refer Ahmar (2011).
4 See Mahapatra (2011).
5 Refer Kumar (2015).
6 Source: UNCTAD Stat.
7 Trade intensity is calculated as total trade of country i with China divided by total trade of country i with the world.
8 World Investment Report (2015).
9 See Cruz et al. (2014).
10 Source: Shanghai Stock Exchange.
11 Source: World Federation of Exchanges.
12 Source: World Federation of Exchanges.
13 Daily stock market benchmark index closing prices of the USA are taken as a proxy for global factor.
14 Monthly 10-year government securities yield of the USA are taken as a proxy for global factor.
15 Source: PTI (2016). China's investments in South Asia climbs to USD 12.29 bn. Retrieved from http://www.business-standard.com/article/pti-stories/china-s-investments-in-south-asia-climbs-to-usd-12-29-bn-116050501430_1.html.
16 Source: SWIFT (2016).

Appendix A

SPATIAL ECONOMETRIC MODEL

We briefly explain the spatial econometric model adopted. Following Martinez-Zarzoso (2003), Anderson and van Wincoop (2004), Rose (2004) and Chou et al. (2015), we specify the spatial econometric model in the following manner. As existing studies have noted, spatial dependence can be modelled in various ways, depending on the nature of the relationship between the dependent and independent variables. Specifically, following Elhorst (2012) and Chou et al. (2015), we apply three versions of the spatial model to estimate the spatial panel data models. These three models are a spatial autoregressive model (SAR), spatial error model (SEM) and spatial Durbin model (SDM).

We have specified the models in the following equations:

$$\text{Export}_{ijt} = \rho(W * \text{Export})_{ijt} + \beta X_{ijt} + \gamma(W * X)_{ijt} + \varepsilon_{ijt}$$
$$\varepsilon_{ijt} = \lambda(W * \varepsilon_{ijt}) + \eta_{it} \tag{1}$$

$$\text{Import}_{ijt} = \rho(W * \text{Import})_{ijt} + \beta X_{ijt} + \gamma(W * X)_{ijt} + \varepsilon_{ijt}$$
$$\varepsilon_{ijt} = \lambda(W * \varepsilon_{ijt}) + \eta_{it} \tag{2}$$

where Exp_{ijt} and Imp_{ijt} are export and import prices of sample SAARC countries and their counterparts.

$$X_{ijt} = X_{ijt} \begin{pmatrix} \text{GDP}_i, \text{rfe}, \text{pop}_i, \text{open}_i, \text{exchange}_i, \text{remit}_i, M_{2i}, \text{private}_i, \\ \text{govt}_i, \text{socio}_i, \text{Inv}_i, \text{internal}_i, \text{external}_i, \\ \text{corrupt}_i, \text{law}_i, \text{democrat}_i, \text{burea}_i, \text{hdi}_i \end{pmatrix}$$

All variables are also repeated with j subscript to explain the bilateral dependence.

W represents the spatial weight matrix.

In Eqs. (1 and 2), dependent variables are bilateral exports and imports of sample SAARC countries, expressed in logarithmic terms. All the explanatory variables represented by the matrix X_{ijt} are in logarithmic terms.

In Eqs. (1 and 2), $\rho*(W*\text{Import})$ and $\rho*(W*\text{export})$ indicate that the sample data is spatially autoregressive under the spatial Durbin framework. $\gamma(W*X)$ captures the exogenous dependence with γ the spatially lagged independent coefficient, and $\lambda(W*\varepsilon_{ijt})$ indicates the innovation terms with λ explaining the spatial errors interaction effects (see Chou et al. 2015). W represents the spatial weight matrix that explains the geospatial relationship among sample SAARC countries. ρ shows the estimated coefficient.

The rationale behind using a spatial lag variable is to understand whether the exports/imports of sample SAARC countries are positively or negatively impacted their exports/imports to other partner countries. Another dimension of the spatial econometrics that needs special mention is about the spatial weight (W) which can be expressed as a block diagonal matrix in Eqs. (1 and 2). According to Anselin et al. (2014), the block diagonal matrix of spatial weight is specified as the number of sample years as the diagonal elements.[1] In our case, it is varying between 1980 and 2015. We adopt the standard spatial econometric analysis as widely used by existing studies. For both the exports and imports equations of sample SAARC nations, we specify the spatial weight based on contiguity, i.e. whether or not two space units are contiguous to each other,

$$W_{ij} = \left\{ \begin{array}{l} 1 \\ 0 \end{array} \right. ;$$

1 denotes that the countries i and j are neighbours and share common border and 0 otherwise. For an illustrative explanation of weight matrix construction in an origin-destination flow system, an astute reader is referred to LeSage and Pace (2008) and Metulini (2013).

Appendix B

DIEBOLD & YILMAZ
METHODOLOGY

Following Diebold and Yilmaz (2012), the shocks are decomposed using generalized vector autoregressive framework of Koop et al. (1996) and Pesaran and Shin (1998) in order to avoid the sensitivity of the order of the variables. This methodology is superior to VAR methodology earlier proposed by Sims (1980) as it can be used to measure the return spillovers both within and across countries, revealing spillover trends, cycles, bursts, etc. Cross-variance share or cross-market directional spillovers measure the forecast error variance of a variable that is attributable to shocks from another variable(s). The fraction of forecast error variance of variable i due to shocks from variable i represents the own variance share. Total spillover index is the average of spillovers from shocks to all other variables to the total forecast error variance. For each variable i, in an N-variable VAR, the measure of connectedness is the sum of the shares of its forecast error variance coming from shocks to asset j represented as a percentage, for all $j \neq i$. Consider a p order, N-variable VAR model:

$$x_t = \sum_{i=1}^{p} \phi_i \, x_{t-i} + \varepsilon_t \quad \text{where} \quad \sum \quad \text{is the variance of the error terms which}$$

are i.i.d. It can be also written in moving average form as $x_t = \sum_{i=1}^{\infty} A_i \, \varepsilon_{t-i}$

where $A_i = \sum \phi_j \, A_{i-j}$ and $j = 1,\ldots,p$. The H step ahead forecast error variance decomposition $\left(\theta_{ij}^g \, (H) \right)$ is defined as follows:

$$\theta_{ij}^g \, (H) = \frac{\sigma_{ii}^{-1} \sum_{h=0}^{H-1} \left(e'_i \, A_h \sum e_j \right)^2}{\sum_{h=0}^{H-1} \left(e'_i \, A_h \sum A'_h \, e_j \right)}$$

where $\sum$ is the variance matrix for the error term of VAR, σ_{ij} is the standard deviation of the error term for the ith equation and e_i is the selection vector with 1 for the ith element and 0 otherwise. Each forecast error variance decomposition is normalized by the row sum as:

$$\tilde{\theta}_{ij}^g (H) = \frac{\theta_{ij}^g (H)}{\sum_{j=1}^{N} \theta_{ij}^g (H}$$

Following Diebold and Yilmaz (2012), the total spillover index is calculated as:

$$S(H) = \frac{\sum_{j=1, i\neq j}^{N} \tilde{\theta}_{ij}^g(H)}{N} \times 100$$

Total spillover index is the sum of cross-variance shares, which are the fraction of the H step ahead error variances in forecasting x_i due to shocks to x_j.

Directional spillover is measured as the sum of the proportions of the forecast error variance of variable i due to shocks to $j \ \forall \ i\neq j$. The directional spillover from variable i to all other variables is calculated as:

$$S_{i0} (H) = \frac{\sum_{j=1, i\neq j}^{N} \tilde{\theta}_{ij}^g(H)}{\sum_{j=1}^{N} \tilde{\theta}_{ij}^g(H)} \times 100$$

It is noteworthy that directional spillover measures are not order sensitive. In similar vein, directional spillover to variable i from all other variables is obtained as:

$$S_{0i} (H) = \frac{\sum_{j=1, i\neq j}^{N} \tilde{\theta}_{ij}^g(H)}{\sum_{j=1}^{N} \tilde{\theta}_{ij}^g(H)} \times 100$$

Lastly, Net Spillover can be obtained by simply taking the difference between directional spillovers to and directional spillovers from all other variables:

$$S_i (H) = S_{i0} (H) - S_{0i} (H)$$

The diagonal entries of the spillover matrix represent the own variance share of the sample countries, and the off-diagonal elements show the cross-market spillovers, i.e. contribution to the forecast error variance of country i coming from shocks to country j. The last column of the matrix ("from others") highlights the directional returns spillover to the country from rest of the countries. The second last row ("to others") indicates the directional spillover from a country to rest of the countries.

Appendix C

COPULA MODELS FOR DEPENDENCE

Empirical literature uses Multivariate GARCH (MGARCH) models to model dependences between two time series. Copula models have been preferred over MGARCH models to model the dependence as the dependence structure estimated via copulas (which captures nonlinear dependence) is more robust, computationally inexpensive and estimation process more flexible because it separates the dependence structure from the choice of margins (Da Silva Filho et al. 2012; Sklar, 1959). The multivariate normality assumption made in MGARCH models is also not suitable for measuring the linkages of equity markets when it comes to asymmetric co-movements (Longin and Solnik, 2001; Poon et al. 2004). Traditional multivariate GARCH models (DCC GARCH, ADCC GARCH, etc.) require that all random variables have the same marginal distribution and also some assumptions of the margins which restraint their usage. Other advantages of using copula models is that tail dependence measured by copulas allows investors to measure the probability of simultaneous extreme losses (Ning, 2010). Furthermore, copulas are invariant to increasing and continuous transformations and the results are the same for the asset returns as for the logarithm of the returns (Reboredo, 2011). At the same time, the copula function can provide us not only the degree of the dependence, but also the structure of the dependence between financial assets (Ning, 2010). Patton (2006) extended this methodology by adding a time-varying specification to capture the dependence over time.

Because the nature of copulas can be either static or time-variant, we discuss in brief about both of them.

Time-Invariant Copula Models

a.   Gaussian Copula: Following Patton (2006a), the dependence parameter of Gaussian process is

$$
\begin{aligned}
C_{Ga}\left(u,v;\rho\right) &= \int_{-\infty}^{\phi^{-1}(u)} \int_{-\infty}^{\phi^{-1}(v)} \frac{1}{2\pi\sqrt{1-\rho^2}} \exp\left(-\frac{x_1^2 - 2\rho x_1\ x_2 + x_2^2}{2(1-\rho^2)}\right) dx_1 dx_2 \\
&= \phi_p\left(\phi^{-1}(u), \phi^{-1}(v); \rho\right)
\end{aligned}
$$

where u and v are cumulative distribution functions of standardized residuals, subjected to a uniform distribution between 0 and 1, ρ is Pearson's linear correlation, ϕ^{-1} is the inverse cumulative distribution function of a standard normal distribution.

    b. T-Copula: The dependence parameter of t copula follows from Fernandez (2008):

$$C(\mathbf{u},\mathbf{v}) = \int\limits_{-\infty}^{T_v^{-1}(u)} dx \int\limits_{-\infty}^{T_v^{-1}(v)} dy \frac{1}{2\pi\sqrt{1-\rho^2}} \left[1 + \frac{x^2 - 2\rho xy + y^2}{v(1-\rho^2)}\right]^{-\frac{v+2}{2}}$$

$$T_v(x) = \int\limits_{-\infty}^{x} \frac{\Gamma\left(\dfrac{v+1}{2}\right)}{\sqrt{\pi v}\,\Gamma\left(\dfrac{v}{2}\right)} \left(1 + \frac{z^2}{v}\right)^{-\frac{v+1}{2}} dz$$

T is the student t-distribution with degrees of freedom v and Pearson's correlation ρ. In comparison with Gaussian copula, t copula captures the tail dependence.

    c.   Gumbel Copula: The dependence parameter (Gumbel, 1960) can capture the upper tail dependence:

$$C_{Ga}(\mathbf{u},\mathbf{v};\theta) = \exp\left(\left(-(-\ln \mathbf{u})^\theta + (-\ln \mathbf{v})^\theta \right)^{\frac{1}{\theta}} \right)$$

where $1 \le \theta < +\infty$; upper limit in Gumbel copula is ∞.

    d.   Clayton Copula: The dependence parameter (Clayton, 1978) captures the lower tail dependence:

$$C_{CL}(\mathbf{u},\mathbf{v};) = \left(\mathbf{u}^{-\theta} + \mathbf{v}^{-\theta} - 1 \right)^{-1/\theta}$$

where $0 \le \theta < +\infty$;

Time-varying copula models

Time-varying copulas can be considered as dynamic generalization of a Pearson's correlation or Kendall's tau but it is difficult to find causal variables to explain such characteristics (Patton, 2006a, b). In practice though, time-varying copulas are operationalized to follow autoregressive moving average (ARIMA) (p,q) process.

    a.   Time-varying Gaussian Copula (Patton, 2006a) uses a coefficient ρ_t to study the dependence dynamics defined as:

$$\rho_t = \tilde{\Lambda}\left(\omega_N + \beta_{N1}.\rho_{t-1} + \ldots\ldots + \beta_{Np}.\rho_{t-p} + \alpha_N, \frac{1}{q}\sum_{j=1}^{q}\phi^{-1}v_{t-j} \right)$$

where $\tilde{\Lambda}(x)$ is a logistic transformation which is defined as $\tilde{\Lambda}(x) = (1 - e^{-x})(1 - e^{-x})^{-1}$

b.   Time-varying T copula (Patton, 2006b) uses the following to study the dependence process:

c.

$$\rho_t = \tilde{\Lambda}\left(\omega_T + \beta_{T1}.\rho_{t-1} + \ldots + \beta_{Tp}.\rho_{t-p} + \alpha_T.\frac{1}{q}\sum_{j=1}^{q}T^{-1}\left(u_{t-j};\text{DoF}\right). \atop T^{-1}\left(v_{t-j};\text{DoF}\right) \right)$$

where T^{-1} is the inverse function of the student t-distribution with given degrees of freedom (DoF).

d.   Time-varying Gumbel copula studies the dependence using θ_t corresponding to $\tau_t = 1 - 1/\theta_t$ defined as:

$$\tau_t = \Lambda\left(\omega_G + \beta_{G\,1}.\,\tau_{t-1} + \ldots + \beta_{G\,p}.\,\tau_{t-P} + \alpha_G\,.\,\frac{1}{q}\sum_{j=1}^{q}\left|u_{t-j} - v_{t-j}\right| \right)$$

where $\Lambda(x) = \left(1 + e^{-x}\right)^{-1}$.

e.   Time-varying Clayton copula uses θ_t corresponding to $\tau_t = \theta_t/(2 + \theta_t)$ to find the dependence defined as:

$$\tau_t = \Lambda\left(\omega_C + \beta_{C1}\cdot\tau_{t-1} + \ldots + \beta_{Cp}.\tau_{t-P} + \alpha_{C1}\cdot\left|u_{t-1} - v_{t-1}\right| + \alpha_{Cq}\cdot\left|u_{t-q} - v_{t-q}\right| \right)$$

The Elliptical copula models (Gaussian and Student t) are most popular in finance literature due to the ease with which they can be implemented. Gaussian copula is symmetric and has no tail dependence, whereas Student t copula can capture extreme dependence between variables. The Gumbel copula exhibits greater dependence in the upper tail than in the lower, whereas the Clayton copula exhibits greater dependence in the negative tail than in the positive tail.

Note

1 See Chou et al. (2015) for further specification details. First, we created $n \times n$ weight matrix (W_0) for n sample countries based on the contiguity. We assign 1 to those who share common border and 0 otherwise. In furtherance we make it row standardized. Since this study is an inflow and outflow-based study (*diad*-system), we obtain $n^2 \times n^2$ weight matrix (W) as a Kroeneker product of W_0 itself. In the consequence, we use it in the further analysis. For elusive explanation please see LeSage and Pace (2008).

REFERENCES

Abad, P., & Chuliá, H. (2014). European government bond market integration in turbulent times. *IREA Working Paper 2014/24*, University of Barcelona.

Abad, P., Chuliá, H., & Gómez-Puig, M. (2010). EMU and European government bond market integration. *Journal of Banking & Finance*, 34(12), 2851–2860.

Adam, K., Jappelli, T., & Menichini, A., et al. (2002). Analyse compare and apply alternative indicators and monitoring methodologies to measure the evolution of capital market integration in the European Union. *CESF*.

ADB. (2015). *Asian Development Bank Outlook 2015: Financing Asia's Future Growth*. Manila: Asian Development Bank.

Agénor, P.-R., McDermott, C. J., & Prasad, E. S. (2000). Macroeconomic fluctuations in developing countries: Some stylized facts. *The World Bank Economic Review*, 14, 251–285.

Ahmad, M. H., & Ahmed, Q. M. (2014). Does the institutional quality matter to attract the foreign direct investment? An empirical investigation for Pakistan. *South Asia Economic Journal*, 15(1), 55–70.

Ahmad, W. (2017). On the dynamic dependence and investment performance of crude oil and clean energy stocks. *Research in International Business and Finance*, 42, 376–389.

Ahmad, W., Rais, S., & Shaik, A. R. (2017). Modelling the directional spillovers from DJIM Index to conventional benchmarks: Different this time? *The Quarterly Review of Economics and Finance*, 67, 14–27.

Ahmad, W., & Sehgal, S. (2017). Business cycle and financial cycle interdependence and the rising role of China in SAARC. *Journal of Quantitative Economics*, 16, 337–362.

Ahmad, W., Sehgal, S., & Bhanumurthy, N. R. (2013). Eurozone crisis and BRIICKS stock markets: Contagion or market interdependence? *Economic Modelling*, 33, 209–225.

Ahmad, W., & Sharma, S. K. (2017). Testing output gap and economic uncertainty as an explicator of stock market returns. *Research in International Business and Finance*, 45, 293–306.

Ahmar, M. (2011). 'China in SAARC? To what effect?': A Pakistani perspective. *Strategic Analysis*, 35(3), 508–510.

Ahmed, N. (2000). Export response to trade liberalization in Bangladesh: A cointegration analysis. *Applied Economics*, 32(8), 1077–1084.

Ahmed, S., & Kumar, S. (2014). Services trade in South Asia: An assessment. *Towards South Asia Economic Union (Ed.), RIS*, Proceedings of the 7th South Asia Economic Summit (SAES), 83–102.

Ahmed, S. M., & Ansari, M. I. (1998). Financial sector development and economic growth: The South-Asian experience. *Journal of Asian Economics*, 9(3), 503–517.

Aidt, T. S., & Gassebner, M. (2010). Do autocratic states trade less? *The World Bank Economic Review*, 24(1), 38–76.

Akhter, N., & Ghani, E. (2010). Regional integration in South Asia: An analysis of trade flows using the Gravity model. *The Pakistan Development Review*, 49(2), 105–118.

Anderson, J. E., & van Wincoop, E. (2004). Trade costs. *Journal of Economic Literature*, 42(3), 691–751.

Anselin, L., Rey, J. S., & Li, W. (2014). Metadata and provenance for spatial analysis: The case of spatial weights. *International Journal of Geographical Information Science*, 28(11), 2261–2280.

Antonakakis, N. (2012). Exchange return co-movements and volatility spillovers before and after the introduction of euro. *Journal of International Financial Markets, Institutions and Money*, 22(5), 1091–1109.

Antonakakis, N., & Vergos, K. (2013). Sovereign bond yield spillovers in the Euro zone during the financial and debt crisis. *Journal of International Financial Markets, Institutions and Money, 26*, 258–272.

Antonakakis, N., Chatziantoniou, L., & Filis, G. (2013). Dynamic co-movements of stock market returns, implied volatility and policy uncertainty. *Economics Letters, 120*(1), 87–92.

Antonakakis, N., Breitenlechner, M., & Scharlerc, J. (2015). Business cycle and financial cycle spillovers in the G7 countries. *The Quarterly Review of Economics and Finance*, 58, 154–162.

Antonakakis, N., & Kizys, R. (2015). Dynamic spillovers between commodity and currency markets. *International Review of Financial Analysis*, 41, 303–319.

Arfaoui, M., & Abaoub, E. (2010). On the determinants of international financial integration in the global business area. *Journal of Applied Economic Sciences*, 5(3), 153–172.

Arora, R. U., & Ratnasiri, S. (2014). Financial integration of South Asia: An exploratory study. *New Zealand Journal of Asian Studies*, 16(1), 39–60.

Asiedu, E., & Lien, D. (2011). Democracy, foreign direct investment and natural resources. *Journal of International Economics*, 84(1), 99–111.

Baele, L., Ferrando, A., & Hordahl, P., et al. (2004). Measuring financial integration in the Euro-Area. *European Central Bank (ECB) Occasional Paper Series*, no. 14, April.

Bahadur, K. (1998). *Democracy in Pakistan: Crises and Conflicts*. New Delhi: Har-Anand Publication Pvt Ltd.

Baker, S. R., Nicholas, B., & Steven, D. (2016). Measuring economic policy uncertainty. *The Quarterly Journal of Economics*, 131(4), 1593–1636.

Balach, R., & Law, H. S. (2015). Effects of financial development, institutional quality, and human capital on economic performance in SAARC countries. *The Empirical Economics Letters*, 14(2), 131–141.

Balaji, M. S. (2016). *India–Bangladesh Relations: An Enduring Economic Partnership*. New Delhi: Vivekananda International Foundation.

Balassa, B. (1961). Towards a theory of economic integration. *Kyklos*, 14(1), 1–17.

Balli, F., Basher, S. A., & Balli, H. O. (2013). International income risk-sharing and the global financial crises of 2008–2009. *Journal of Banking and Finance*, 37(7), 2303–2313.

Baltagi, B. H. (2001). *Econometric Analysis of Panel Data*. Boston, MA: Kluwer Academic Publishers.

Baltagi, B. H., Egger, P., & Pfaffermayr, M. (2003). A generalized design for bilateral trade flow models. *Economics Letters*, 80, 391–397.

Bandara, J. S., & McGillivray, M. (1998). Trade policy reforms in South Asia. *World Economy*, 21(7), 881–896.

Banik, N., & Gilbert, J. (2008). Regional integration and trade costs in South Asia. *Working Paper No. 127*, Asian Development Bank Institute, Japan.

Bartram, S., Taylor, S. J., & Wang, Y. (2007). The Euro and European financial market dependence. *Journal of Banking and Finance*, 51(5), 1461–1481.

Batten, A., Doung, P., & Enkhbold, E., et al. (2015, September). The financial systems of financially less developed Asian economies: Key features and reform priorities. *ADB Economics Working Paper Series, No 450*, 1–22.

Baunsgaard, T., & Keen, M. (2005). Tax revenue and (or?) trade liberalization. *IMF Working Paper No. 05/112* Washington: IMF.

Baxter, M., & Kouparitsas, M. (2004). Determinants of business cycle commovement: A robust analysis. *NBER Working Paper No. 10725*.

Baysan, T., Panagariya, A., & Pitigala, N. (2006). Preferential trading in South Asia. *World Bank Policy Research Working Paper No. 3813*. Retrieved from SSRN: https://ssrn.com/abstract=875665.

Beck, T., Demirgüç-Kunt, A., & Levine, R. (2000). A new database on financial development and structure. *World Bank Economic Review*, 14, 597–605.

Beckley, M. (2012). China and Pakistan: Fair-weather friends. *Yale Journal of International Affairs*, 7(1), 9–22.

Bekaert, G., Campbell, R. H., Christian, L., & Stephan, S. (2011a). What segments equity markets? *Review of Financial Studies*, 24, 3847–3890.

Bekaert, G., Campbell, R. H., & Christian, L. (2011b). Financial openness and productivity. *World Development*, 39, 1–19.

Bekaert, G., Harvey, C. R., & Ng, A. (2005). Market integration and contagion. *Journal of Business*, 78, 39–69.

Bekiros, S., & Marcellino, M. (2013). The multiscale causal dynamics of foreign exchange markets. *Journal of International Money and Finance*, 33, 282–305.

Berger, N. A., & Udell, F. G. (1998). The economics of small business finance: The roles of private equity and debt markets in the financial growth cycle. *Journal of Banking & Finance*, 2(6–8), 613–673.

Bernanke, B., & Gertler, M. (1989). Agency costs, net worth, and business fluctuations. *The American Economic Review*, 79(1), 14–31.

Bernanke, B., Gertler, M., & Gilchrist, S. (1996). The financial accelerator and the flight to quality. *The Review of Economics and Statistics*, 78(1), 1–15.

Bernanke, B., Gertler, M., & Gilchrist, S. (1999). The financial accelerator in a quantitative business cycle framework. In M. J. B. Taylor, *Handbook of Macroeconomics. Vol. 1 of Handbook of Macroeconomics* (pp. 1341–1393). Amsterdam: Elsevier.

Bhagwati, J. (1991). *The World Trading System at Risk*. Princeton, NJ: Princeton University Press.

Bhaskaran, M., & Ghosh, R. (2010). Impact and policy responses: Bangladesh, Sri Lanka, Nepal, Bhutan and Maldives. In H. S. Sharma, *A Resilient Asia Amidst Global Financial Crisis: From Crisis Management to Global Leadership* (pp. 1–417). New Delhi: Sage Publications India Pvt Ltd.

Bilson, C. M., Brailsford, T. J., & Hooper, V. C. (2002). The explanatory power of political risk in emerging markets. *International Review of Financial Analysis*, 11(1), 1–27.

Brunjes, E., Levine, N., & Palmer, M. (2013). *China's Increased Trade and Investment in South Asia*. Madison: U.S. Government Office of South Asia Policy, University of Wisconsin System.

Brunnermeier, M. K., Nagel, S., & Pedersen, L. H. (2008). Carry trades and currency crashes. *NBER Macroeconomics Annual*, 23, 313–347.

Brunnermeier, M. K., & Pedersen, L. H. (2009). Market liquidity and funding liquidity. *Review of Financial Studies*, 22(6), 2201–2238.

Buch, C. M., & Heinrich, R. P. (2002). European financial integration and corporate governance. *Dt. Bank Research*.

Buch, M. C., & Lipponer, A. (2005). Business cycles and FDI: Evidence from German sectoral data. *Review of World Economics*, 2005(141), 732–759.

Buchholz, M., & Tonzer, L. (2016). Sovereign credit risk co-movements in the Eurozone: simple interdependence or contagion? *International Finance*, 19(3), 246–268.

Burger, J. D., Warnock, F. E., & Warnock, V. C. (2015). Bond market development in developing Asia. *Asian Development Bank Economics Working Paper Series, 448*.

Büttner, D., & Hayo, B. (2010). News and correlations of CEEC-3 financial markets. *Economic Modelling*, 27(5), 915–922.

Büttner, D., & Hayo, B. (2011). Determinants of European stock market integration. *Economic Systems*, 35(4), 574–585.

Cavoli, T., Rajan, R. S., & Siregar, R. (2004). A survey of financial integration in East Asia: How far? How much further to go. *University of Adelaide, Discussion paper, 0401*.

CBS. (2008). *SAARCFINANCE: Governors' Symposium "South Asia's Recent Growth and Future Prospects"*. Colombo: Central Bank Printing Press.

Cerqueira, P. A., & Martins, R. (2009). Measuring the determinants of business cycle synchronization using a panel approach. *Economics Letters*, 102(2), 106–108.

Chaudhari, K. S. (1995). Cross border trade between India and Bangladesh. *Working Paper 58*. New Delhi: National Council of Applied Economic Research.

Chou, K.-H., Chen, C.-H., & Mai, C.-C. (2015). Factors influencing China's exports with a spatial econometric model. *The International Trade Journal*, 29(3), 191–211.

Ciner, C. (2011). Information transmission across currency futures market: Evidence from frequency domain tests. *International Review of Financial Analysis*, 20, 134–139.

Claessens, S., Kose, M. A., & Terrones, M. E. (2012). How do business and financial cycles interact? *Journal of International Economics*, 87(1), 178–190.

Clark, T. E., & Wincoop, V. E. (2001). Borders and business cycles. *Journal of International Economics*, 55(1), 59–85.

Clayton, D. G. (1978). A model for association in bivariate life tables and its application in epidemiological studies of familial tendency in chronic disease incidence. *Biometrika*, 65, 141–152.

Cohen, D., & Soto, M. (2007). Growth and human capital: good data good results. *Journal of Economic Growth*, 51(12), 76.

Council, T. P. (2015). *An Assessment of the Pakistan–Sri Lanka Free Trade Agreement*. Karachi: The Pakistan Business Council.

Cronbach, L. J. (1951). Coefficient alpha and the internal structure of tests. *Psychometrika*, 16(3), 297–334.

Cronin, D. (2014). The interaction between money and asset markets: A spillover approach. *Journal of Macroeconomics*, 39(A), 185–202.

Crosby, M. (2003). Business cycle correlations in Asia–Pacific. *Economics Letters*, 80(1), 35–44.

Csonto, B., & Ivaschenko, I. (2013). Determinants of sovereign bond spreads in emerging markets: Local fundamentals and global factors vs ever-changing misalignments. *IMF Working Paper, WP/13/164*, 1–42.

Da Silva Filho, O. C., Ziegelmann, F. A., & Dueker, M. J. (2012). Modeling dependence dynamics through copulas with regime switching. *Insurance: Mathematics and Economics*, 50, 346–356.

Dabla-Norris, E., Ho, G., & Kyobe, A. (2016). Structural reforms and productivity growth in emerging market and developing economies. *IMF Working Paper, WP/16/15*, 1–34.

Dai, Y. (2014). Business cycle synchronization in Asia: The role of financial and trade linkages. *ADB Working Paper Series on Regional Economic Integration (139)*.

Dash, K. C. (1996). The political economy of regional cooperation in South Asia. *Pacific Affairs*, 69, 185–209.

Dayal, P., Das, A., & Banga, R., et al. (2008). *Quantification of Benefits from Economic Cooperation in South Asia*. New Delhi: Macmillan.

De, P. (2011). Why is trade at borders a costly affair in South Asia? An empirical investigation. *Contemporary South Asia*, 19(4), 441–464.

De Haan, J., Inklaar, R., & Jong-A-Pin, R. (2008). Will business cycles in the Euro area converge? A critical survey of empirical research. *Journal of Economic Surveys*, 22(2), 234–273.

De Brouwer, G. (1999). *Financial Integration in East Asia*. Cambridge: Cambridge University Press.

Demir, F., & Duan, Y. (2018). Bilateral FDI flows, productivity growth, and convergence: The North vs. The South. *World Development*, 101, 235–249.

Diamonte, R. L., Liew, J. M., & Stevens, R. L. (1996). Political risk in emerging and developed markets. *Financial Analysts Journal*, 52(3), 71–76.

Didier, T., & Schmukler, S. L. (2013). The financing and growth of firms in China and India: Evidence from capital markets. *Journal of International Money and Finance*, 39, 111–137.

Diebold, F. X., & Yilmaz, K. (2009). Measuring financial asset return and volatility spillovers with application to Global Equity Markets. *The Economic Journal*, 119, 158–171.

Diebold, F. X., & Yilmaz, K. (2012). Better to give than to receive: Predictive directional measurement of volatility spillovers. *International Journal of Forecasting*, 28(1), 57–66.

Dornbusch, R., Park, Y. C., & Claessens, S. (2000). Contagion: Understanding how it spreads. *World Bank Research Observer*, 15, 177–198.

Dubey, M. (2007). SAARC and South Asian economic integration. *Economic and Political Weekly*, 42, 1238–1240.

Dutta, S. (2011). China in SAARC? To what effect? *Strategic Analysis*, 35(3), 493–501.

ECB. (2004). *Measuring Financial Integration in Euro-Area*. Frankefurt: European Central Bank (ECB).

Egger, P. (2002). An econometric view on the estimation of gravity models and the calculation of trade potentials. *The World Economy*, 25(2), 297–312.

Eichengreen, B., & Leblang, D. (2008). Democracy and globalization. *Economics & Politics*, 20(3), 289–334.

Elhorst, J. P. (2003). Specification and estimation of spatial panel data models. *Regional Science Review*, 26(3), 244–268.

Elhorst, J. P. (2012). Matlab software for spatial panels. *International Regional Science Review*, 35(4), 1–17.

Engle, R. (2002). Dynamic conditional correlation: A simple class of multivariate generalized autoregressive conditional heteroskedasticity models. *Journal of Business and Economic Statistics*, 20, 339–350.

Erb, C. B., Harvey, C. R., & Viskanta, T. E. (1996). Political risk, economic risk and financial risk. *Financial Analysts Journal*, 52(6), 29–46.

Estrada, G., Park, D., & Ramayandi, A. (2010, November). Financial development and economic growth in developing Asia. *ADB Economics Working Paper Series No. 233*, 1–55.

Exim Bank. (2014, June). Potential for enhancing intra-SAARC trade: A brief analysis. *Working Paper No. 31, Exim-Bank of India*, 1–87.

Fernandez, V. (2008). Copula-based measures of dependence structure in assets returns. *Physica A: Statistical Mechanics and its Applications*, 387(14), 3615–3628.

Fernández-Rodríguez, F., Gómez-Puig, M., & Sosvilla-Rivero, S. (2015). Volatility spillovers in EMU sovereign bond markets. *International Review of Economics and Finance*, 39, 337–352.

Fernández-Rodríguez, F., Gómez-Puig, M., & Sosvilla-Rivero, S. (2016). Using connectedness analysis to assess financial stress transmission in EMU sovereign bond market volatility. *Journal of International Financial Markets, Institutions and Money*, 43, 126–145.

Forbes, K., & Rigobon, R. (1999). No contagion, only interdependence: Measuring stock market comovements. *NBER Working Paper, No. 7267*, July 1999.

Forhad, M. A. (2014). How many currencies in SAARC countries? A multivariate structural VAR approach. *The Journal of Developing Areas*, 48(4), 265–286.

Fostel, A., & Geanakoplos, J. (2008). Leverage cycles and the anxious economy. *American Economic Review*, 98(4), 1211–1244.

Frankel, A. J., & Rose, K. A. (1998). The endogenity of the optimum currency area criteria. *The Economic Journal*, 108(449), 1009–1025.

Fratzscher, M. (2009). What explains global exchange rate movements during the financial crisis? *Journal of International Money and Finance*, 28(8), 1390–1407.

García-Herrero, A., & Ruiz, J. M. (2008). Do trade and financial linkages foster business cycle synchronization in a small country. *Banco de España Working Paper No. 0810*, 1–29.

Gertler, M., & Kiyotaki, N. (2010). Financial intermediation and credit policy in business cycle analysis. In B. M. Friedman, *Handbook of Monetary Economics. Vol. 3 of Handbook of Monetary Economics* (pp. 547–599). Amsterdam: Elsevier.

Ghani, E., & Ahmed, S. (2009). *Accelerating Growth and Job Creation in South Asia*. New Delhi: Oxford University Press.

Giavazzi, F., & Tabellini, G. (2005). Economic and political liberalizations. *Journal of Monetary Economics*, 52(7), 1297–1340.

Gill, I., Sugawara, N., & Zalduendo, J. (2014). The center still holds: Financial integration in the Euro Area *Comparative Economic Studies*, 56, 351–375.

Gómez-Puig, M., Sosvilla-Rivero, S., & Ramos-Herrera, M. C. (2014). An update on EMU sovereign yield spreads drivers in times of crisis: A panel data analysis. *The North American Journal of Economics and Finance*, 30, 133–153.

Goodhand, J., Korf, B., & Spencer, J. (2011). *Conflict and Peacebuilding in Sri Lanka: Caught in the Peace Trap?* New Delhi: Routledge.

Goyal, A. (2011). Inflationary pressures in South Asia. *Asia-Pacific Development Journal*, 17(2), 1–42.

Guesmi, K., Nguyen, D.-K., & Teulon, F. (2013). Further evidence on the determinants of regional stock markets integration in Latin America. *European Journal of Comparative Economics*, 34(1), 397–413.

Gumbel, E. J. (1960). Bivariate exponential distributions. *Journal of the American Statistical Association*, 55, 698–707.

Gupta, P., Sehgal, S., & Deisting, F. (2015). Time-varying bond market integration integration in EMU. *Journal of Economic Integration*, 30(4), 708–760.

Hassan, K. M. (2001). Is SAARC a viable economic block? Evidence from gravity model. *Journal of Asian Economics*, 12(2), 263–290.

He, D., & Liao, W. (2012). Asian business cycle synchronization. *Pacific Economic Review*, 17(1), 106–135.

Hossain, M., Shinkai, N., & Yunus, M. (2012). Integration of ICT industries and its impact on market access and trade: The case of Bangladesh and India. In S. K.-P. Sultan Hafeez Rahman, *Regional Integration and Economic Development in South Asia* (p. 424). Northampton, MA: Edward Elgar Publishing Ltd.

Hsu, C. C., Woo, J. Y., & Yau, R. (2011). Foreign direct investment and business cycle co-movements: The panel data evidence. *Journal of Macroeconomics*, 33, 770–783.

Huoy, C. W., & Goh, K. L. (2007). The determinants of stock market integration: A panel data investigation. *15th Annual Conference on Pacific Basin Finance, Economics, Accounting and Management*, Ho Chi. Minh City, Vietnam, 20 & 21 July.

Imbs, J. (2004). Trade, finance, specialization and synchronization. *Review of Economics and Statistics*, 86(3), 723–734.

Imbs, J. (2006). The real effects of financial integration. *Journal of International Economics*, 68(2), 296–324.

Imbs, J. (2010). The first global recession in decades. *IMF Economic Review*, 58(2), 327–354.

Imbs, J. (2011). What happened to the East Asian business cycle? In M. Devereux, P. Lane, C. Y. Park, & S. J. Wei, *The Dynamics of Asian Financial Integration* (pp. 284–310). London: Routledge.

Inklaar, R., Pin-A-Jong, R., & Haan, D. J. (2008). Trade and business cycle synchronization in OECD countries—A re-examination. *European Economic Review*, 52(4), 646–666.

Isham, J., & Kaufmann, D. (1999). The forgotten rationale for policy reform: The productivity of investment projects. *Quarterly Journal of Economics*, 114(1), 149–184.

Ismail, S. (2012). Trade induced technology spillover and economic growth: An econometric analysis. In S. Ahmed & S. Ashraf, *International Trade in Emerging Economies* (pp. 183–194). New Delhi: Bloomsbury.

Islam, A., & Salim, R. (2012). Moribund SAFTA and trade policy options for South Asia. In *Proceedings of 7th Asian business research conference* (pp. 1–33). World Business Institute.

Jansen, J. W., & Stockman, A. C. (2004). Foreign direct investment and international business cycle comovement. *De Nederlandsche Bank Monetary & Economic Policy Working Paper 2003–2010*.

Jawaid, S. T., & Raza, S. A. (2016). Effects of workers' remittances and its volatility on economic growth in South Asia. *International Migration*, 54(2), 50–68.

Jayasuriya, S., & Maskay, M. N. (2010). Enhancing economic integration in South Asia: Issues and prospects for closer monetary cooperation. *The Singapore Economic Review*, 55(1), 185–206.

Jermann, U., & Quadrini, V. (2012). Macroeconomic effects of financial shocks. *American Economic Review*, 102(1), 238–271.

Jordà, Ò., Schularick, M., & Taylor, A. M. (2013). When credit bites back. *Journal of Money, Credit and Banking*, 45(s2), 3–28.

Kadirgamar, A. (2016, May 11). *Why India's Big Push for Economic Cooperation in Lanka May Backfire*. Retrieved July 18, 2018, from https://thewire.in/; https://thewire.in/diplomacy/why-indias-big-push-for-economic-cooperation-in-lanka-may-backfire.

Kalegama, S. (2014). China-Sri Lanka economic relations: An overview. *China Report*, 50(2), 131–149.

Kalemli-Ozcan, S., Papaioannou, E., & Peydro, J.-L. (2013). Financial regulation, financial globalization, and the synchronization of economic activity. *The Journal of Finance*, 68(3), 1179–1228.

Kalemli-Ozcan, S., Sørensen, E. B., & Yosha, O. (2003). Risk sharing and industrial specialization: Regional and international evidence. *The American Economic Review*, 93(3), 903–918.

Kanungo, K. A. (2017). Regional integration in services in South Asia: Opportunities & constraints. FREIT *Working Paper Archive WP#1292*, 1–29. Retrieved from http://www.freit.org/WorkingPapers/Papers/TradePolicyRegional/FREIT1292.pdf.

Kelegama, S. (2001). Sri Lankan economy in turbulent times: Budget 2001 and IMF package. *Economic and Political Weekly*, 36(28), 2665–2673.

Khan, M. S., & Khan, S. Z. (2003). Asian economic integration: A perspective on South Asia. *Journal of Asian Economics*, 13(6), 767–785.

Khan, Z. M. (1999). Liberalization and economic crisis in Pakistan. In A. D. Bank, *Rising to the Challenge in Asia: A Study of Financial Markets* (pp. 1–112). Islamabad: Asian Development Bank.

Kharel, S. R., & Pokhrel, R. D. (2012). Does Nepal's financial structure matter for economic growth. *NRB Economic Review*, 24(2), 32–46.

Kilian, L. (2009). Not all oil price shocks are alike: Disentangling demand and supply shocks in the crude oil market. *American Economic Review*, 99(3), 1053–1069.

Kim, S. J., Moshirian, F., & Wu, E., (2005). Dynamic stock market integration driven by the European Monetary Union: An empirical analysis. *Journal of Banking & Finance*, 29(10), 2475–2502, October.

Kim, S., & Kim, H. S. (2013). International capital flows, boom-bust cycles, and business cycle synchronization in the Asia Pacific Region. *Contemporary Economic Policy*, 30(1), 191–211.

Kiran, H., Rehman, S., & Iftikhar, N. M., et al. (2013). Does corruption effects on social sector in SAARC Region? *Journal of Asian Development Studies*, 2(2), 53–59.

Kiyotaki, N., & Moore, J. (1997). Credit cycles. *Journal of Political Economy*, 105(2), 211–248.

Kogan Page. (2003). *Asia and Pacific Review 2003/04*. London: Wolden Publishing Ltd in association with International Chamber of Commerce, The World Business Organization.

Koop, G., Pesaran, M. H., & Potter, S. M. (1996). Impulse response analysis in nonlinear multivariate models. *Journal of Econometrics*, 74(1), 119–147.

Kose, M. A., Otrok, C., & Prasad, E. (2012). Global Business Cycles: Convergence or Decoupling? *International Economic Review, 53*, 511–538.

Krueger, A. O. (1974). The political economy of the rent-seeking society. *American Economic Review*, 64(3), 291–303.

Kruskal, W. H., & Wallis, W. A. (1952). Use of ranks in one-criterion variance analysis. *Journal of the American Statistical Association*, 47(260), 583–621.

Kumar, M. S., & Okimoto, T (2011). Dynamics of international integration of government securities markets. *Journal of Banking and Finance*, 35(1), 142–154.

Kumar, S. (2007). The China–Pakistan strategic relationship: Trade, investment, energy and infrastructure. *Strategic Analysis*, 31(5), 757–790.

Kumar, S., & Ahmed, S. (2015). Gravity model by panel data approach: An empirical application with implications for South Asian Countries. *Foreign Trade Review*, 50(4), 233–249.

Kumar, S. S. (2015). China's SAARC membership: The debate. *International Journal of China Studies*, 6(3), 299.

Lamb, D. R., & Small, A. (2014). *Regional dynamics and strategic concerns in South Asia*. Washington, DC: Center for Strategic & International Studies.

Lane, P. R., & Milesi-Ferretti, G. M. (2003). International financial integration. *IMF Economic Review*, 50(1), 82–113.

Lane, P. R., & Milesi-Ferretti, G. M. (2008). The drivers of financial globalization. *American Economic Review*, 98(2), 327–332.

LeSage, J., & Pace, R. K. (2009). *Introduction to Spatial Econometrics*. Boca Raton, FL: CRC Press.

LeSage, J. P., & Pace, R. K. (2008). Spatial econometric modeling of origin-destination flows. *Journal of Regional Science*, 48(5), 941–967.

Longin, F., & Solnik, B. (2001). Extreme correlation of international equity markets. *The Journal of Finance*, 56(2), 649–676.

Lukmanova, E., & Tondl, G. (2017). Macroeconomic imbalances and business cycle synchronization. Why common economic governance is imperative for the Eurozone. *Economic Modelling*, 62, 130–144.

Mahmood, T., Arby, M. F., & Sherazi, H. (2014). Debt sustainability: A comparative analysis of SAARC countries. *Pakistan Economic and Social Review*, 52(1), 15–34.

Malik, M. J. (2001). South Asia in China's foreign relations. *Global Change Peace & Security*, 13(1), 73–90.

Manova, K. (2013). Credit constraints, heterogeneous firms, and international trade. *The Review of Economic Studies*, 80(2), 711–744.

Manzoor, H. S., & Chaudhary, E. M. (2017). Foreign direct investment in Bangladesh: Some recent trends and implications. *Journal of Business & Economics Research*, 15(1), 1–12.

Méon, P. G., and Sekkat, K. 2004. Does the Quality of Institutions Limit the MENA's Integration in the World Economy? *The World Economy*, 27(10), 1475–1498.

Marjit, S., Mandal, B., & Roy, S. (2014). Trade openness, corruption and factor abundance: Evidence from a dynamic panel. *Review of Development Economics*, 18(1), 45–58.

Martinez-Zarzoso, I. (2003). Gravity model: An application to trade between regional blocs. *Atlantic Economic Journal*, 31(2), 174–187.

Metulini, R. (2013). Spatial gravity models for international trade: a panel analysis among OECD countries. ERSA conference papers ersa13p522. ERSA conference papers ersa13p522. *European Regional Science Association*.

Minetti, R., & ChunZhu, S. (2011). Credit constraints and firm export: Microeconomic evidence from Italy. *Journal of International Economics*, 83(2), 109–125.

Mohanty, S. K. (2014). *India–China Bilateral Trade Relationship*. New Delhi: Research and Information System for Developing Countries.

Moinuddin, M. (2013). Fulfilling the promises of South Asian integration: Gravity estimation. *ADBI Working Paper 415*. Tokyo: Asian Development Bank Institute.

Muhammad, A. S., Rana, M. A., & Akbar, M. (2015). Opportunities and challenges of regional economic interaction: A case study of Pakistan and Nepal. *Pakistan Journal of Social Sciences (PJSS)*, 35(2), 969–980.

Muni, S. D. (2011). 'China in SAARC? To what effect?': A comment. *Strategic Analysis*, 35(3), 505–507.

Mustafa, G., Rizov, M., & Kernohan, D. (2017). Growth, human development, and trade: The Asian experience. *Economic Modelling*, 61, 93–101.

Mylonidis, N., & Kollias, C. (2010). Dynamic European stock market convergence: Evidence from rolling cointegration analysis in the first euro-decade. *Journal of Banking & Finance*, 34, 2056–2064.

Narayan, S., Sriananthakumar, S., & Islam, S. Z. (2014). Stock market integration of emerging Asian economies: Patterns and causes. *Economic Modelling*, 39, 19–31.

Nawaz, S. (2015). Growth effects of institutions: A disaggregated analysis. *Economic Modelling*, 45, 118–126.

Ng, L., Solnik, B., & Wu, E., et al. (2013). Characterizing global financial and economic integration using cash flow expectations. *Working paper of University of Wisconsin – Milwaukee*.

Ning, C. (2010). Dependence structure between the equity market and the foreign exchange market—A copula approach. *Journal of International Money and Finance*, 29, 743–759.

NRB. (2018, June). *A Survey Report on the Foreign Direct Investment in Nepal*. Kathmandu: Research Department, Nepal Rastra Bank.

Nunnally, J. C. (1978). *Psychometric Theory* (2nd ed.). New York: McGraw-Hill.

Oskooee-Bahmani, M., & Shabsigh, G. (1996). On the effects of money on the terms of trade: An empirical investigation. *Applied Economics Letters*, 3, 721–724.

Owen, R. F. (2013). Governance and economic integration: Stakes for Asia. Asian Development Bank Institute, *Working Paper Series, 425*.

Ozaki, M. (2012). Worker migration and remittances in South Asia. *South Asia Working Paper Series*, 12, 1–31.

Pandey, P., & Sehgal, S. (2018). Dynamic currency linkages and their determinants: An empirical study for east asian economic community region. *Emerging Markets Finance and Trade*, 54(7), 1538–1556.

Pandey, P., Sehgal, S., & Ahmad, W. (2019). Dynamics of Banking Sector Integration in South Asia: An Empirical Study. *Indian Growth and Development Review*, 12, 315–332. https://doi.org/10.1108/IGDR-07-2018-0079.

Park, C. Y. (2016). Developing local currency bond markets in Asia. Asian Development Bank Economics. *Working Paper Series, 495*.

Pattanaik, S. S. (2006). Making sense of regional cooperation: SAARC at twenty. *Strategic Analysis*, 30(1), 139–160.

Pattanaik, S. S. (2010). SAARC at twenty-five: An incredible idea still in its infancy. *Strategic Analysis*, 34(5), 671–677.

Patton, A. J. (2006a). Modelling asymmetric exchange rate dependence. *International Economic Review*, 47(2), 527–556.

Patton, A. J. (2006b). Estimation of multivariate models for time series of possibly different lengths. *Journal of Applied Econometrics*, 21(2), 147–173.

Pauer, F. (2005). Financial market integration and financial stability. *Oesterreichische National Bank Monetary Policy & The Economy*, Q, 2, 144–151.

Perego, E. R., & Vermeulen, W. N. (2016). Macro-economic determinants of European stock and government bond correlations: A tale of two regions. *Journal of Empirical Finance*, 37, 214–232.

Pesaran, B., & Pesaran, M. H. (2007). Modelling volatilities and conditional correlations in futures markets with a multivariate t distribution. *Cambridge Working Papers in Economics*, 0734.

Pesaran, H. H., & Shin, Y. (1998). Generalized impulse response analysis in linear multivariate models. *Economics Letters*, 58, 17–29.

Peter, J. P. (1979). Reliability: A review of psychometric basics and recent marketing practices. *Journal of Marketing Research*, 16(1), 6–17.

Petrović, P., & Gligorić, M. (2010). Exchange rate and trade balance: J-curve effect. *PANOECONOMICUS*, 1, 23–41.

Piljak, V. (2013). Bond markets co-movement dynamics and macroeconomic factors: Evidence from emerging and frontier markets. *Emerging Markets Review*, 17, 29–43.

Poon, S.-H., Rockinger, M., & Tawn, J., (2004). Extreme value dependence in financial markets: diagnostics, models, and financial implications. *The Review of Financial Studies*, 17(2), 581–610.

Poonpatpibul, C., Tanboon, S., & Leelapornchai, P. (2006). *The Role of Financial Integration in East Asia in Promoting Regional Growth and Stability*. Mimeo: Bank of Thailand.

Prasad, U. S. (2015). Study of Nepal's economic relations with China. *The Journal of Development and Administrative Studies*, 23(1–2), 23–32.

Pulok, H. M., & Ahmed, U. M. (2017). Does corruption matter for economic development? Long run evidence from Bangladesh. *International Journal of Social Economics*, 44(3), 350–361.

Rahman, M., Shadat, W. B., & Das, N. C. (2006). Trade potential in SAFTA: An application of augmented gravity model. *CPD Occasional Paper No. 61*, CPD, Dhaka.

Rahman, N. M., & Grewal, S. H. (2017). Foreign direct investment and international trade in BIMSTEC: Panel causality analysis. *Transnational Corporations Review*, 9(2), 112–121.

Rajapakse, P., & Arunatilleke, N. (1997). Would a reduction in trade barriers promote intra SAARC trade? A Sri Lankan perspective. *Journal of Asian Economics*, 8(1), 95–115.

Rana, B. P. (2007). Economic integration and synchronization of business cycles in East Asia. *Journal of Asian Economics*, 18(5), 711–725.

Reboredo, J. C. (2011). How do crude oil prices co-move? A copula approach. *Energy Economics*, 33, 948–955.

René, C., & Mollick, A. V. (2012). Convergence rates to output growth in a global world: The roles of openness and government size. *The International Trade Journal*, 26(3), 201–222.

Rime, D., & Schrimpf, A. (2013). The anatomy of the global FX market through the lens of the 2013 Triennial Survey. *BIS Quarterly Review*, December, 27–43.

Rizavi, S. S., Naqvi, B., & Rizvi, S.K.A. (2011). Global and regional financial integration for Asian stock markets. *International Journal of Business and Social Sciences*, 2(9), 82–93.

Rodriguez, J. C. (2007). Measuring financial contagion: A copula approach. *Journal of Empirical Finance*, 14(3), 401–423.

Rodríguez-Delgado, J. D. (2007). *SAFTA: Living in a World of Regional Trade Agreements (No. 7–23)*. Washington: International Monetary Fund.

Rose, A. (2004). Do we really know that the WTO increases trade? *American Economic Review*, 90(1), 98–114.

Roy, R., & Dixon, R. (2016). Workers' remittances and the Dutch disease in South Asian countries. *Applied Economics Letters*, 23(6), 407–410.

Sahoo, P. (2013a). Economic relations with Bangladesh: China's ascent and India's decline. *South Asia Research*, 33(2), 123–139.

Sahoo, P. (2013b). The growing dominance of China in South Asia: An Indian perspective. *The International Trade Journal*, 27(2), 111–141.

Saini, G. (2011). Prospects of regional economic cooperation in South Asia. In G. Saini, *Chapter 5: Gravity Analysis of South Asia's Free Trade*. Sawston: Chandos Publishing.

Salim, R., & Kabir, S. (2010). The immediate impact of euro on intra-regional trade: An event study approach. *Journal of Economic Development*, 35(3), 43–55.

Sally, R. (2006). FTAs and the prospects for regional integration in Asia. *European Centre for International Political Economy Working Paper, 1.*

Samaratunga, R. H. (1999). *Essays in trade policy and economic integration with special reference to South Asia*. Melbourne: PhD Thesis, La Trobe University.

Saxena, C. S. (2005). Can South Asia adopt a common currency? *Journal of Asian Economics*, 16(4), 635–662.

Sehgal, S., Ahmad, W., & Deisting, F. (2015). An investigation of price discovery and volatility spillovers in India's foreign exchange market. *Journal of Economic Studies*, 42(2), 261–284.

Sehgal, S., Ahmad, W., & Deisting, F. (2014). An empirical examination of the process of information transmission in India's agriculture futures markets. *Journal of Quantitative Economics*, 12(1), 96–125.

Sehgal, S., Gupta, P., & Deisting, F. (2016a). Assessing time varying stock market integration in Economic and Monetary Union for normal and crisis periods. *The European Journal of Finance*, 23, 1025–1058. https://doi.org/10.1080/135 1847X.2016.1158727.

Sehgal, S., Gupta, P., & Deisting, F. (2016b). Integration from retail banking to non-financial Corporations in EMU. *Journal of Economic Integration*, 31, 674–735.

Sehgal, S., Pandey, P., & Diesting, F. (2018a). Examining dynamic currency linkages amongst South Asian economies: An empirical study. *Research in International Business and Finance*, 42, 173–190.

Sehgal, S., Pandey, P., & Deisting, F. (2018b). Stock market integration dynamics and its determinants in the East Asian Economic Community Region. *Journal of Quantitative Economics*, 16(2), 389–425.

Sehgal, S., Pandey, P., & Deisting, F. (2018c). Time varying integration amongst the South Asian equity markets: An empirical study. *Cogent Economics & Finance*, 6(1), 1452328.

Sehgal, S., Pandey, P., & Saini, S. (2018d). Dynamics of short and long term debt market integration in the South Asian economies. *Theoretical Economics Letters*, 8, 2416–2443.

Sen, A. (2018, January 12). *Trade pact: India, Sri Lanka to iron out differences in services, rules of origin*. Retrieved July 12, 2018, from https://www.thehindubusinessline.com/economy/trade-pact-india-sri-lanka-to-iron-out-differences-in-services-rules-of-origin/article9510053.ece.

Sengupta, J. (2007, August). Time to boost India-Bangladesh trade and economic relations. *ORF ISSUE BRIEF*, 10, 1–4.

Serlenga, L., & Shin, Y. (2007). Gravity models of intra-EU trade: Application of the CCEP-HT estimation in heterogeneous panels with unobserved common time-specific factors. *Journal of Applied Econometrics*, 22(2), 361–381.

Sethapramote, Y. (2015). Synchronization of business cycles and economic policy linkages in ASEAN. *Journal of Asian Economics*, 39, 126–136.

Shahid, A., Saeed, H., & Tirmizi, A. M. (2015). Economic development and banking sector growth in Pakistan. *Journal of Sustainable Finance & Investment*, 5(3), 121–135.

Sims, C. A. (1980). Macroeconomics and reality. *Econometrica*, 48, 1–48.

Sklar, A. (1959). Fonctions de répartition à n dimensions etleursmarges. *Publications de l'Institut de Statistique de Paris*, 8, 229–231.

Sowmya, S., Prasanna, K., & Bhaduri, S. (2016). Linkages in the term structure of interest rates across sovereign bond markets. *Emerging Markets Review*, 27, 118–139.

Srinivasan, T. N. (1994). Regional trading arrangements and beyond: Exploring some options for South Asia – theory, empirics and policy. *Internal discussion paper; no. IDP 142.*

Srinivasan, T. N., & Canonero, G. (1995). *Preferential Agreements in South Asia: Theory, Empirics and Policy*. Mimeo: Yale Growth Center, Yale University.

State Bank of Pakistan. (2014). *Monetary Policy Frameworks in the SAARC Region*. Karachi: State Bank of Pakistan, Monetary Policy Department.

SWIFT. (2016). RMB adoption improves across India. Retrieved from https://www.swift.com/insights/press-releases/rmb-adoption-improves-across-india.

Taneja, N. (2002). *India's Informal Trade with Sri Lanka*. New Delhi: International Council for Research on International Economic Relations.

Taneja, N. (2004). Informal trade in the SAARC region: Implications for FTAs. *Economic and Political Weekly*, 39(51), 5367–5371.

Taneja, N., & Bimal, S. (2016). *India's Informal Trade with Pakistan*. New Delhi: Indian Council for Research on International Economic Relations.

Taneja, N., Mehra, M., & Mukherjee, P., et al. (2013). *Normalizing India Pakistan Trade*. New Delhi: Indian Council for Research on International Economic Relations.

Taneja, N., Ray, S., & Devyani, P. (2016). *India-Pakistan Trade: Textiles and Clothing*. New Delhi: Indian Council for Research on International Economic Relations.

Taylor, A. M., & Schularick, M. (2012). Credit booms gone bust: Monetary policy, leverage cycles, and financial crises 1870–2008. *American Economic Review*, 102(2), 1029–1061.

The Asia Foundation. (2016). Intra-Regional Trade in South Asia. Retrieved from http://asiafoundation.org/publication/intra-regional-trade-south-asia/.

Tsiang, S. C. (1961). The role of money in trade-balance stability: Synthesis of the elasticity and absorption. *The American Economic Review*, 51(5), 912–936.

Uddin, B. M., & Murshed, M. S. (2017). International transfers and Dutch Disease: Evidence from South Asian countries. *Journal of the Asia Pacific Economy*, 22(3), 486–509.

Uddin, S. G., Kyophilavong, P., & Sydee, N. (2012). The causal nexus of banking sector development and poverty reduction in Bangladesh. *International Journal of Economics and Financial Issues*, 2(3), 304–311.

UNESCAP. (2016). Achieving the sustainable development goals in South Asia: Key policy priorities and implementation challenges. Retrieved from http://www.unescap.org/sites/default/files/SDGs%20South%20Asia%20report%20 2016%20rev%2014%20April%202016.pdf.

UNESCAP. (2017). Unlocking the potential of regional economic cooperation and integration in South Asia: Potential, challenges and the way forward. Retrieved from http://www.unescap.org/sites/default/files/publications/Report_Regional_Economic_Cooperation_and_Integration_in_South_Asia_12052017.pdf.

Valentina, M., Alvaro, C. C., & Chuck, K. C. (2013). The impact of conflict types and location on trade. The *International Trade Journal*, 27(3), 197–224.

Villasenor, D. J., West, M. D., & Lewis, J. R. (2016, August). *The 2016 Brookings Financial and Digital Inclusion Project Report*. Washington, DC: Center for Technology Innovation at Brookings.

Vo, X. V., & Daly, K. J. (2007). The determinants of international financial integration. *Global Finance Journal*, 18(2), 228–250.

Volz, U. (2010). *Prospects for Monetary Cooperation and Integration in East Asia*. Cambridge: MIT Press.

Wang, P., & Moore, T. (2008). Stock market integration of the transition economies: Time-varying conditional correlation approach. *The Manchester School*, 76(Supplement s1), 116–133.

World Bank. (2009). *Impact of Global Financial Crisis on South Asia*. Washington: South Asia Region, The World Bank Group. Retrieved October 21, 2017, from http://siteresources.worldbank.org/SOUTHASIAEXT/Resources/223546-1171488994713/3455847-1232124140958/gfcsouthasiafeb172009.pdf.

World Bank. (2014a). Finance and growth in China and India.

World Bank. (2014b). *South Asia Regional Brief*. Retrieved from http://www.worldbank.org/en/news/feature/2014/03/24/south-asia-regional-brief.

World Bank. (2016a). South Asia Economic Focus, Spring 2016: Fading Tailwinds. *World Bank*. https://openknowledge.worldbank.org/handle/10986/24016 License: CC BY 3.0 IGO.

World Bank. (2016b). South Asia Economic Focus, Fall 2016: Investment Reality Check. *World Bank*. https://openknowledge.worldbank.org/handle/10986/25096 License: CC BY 3.0 IGO.

World Bank. (2017). *South Asia Economic Focus: Globalization Backlash*. Washington: World Bank.

Wu, H. L., Chen, C. H., and Chen, L. T. 2007. Foreign Trade in China's Electronics Industry. *Eurasian Geography and Economics*, 48(5), 626–642.

Yang, L., & Hamori, S. (2014). Dependence structure between CEEC-3 and German government securities markets. *Journal of International Financial Markets, Institutions and Money*, 29, 109–125.

Yilmaz, K. (2009). International business cycle spillovers. *Koc University-TUSIAD Economic Research Forum Working Papers 0903*. Koc University-TUSIAD Economic.

Yu, I., Fung, L., & Tam, C. (2010). Assessing financial market integration in Asia-equity markets. *Journal of Banking and Finance*, 34(12), 2874–2885.

Yu, M. (2007). Political competition and bilateral direct investment. *Frontiers of Economics in China*, 2(2), 250–274.

Yuan, J.-D. (2007). The dragon and the elephant: Chinese–Indian relations in the 21st century. *The Washington Quarterly*, 30(3), 131–144.

INDEX

Note: **Bold** page numbers refer to tables; *Italic* page numbers refer to figures and page numbers followed by "n" denote endnotes.

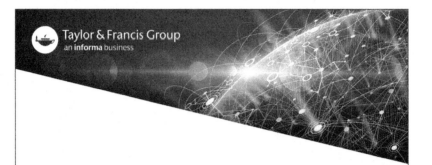

Printed in the United States
By Bookmasters